The EU Race Directive

In 2000, the European Union adopted a Directive against discrimination on the grounds of racial or ethnic origin. This book provides an in-depth evaluation of the Race Directive and its effects, questioning how successful the Race Directive has been.

The EU Race Directive discusses the history of the fight against racial discrimination in the EU and the equality clauses in international Human Rights instruments. It then examines the terms race, racism and racial discrimination in the Directive. The book also looks at the concepts of equality which can be distinguished in the Race Directive and in the subsequent developments at EU level. Examining whether the Directive has improved the protection against racial or ethnic origin discrimination for people within the EU, the book concludes with an assessment of how far the EU has come on the road to racial equality with the adoption of the Race Directive and the subsequent developments. It also contains proposals for possible improvements. The comprehensive and up-to-date analysis in this book goes beyond most other books written on the subject and the specific focus on racism and racial discrimination means a more thorough examination than most texts focusing on discrimination on a larger number of grounds.

This book will be of great value to students and academics in (European) law, social sciences and human rights, researching racism, racial discrimination, ethnicity and race relations. It will also be useful for policy makers.

Erica Howard is a Senior Lecturer in Law at Middlesex University.

The EU Race Directive

Developing the protection against racial discrimination within the EU

Erica Howard

Routledge
Taylor & Francis Group
LONDON AND NEW YORK

First published 2010
by Routledge
2 Park Square, Milton Park, Abingdon, Oxon OX14 4RN

Simultaneously published in the USA and Canada
by Routledge
270 Madison Avenue, New York, NY 10016

Routledge is an imprint of the Taylor & Francis Group, an informa business

Typeset in Garamond by
Keyword Group Ltd.
Printed and bound in Great Britain by
MPG Books Ltd, Bodmin, Cornwall

British Library Cataloguing in Publication Data
A catalogue record for this book is available from the British Library

Library of Congress Cataloging in Publication Data
The EU race directive : developing the protection against racial discrimination within the EU / Erica Howard.
p. cm.
Includes bibliographical references.
ISBN 978-0-415-54373-6
1. Council of the European Union. Council directive 2000/43/EC.
2. Race discrimination—Law and legislation—European Union countries. 3. Equality before the law—European Union countries. I. Title. II. Title: European Union race directive.
KJE5142.H69 2009
342.2408'73—dc22 2009019013

ISBN10: 0-415-54373-8 (hbk)
ISBN10: 0-203-86621-5 (ebk)

ISBN13: 978-0-415-54373-6 (hbk)
ISBN13: 978-0-203-86621-4 (ebk)

In memory of my parents

Contents

Acknowledgements

The research for this book started with a PhD study completed in 2007 at Queen Mary, University of London and is partly based on the thesis for this study. Thanks should go out to a number of people without whom the PhD study and this book would not have been possible. A special thank you to my PhD supervisor, Dr. Prakash A. Shah, for his comments, recommendations, support and lively discussions throughout the PhD studies.

Thank you to everyone at Routledge, who have given me help and support both during the proposal stage and since then. I also thank the anonymous reviewers for their constructive comments and suggestions on the book proposal.

Thank you to my family who have been very patient, understanding and supportive during the time it took me to complete the thesis and the book. Thank you to my husband, Chris, for his proof reading, editing, formatting, trouble shooting, encouragement and support, but most of all for believing in me. Thank you also to my sons, Mark and Ben, for their support, help in solving computer problems, occasional meals and endless cups of tea.

Thank you to my colleagues at Middlesex University for their encouragement and support and for creating a friendly environment.

And, last but not least, thank you to my parents, with whom it all began. This book is dedicated to their memory.

Table of cases

European Court of Justice

European Court of Human Rights

UK Courts

Introduction

In 2000, the EU adopted a Directive against discrimination on the grounds of racial or ethnic origin.[1] This Directive was one of the first legislative measures taken by the EU in the fight against racism and racial discrimination. This fight had been part of the discussions within the EU since the mid 1980s, but no legislative action was taken until the Treaty of Amsterdam of 1997 established the Community competence to do so by inserting Article 13 into the EC Treaty. However, once it was given the competence, the EU adopted the Race Directive in record time.

This book aims to identify whether the Race Directive improves the protection against discrimination on the grounds of racial or ethnic origin for people within the EU by an in-depth analysis and evaluation of the Directive. It starts from the assumption that anti discrimination legislation needs to be studied within the wider conceptual, historical and societal context. For a proper understanding of the Race Directive, it is important to study it in the contexts of the history of the fight against racism and racial discrimination in the EU; of the anti discrimination provisions and equality clauses in international human rights instruments; of theories about race and racism; and of concepts of equality. All these contexts are important because they have been influential on the development of the provisions of the Directive. These contexts are also all interrelated and can be seen as mutually influencing each other. They help explain why the Directive was adopted, why it covers particular grounds and areas and, ultimately, why and where its effectiveness is limited. Therefore, these contexts provide both a framework and a set of standards for the examination of the Race Directive and its effectiveness in protecting all people within the EU against racial and ethnic origin discrimination.

The literature on the Race Directive suggests, on the one hand, that overall the Directive is considered to be a very positive development in the fight against racial and ethnic origin discrimination within the EU and its Member States.

1 Council Directive 2000/43/EC. This Directive will be referred to as the Race Directive throughout this book.

On the other hand, many writers are also highly critical of a number of its provisions because they are falling short of providing comprehensive protection for all. However, this literature has often looked at one or more separate issues or provisions of the Race Directive in isolation, without giving enough detailed attention to the historical, social and political backgrounds which have made the Directive into what it is today. This book, on the other hand, analyzes and critiques the Directive using the contexts mentioned to explain its strengths and weaknesses.

Racism and racial discrimination are by no means recent problems but, at the international level, the fight against these came to the fore after World War II. In the war, theories about the existence of different races and the superiority of some over others had led to genocide and persecution. The feeling was that states should work together to avoid a repetition of the war. To further this aim, the United Nations was formed in 1945 and the Council of Europe in 1949. Fundamental human rights were seen as vitally important to achieve greater unity between nations and, therefore, the United Nations agreed the Universal Declaration of Human Rights (UDHR) in 1948 and the Council of Europe adopted the European Convention on Human Rights and Fundamental Freedoms (ECHR) in 1950. Both include a prohibition of discrimination in the enjoyment of the rights protected in the instrument on a large number of grounds, including race, colour, religion and national origin. Thus, after World War II, the fight against racism and racial discrimination developed at the international and the wider European level, both of which affected the European states (Banton 1996 and 2002a; van Boven 2001: 127–9; Boyle and Baldaccini 2001; Niessen and Chopin 2004: *vii–xi*).

Many of these European states already had a plural society made up of people of different descent, ancestry or culture, even before the large-scale immigration that took place after World War II. Some of these states were colonial powers and had people of their former colonies, often with citizenship rights, living within their territory. Others had taken in people fleeing persecution on the grounds of their religion, race or ethnic origin and economic migrants who came to work in the industries in these countries and then settled there. Most European States, therefore, have had a very mixed, plural society for a long time (MacEwen 1995: 1–8 and 176–9; Spencer 1995: 137–40; Duncan 1997b: 183–5; Martiniello 2004). However, the numbers of people from other states have risen sharply since 1945. All countries were building up their economies again after the war and many new industries were established. For these, large numbers of workers were needed and many countries could not fill this need from the people already living within their borders, so most looked further afield and brought in people from elsewhere. The present situation in most EU countries is that these people who came to work there and who, originally, may have had no intention to stay, did in the end settle and brought their families to the new country as well (MacEwen 1995: 3–6; Duncan 1997b; Alibhai-Brown 2000: 178–95; Bell 2002a: 55–9;

Niessen and Chopin 2004: *vii–viii*). Once the economic situation deteriorated, their presence started to lead to resentment in the people who were already in the country as they saw these new settlers as taking their jobs, housing, benefits, etc. All this had an effect on racial and ethnic relations because the newcomers were often of a different race, ethnic origin and/or religion, and hatred and distrust of these people took on the form of discrimination on these grounds and of racism. Many states looked to control the situation through their immigration and asylum policies. Alongside these policies, anti race discrimination laws were often developed as well. The latter were enacted to lighten or soften the impact of harsh immigration and asylum rules and to show that something was being done about racism and racial discrimination. States wanted to restrict immigration, but, on the other hand, they did not want to be seen to be racist, either at home or on the international scene (King 1995; MacEwen 1995: 67–70; Gearty 1999; Hervey 1999; Dummett 2000).

The September 11th, 2001 attacks on New York and the Madrid, London and Bali bombings have escalated the antagonism towards people perceived to be of certain races and religions who are linked to terrorism. Almost all European States are now considering tightening up their entry requirements for immigrants and asylum seekers and their conditions for acquiring citizenship, or have already done so.

The Member States joining the EU in 2004 and in 2007 have brought their own problems in this area. They might not all have as many economic migrants as the old Member States, but many of the Eastern European states have national minority populations and a considerable number of people of Roma origin, both of which have been discriminated against for many years and on a large scale.

Because all the EU Member States have faced similar problems, cooperation and policy coordination in immigration appeared on the EU Agenda in the early 1990s, and this was one of the factors which led to the development of measures against racism and discrimination. As Bell mentions, 'the restrictive trend of EU immigration policy acted as a catalyst for EU policy to combat racism'. Civil society was galvanized into transnational action for anti racism measures at EU level, 'so as to ameliorate the effects of immigration policies' (Bell 2002a: 67). There was pressure 'to improve the image of EU immigration policies' (Ibid: 69).

The above provides the backdrop for the analysis of the Race Directive in this book. In Chapter 1, the Directive is placed within its historical context by looking at the developments that led up to its adoption. We examine how the fight against racism and racial discrimination entered the discussions at EU level, and who played a role in bringing about the insertion of Article 13 EC by the Treaty of Amsterdam and the speedy adoption of the Directive following this. We discuss why the Directive was adopted so quickly and what happened in relation to implementation. New developments within the EU since the Directive's adoption are also examined.

We explore the international context of the Race Directive in Chapter 2. A number of international measures, most of which are signed and ratified by all EU Member States, contain equality guarantees and anti discrimination clauses. These instruments set minimum standards of human rights at international level, and these minimum standards are recognized by the EU as the EU Treaties and other legislative measures refer to these international human rights instruments. Moreover, the European Institutions have, from the very first discussions on the fight against racism, placed the right to equality and the right not to be discriminated against firmly within a wider human rights context. This right is also recognized by the European Court of Justice (ECJ) as a fundamental principle of Community law. The Race Directive also places itself within this wider human rights context by referring to a number of international instruments in Recital 3 of its Preamble. An overview of equality and/or anti discrimination clauses in the main global instruments is followed by a more extensive discussion of the International Convention on the Elimination of all Forms of Racial Discrimination (ICERD) and two instruments of the Council of Europe: Article 14 of the ECHR and Protocol 12 to the ECHR.

In our analysis of the Race Directive, a number of concepts are used – race, racism, (racial) discrimination, ethnic (origin) and ethnicity, xenophobia and equality – and it is important to make clear at the start what is to be understood by these concepts. In Chapter 3, we examine these key concepts, except for the concept of equality, which warrants a chapter of its own and will thus be discussed in Chapter 5. We point out possible pitfalls that should be avoided. All these concepts can be, and have been, defined in very different ways, and it is, therefore, easy to get confused about what exactly is meant by these terms. Thinking about these terms has also changed over time and thus their development in history needs to be examined to get an idea of their current meaning. The latter is especially true of the terms race and racism. Furthermore, the terms racism and (racial) discrimination have, over time, acquired a negative connotation and are linked to a moral judgment that they are 'bad'.

In Chapter 4, we examine the way the Race Directive has dealt with the concepts of race, racism and racial discrimination discussed in Chapter 3. The Directive itself does not define many of the key terms and, therefore, there are a number of questions as to how these will be interpreted. We examine the possible problems this may cause and in what ways this weakens the Directive and we suggest examples of definitions or interpretations that the Member States and the ECJ could follow. The reason for the omission of these definitions is discussed, as is the question whether the Directive should cover more than racial or ethnic origin. The history of the fight against racism and racial discrimination within the EU and the developments that led up to the adoption of the Directive will be referred to where this is useful to explain the provisions of the Race Directive.

There is also confusion about the meaning of the concept of equality, which appears to be used to indicate any of the following four notions: formal equality or equality of treatment; equality of opportunity and equality of results, which both can be seen as substantive as opposed to formal concepts of equality; and, pluralism. Equality is a key concept in any study of discrimination because the right not to be discriminated against is a human right based on the equality of all humans. In Chapter 5, we examine the four types of equality as they can all be the objective of anti discrimination legislation. The aim(s) pursued will likely influence not only the measures laid down, but also the enforcement procedures and remedies made available. In other words, different aims call for different provisions, remedies and enforcement strategies and, therefore, it is important to know which concept of equality the legislation is aiming for. Legislation aiming at formal equality prohibits unequal treatment of people in the same or similar situations. Legislation aiming at equality of opportunity tries to equalize the starting point for everyone, so everyone can compete on an equal footing. Laws aiming at equality of results attempt to achieve a fairer distribution of goods, resources and opportunities in society and equal participation of all. And, legislation with a pluralist approach to equality as objective aims to create a society that welcomes and celebrates diversity.

Chapter 6 is devoted to a detailed analysis of the Race Directive in relation to the concepts of equality discussed in Chapter 5. We discuss which of these concepts can be detected in the Directive and whether the EU legislation against racial or ethnic origin discrimination goes beyond a formal concept of equality to promote equality of opportunity, equality of results and/or pluralism. We also discuss other measures and developments within the EU since the Directive was adopted and which concept of equality these measures can be seen to be aiming at. There appears to be a shift in the language at EU level from formal equality towards more substantive concepts and we discuss this shift and the likelihood of legislative or other changes in EU measures and policies in the near future.

Chapter 7 is divided up into three parts. The first part contains conclusions from the previous chapters, including the gaps detected in the protection provided against racial or ethnic origin discrimination by the Directive. In the second part, we discuss what the results of the analysis have revealed about the Race Directive and apply these results to answer the question whether it provides increased protection against racial or ethnic origin discrimination for people within the EU. From the preceding analysis it will be clear that the Race Directive should not be seen in a vacuum, but should be placed within the many different contexts which have all played a role in its development and its drafting process and which will, no doubt, play a further role in its interpretation and in the future of anti race discrimination measures in the EU.

The concluding part of Chapter 7 will suggest a number of changes which can be made to the Race Directive to make it a more effective tool to fight racism and racial and ethnic origin discrimination in the EU and discuss the case law of the ECJ on the Race Directive and the Framework Directive,[2] the Directive that was proposed at the same time as the Race Directive and adopted just a few months after that Directive. It prohibits discrimination on the grounds of religion or belief, disability, age and sexual orientation. Because these two Directives contain many definitions which are the same or very similar, the interpretations given by the ECJ are important for both Directives.

2 Council Directive 2000/78/EC. Throughout this book, this Directive will be referred to as the Framework Directive.

1 The EU and the fight against racial discrimination

1.1 Introduction

For a proper analysis of the Race Directive, the history of the fight against racism and racial discrimination within the EU and the developments which led up to its adoption are important. In this Chapter, the Directive is placed within its historical context by reviewing how and when the problem of racism and racial discrimination entered the discussions at EU level; and, identifying who played a role in bringing about the insertion of Article 13 EC by the Treaty of Amsterdam and the speedy adoption of the Race Directive once this Article came into force. Since the mid-1980s, the problems of racism and racial discrimination have been debated within the Union and repeated calls for legislative action were made. However, legal measures at Union level were not taken until June 2000, when the Race Directive was adopted. Despite a number of suggestions and proposals for a directive or for treaty amendment made over the years, it was said that the Union did not have the competence to adopt legislative measures. This competence was given by the Treaty of Amsterdam, which came into force on 1 May 1999 and introduced Article 13 into the EC Treaty.

Once the competence was established, the Commission acted quickly and issued, in November 1999, three proposals based on Article 13: COM (1999) 565, proposing a general framework directive for equal treatment in employment and occupation; COM (1999) 566, proposing a directive on equal treatment irrespective of racial or ethnic origin; and COM (1999) 567, proposing a Community action programme to combat discrimination. In June 2000, the Race Directive was adopted, followed in November 2000 by the Framework Directive and the Action Programme.[1]

In this Chapter we look at the history of anti race discrimination measures at the EU level because this will help explain why the Race Directive is formulated as it is, why it was adopted in the first place and why it was adopted so quickly. We start with a discussion of the developments that led to the adoption of Article 13 EC and the Directives based on that Article.

1 Council Decision 2000a. Hereafter referred to as the Action Programme.

We also study Article 13 and the criticism levelled against it, the state of play as regards implementation and further action taken by the EU and the announcement of new developments in this field.

1.2 History of the fight against racial discrimination in the EU

1.2.1 Up to the early 1990s

The problems of racism and racial discrimination have been discussed within the EU since the mid-1980s. The European Parliament has been particularly active in this field. In 1985, it adopted the first Report of the Committee of Inquiry on the Rise of Fascism and Racism in Europe, which recommended, among other things, that 'an effort must be made to define more broadly Community powers and responsibilities in the area of race relations' in a number of ways, and 'if necessary, by revision of the Treaties' (European Parliament 1985: 95, 6.1(j)). The following year, after two Resolutions of the Parliament (Resolutions 1986) calling for a Declaration, the Community institutions adopted a Joint Declaration (Joint Declaration 1986). The institutions recognized the growth of xenophobia in the Community; vigorously condemned intolerance and hostility on the grounds of racial, religious, cultural, social or national differences; and affirmed their resolve to protect individuality and dignity and to reject segregation. This Declaration, therefore, did not contain any proposals for action and merely stated a resolve, but it is important because it is the first coordinated joint statement by the Council, the Commission and the Parliament against racism and xenophobia.

The Parliament adopted two more measures (Resolutions 1987 and 1988) before the Commission brought out COM (1988) 318, a Proposal for a Council Resolution in which it considered that the introduction of an education and information programme was urgently required. Both the Economic and Social Committee (Opinion 1989) and the Parliament (European Parliament Resolution 1989) stated that this proposal did not go far enough and that there was a need for some form of legislation. The following year, the Community brought out a Community Charter of Fundamental Social Rights (COM (1989) 471), which stressed the importance of combating every form of discrimination, including discrimination on grounds of sex, colour, race, opinions and beliefs. The Council adopted a Resolution in 1990, but this Resolution was even weaker than the 1988 Proposal and again did not really contain any proposals for action. One interesting point was that it stressed 'the importance of all appropriate forms of cooperation between the Community and the Council of Europe' (Council Resolution 1990: point 5).[2]

2 The Council of Europe is an international organization focusing on human rights within Europe which adopted the ECHR. The Council and the ECHR are discussed in more detail in Chapter 2.

In that same year, the Parliament adopted the Report of the Committee of Inquiry on Racism and Xenophobia. One of its recommendations was for 'a draft directive, to be prepared by 31 March 1991, to provide a Community framework of legislation against any discrimination connected with belonging or not belonging to an ethnic group, nation, region, race or religion, covering all Community residents' (European Parliament 1990a: Recommendation 31). This shows that the Committee of Inquiry considered that the Community had the competence to draft such a directive.

In 1990, the Parliament again brought out a number of resolutions (European Parliament Resolutions 1990b,c and d). The last one of these contained draft amendments which would add a Declaration of Fundamental Rights to the EC Treaty. Article 3, headed 'Equality before the law', stated that:

> In the field of application of Community law, everyone shall be equal before the law.
>
> Any discrimination on grounds such as race, colour, sex, language, religion, political or other opinions, national or social origin, association with a national minority, property, birth or other status, shall be prohibited.

This Article thus established everyone's right to equality before the law and to protection against discrimination. The grounds mentioned are the same as those mentioned in Article 14 ECHR, which also contains a prohibition of discrimination. Article 8e, entitled 'Racism and xenophobia', also contained an amendment:

> The Community and its Member States, acting in those areas to which their respective authorities apply, shall take the necessary measures to avert, and where necessary to prohibit, all forms of intolerance, hostility or violence against persons or groups of persons inspired by racial, religious, cultural, linguistic, social or national differences, and to prevent any form of segregation against such persons or groups of persons.

So, as early as 1990, the Parliament suggested the incorporation of a Declaration of Fundamental Rights into the EC Treaty and to add an article to confer competence on the Community to take measures to avert or prohibit racism and intolerance. In these early years, there were a number of suggestions for legislative action against discrimination and for Treaty amendment, but there did not appear to be any great desire within the Council to act on these. Bell (2002a: 62–3), describing the evolution of EU law and policy in the field of racial discrimination, notes that, although racism entered into the debates in the mid-1980s, no significant progress was made because of the opposition in the Council. He writes:

> Symbolic statements of commitment were not underpinned by a genuine desire to develop common measures against race discrimination.

> The Council relied on the absence of any specific EC Treaty provision on racism to insist that this was not within the Community's legal competence. In this way, the question of competence became a kind of filter mechanism, a device to keep off the agenda issues the Council did not wish to address.

As Bell mentions, if the Member States really had wanted to take action they could have amended the Treaty to give the Community legal competence in this field, but they did not do so in either the Single European Act in 1986 or the Treaty on European Union (TEU) in 1992. MacEwen (1995: 75) notes that there was 'a lack of resolve, particularly by the Council of Ministers, to secure the promotion of Community legislation against racial discrimination'. Therefore, the Member States appear to have been reluctant to take anti race discrimination measures at EU level, despite the opinion often expressed by the European Parliament and by many non-governmental organizations (NGOs) that this was necessary. The statements by the Council about its commitment to fighting racism and xenophobia can be said to be hollow statements, because they were not followed up by concrete action. MacEwen suggests as a reason for this reluctance that a Community directive could be argued to be superfluous, because of extensive membership of the ICERD and recognition of the ECHR by Member States and Community institutions or because of a growing body of legislation at national level. Member States might also have considered that action against racial discrimination was a matter for national legislation. However, some other, more hidden, reasons might also have played a role. Member States might have been reluctant to acknowledge that the problem of racism and racial discrimination existed within their borders and might have considered it a problem affecting other states. The denial could have been exacerbated by the fact that, in some Member States, the subjects of race and racism and the use of these terms with their negative connotations was and is a sensitive issue. Taking action against racism and racial discrimination might also have been considered not politically beneficial, as it was not an issue that would win many votes.

1.2.2 From early 1990s until the 1997 Treaty of Amsterdam

The situation started to change in the early 1990s, and support for community action grew in many different quarters, including in the European Council. Bell (2002a: 63–9) mentions three principal reasons for this: first, the development of cross-border racism and the realization that this might affect the functioning of the internal market; second, the spill-over effects from EU immigration and asylum policies; and, third, the establishment of an effective European lobby against racism. The EU immigration and asylum policies 'galvanised national and European civil society into transnational action for anti-racism measures at the EU level, so as to ameliorate the effects of the immigration policies' (Ibid: 67). In 1991, a number of these groups formed the 'Starting Line Group', an informal network of NGOs, semi-official organizations, trade unions, churches, independent experts and academics in the EC. The group's aim was to promote legal measures to combat racism and xenophobia in the EC.

During 1991 and 1992, the European Parliament affirmed its commitment to combating racism and xenophobia in five Resolutions (1991 and 1992a,b,c and d) and the Council mentioned the importance of the fight against racism and xenophobia at the Maastricht Summit in 1991, the Edinburgh Summit in 1992 and the Copenhagen Summit in 1993.[3]

In 1993, the Starting Line Group launched the Starting Line, a proposal for a draft Council directive concerning the elimination of racial discrimination, which covered race, colour, descent, nationality, national and ethnic origin (Dummett 1994). It considered Community action against racism necessary, first, because the Community's own acknowledged respect for human rights and the general principles of law required action on the obvious breaches of human rights which racism and xenophobia were causing. Second, in the single market, unjust discrimination would interfere with the free movement of persons and services because it would prevent people who suffer discrimination from obtaining the jobs, housing or services they seek. Third, variations between national levels of protection would discourage persons likely to suffer discrimination from moving to those states where protection is small or non-existent. And, fourth, the proper functioning of the single market required prompt action: a Community directive would force Member States to produce their own legislation within a certain time limit. It would lay down a common pattern, providing some guarantee of a legal remedy in any part of the EC.

The group based the Community competence to legislate in this field on Article 235 EC (now 308 EC). The proposal was offered as a basis for discussion and lobbying, but the ultimate aim remained to obtain a directive. The proposal recognized that it might be necessary to aim first at Treaty amendment to ensure that the Community had the competence to produce such legislation. The European Parliament also called again for a directive (Resolution 1993).

At the 1994 Corfu Summit,[4] the European Council, acting on a Franco-German initiative, decided to set up a Consultative Commission on Racism and Xenophobia to make 'recommendations ... on co-operation between governments and the various social bodies in favour of encouraging tolerance, understanding and harmony with foreigners' (Ibid: III, 1).[5] It also agreed to develop a global strategy at Union level to combat acts of racist and

3 See EC Bulletins, 12–1991, 12–1992 and 6–1993.

4 For the conclusions see: www.europarl.eu.int/summits/cor1_ www.europarl.eu.int/summits/cor1_en.htm#justice (accessed 1 April 2009)

5 This Commission was chaired by Jean Kahn and it is therefore often referred to as the Kahn Commission.

xenophobic violence. At the Essen summit[6] in the same year, the Council asked the Commission 'to step up its discussions in particular in the various areas of education and training, information and the media, and in the areas of police and justice'. In its White Paper on Social Policy, the Commission announced its intention to 'press for specific powers to combat racial discrimination to be included in the Treaty' (COM (1994): 333).

Also in 1994, the Starting Line Group issued a proposal for amending the European Community Treaty, called 'The Starting Point' (Starting Line Group 1997). Their aim was to remedy what they saw as an obvious defect in the original Treaty of Rome, namely that it did not contain anything on racism or xenophobia. The group proposed to add Article 3(u) to the present Article 3 EC (... 'the activities of the Community shall include ...'):

> the elimination of discrimination against persons or groups of persons, whether citizens of the European Union or not, on the grounds of race, colour, religion, or national, social or ethnic origin, and the promotion of harmonious relations between such persons or groups of persons.

The EU would make an unequivocal statement of principle by adding the elimination of discrimination to the guiding aims of the Union, which the group saw as an urgent requirement. As mentioned, the 'Starting Line', the group's proposal for a directive, was based on the presumption that the Community had the competence to issue a directive under Article 235 EC (now 308 EC). Because it was not clear if this competence actually existed, the group also proposed to add an article to the Treaty to allow the Council to issue directives or regulations in this field. At the end of that year another resolution of the Parliament (Resolution 1994) again urged the Commission to draw up a directive.

In 1995, the final Report of the Kahn Commission (European Council 1995) was adopted. The Commission proposed the establishment of a European Observatory on racism and xenophobia (Ibid: 16–22). As regards police and justice, the Commission recommended that fundamental human rights be accorded to all individuals, regardless of their race, religion, colour, or ethnic or national background or residential status; and that the freedom of movement provisions of the treaty should be extended to those members of minorities who had been legally resident within a EU Member State for five years or more. The Commission stated that consideration should be given to an extension of citizenship of the EU to such persons. It further recommended that a clear prohibition of incitement to racial hatred, holocaust denial and trivialization of crimes against humanity should be included

6 For the conclusions of this summit see: www.europarl.eu.int/summits/ess1_en.htm#jha (accessed 1 April 2009).

explicitly in the criminal law of the Member States; and that the criminal law should provide for penalty enhancement for racially motivated crimes (Ibid: 36–7 and 46–56).

As regards employment, the principle should be that 'all individuals regardless of their colour, race, nationality, ethnic or national origins or religion, should have the right of equal access to employment, equal pay and fair treatment from an employer'. The Commission proposed that Member States should introduce proposals to make racial discrimination in employment unlawful and that racial discrimination should include direct and indirect discrimination and victimization; that, once a *prima facie* case of discrimination has been established, the burden of proof should be reversed; that tribunals should be able to order compensation, certain courses of action and reinstatement; and, that only limited exceptions for genuine qualifications for a job would be allowed (Ibid: 39–45).

The Commission concluded that 'amendment of the Treaty to provide explicitly for Community competence must be regarded as an essential element in any serious European strategy aimed at combating racism and xenophobia'. The Commission saw this as 'the clearest expression of the European Union's real intention of combating, not merely protesting against, the rising tide of racism and xenophobia' (Ibid: 57). The Commission considered that the question of amendment of the Treaty should be formally placed on the agenda of the Intergovernmental Conference in 1996 and that:

> The amendment should be directed towards the elimination of all forms of discrimination against persons or groups of persons, whether citizens of the EU or not, on grounds of race, skin colour, birth, religion, language, or national, social or ethnic origin. This should be without prejudice to measures adopted for the purpose of redressing disadvantages or removing existing inequalities affecting such persons and groups. The amendment should impose an obligation on Member States to ensure the elimination of such discrimination.
>
> (Ibid: 59–60)

The Kahn Report is important because it was a report from a body appointed by the European Council and consisting of representatives of the Member States themselves. It shows clearly that the mood within the EU had changed in favour of taking legislative measures against racism and racial discrimination at EU level. The Report was followed by two European Parliament Resolutions, calling on the Commission to introduce a proposal for an anti discrimination directive (Resolutions 1995a and b).

At the end of 1995, the Commission issued a communication on racism, xenophobia and anti-Semitism, together with a proposal to designate 1997 as European Year against Racism (COM (1995) 653). In the communication, the Commission considered that non-discriminatory application of Community law could be guaranteed, either by incorporating in the Treaty a general non-discrimination clause which would apply to all Community legislation, or by adopting Community legislation against discrimination.

The Intergovernmental Conference was inaugurated at the European Council in Turin of 29 March 1996 and lasted until 17 June 1997. It was concluded with the Council meeting in Amsterdam and led to the Treaty of Amsterdam.

In July 1996, the Council adopted a Joint Action (96/433/JHA) concerning action on co-operation in criminal matters, aiming to ensure effective judicial cooperation to avoid that people who perpetrate racist or xenophobic offences can escape prosecution by travelling from one Member State to another. This plan, which aimed at 'action to combat racism and xenophobia', as it title states, includes religious discrimination and acts of religious hatred in this fight against racism and xenophobia. This is clear from the following. The plan determines that cooperation should take place in respect of offences based on a number of types of behaviour, among which are:

> (a) public incitement to discrimination, violence or racial hatred, in respect of a group of persons or a member of such a group defined by reference to colour, race, religion or national or ethnic origin; and ...
>
> (e) participation in activities of groups, organizations or associations, which involve discrimination, violence or racial, ethnic or religious hatred.

In the same period, the Council decided that 1997 would be the European Year against Racism (Resolution 1996). Also, the Kahn Commission completed its feasibility report on a European Monitoring Centre on Racism and Xenophobia and expressed a strong preference for a very active role for such a centre, including the right to make policy recommendations for both the EU and the Member States. The Council, in its meeting in Florence in June 1996, asked the Commission to continue its work until the centre was established.

The Irish Government, holder of the Council Presidency in the second half of 1996, prepared an outline for a draft revision of the Treaties as the basis for negotiations at the Dublin Summit of December 1996. It proposed a new Article 6a in the EC Treaty:

> Within the scope of application of this Treaty and without prejudice to any special provisions contained therein, the Council, acting unanimously on a proposal from the Commission and after consulting the European Parliament, may take appropriate action to prohibit discrimination based on sex, racial, ethnic or social origin, religious belief, disability, age or sexual orientation.
>
> (CONF/2500/96)

This would thus establish the competence of the Community to enact legislation against discrimination on the grounds mentioned.

The year 1997 was designated European Year against Racism. In a Resolution in 1997, the European Parliament called 'once more for binding legal instruments to combat racism and xenophobia at European level' and stated that:

> ... the European Union should be given responsibility for the development of measures against racism and xenophobia, so that the Commission is given the right to initiate measures, the Council decides by majority voting and the European Parliament acquires powers of co-decision, in order that ... an anti-discrimination Directive can be drawn up as soon as possible.
>
> (European Parliament 1997: para 14)

The Parliament also clearly expressed its opposition to the requirement of unanimity in the Council (para 19).

At the Opening Conference of the European Year against Racism, the Presidents of the Council, the Parliament and the Commission made a declaration of intent called 'Europe against Racism' (Report from the Opening Conference 1997). Many of the speakers at the opening conference called upon the Intergovernmental Conference, which was preparing the Treaty of Amsterdam, to strengthen legal instruments to combat racism and xenophobia by including a strong anti discrimination clause in the treaty.

At the end of 1996, the Commission had proposed the establishment of a European Monitoring Centre on Racism and Xenophobia (COM (1996) 615). This Centre was established by a Council Regulation in June 1997 (Council Regulation 1035/97/EC). The prime objective of the Centre, according to Article 2, was to provide the Community and the Member States with objective, reliable and comparable data at European level on the phenomena of racism, xenophobia and anti-Semitism. Article 2 also required the Centre to study the extent and development of these phenomena, analyze their causes and effects and examine examples of good practice in dealing with them. Article 7(3) prescribed that the Centre shall enter into an agreement with the Council of Europe 'for the purpose of establishing close cooperation between the latter and the Centre' (Agreement 1999).

1.2.3 From the 1997 Treaty of Amsterdam until the Article 13 proposals

The major event in June 1997 for our subject was the European Council meeting in Amsterdam, leading to the Treaty of Amsterdam. However, the Treaty did not come into force until 1 May 1999. The Treaty made a number of changes in the EC Treaty and the TEU. The Treaty added 'preventing and combating racism and xenophobia' to Article 29 TEU, as one of the means by which the Union shall provide citizens with a high level of safety within an area of freedom, security and justice. It also added a mention of equality between men and women to Articles 2 and 3 EC. But the most important change for our purpose was the addition of Article 13 EC. This Article reads:

> Without prejudice to the other provisions of this Treaty and within the limits of the powers conferred by it upon the Community, the Council, acting unanimously on a proposal from the Commission and after consulting the European Parliament, may take appropriate action to combat discrimination based on sex, racial or ethnic origin, religion or belief, disability, age or sexual orientation.

Therefore, this established the competence of the Community to take measures against discrimination. There are, however, a number of points to be made about this article. The Irish proposal of 1996 followed the opening part of Article 12 EC, which prohibits discrimination on the ground of nationality: 'within the scope of application of this Treaty, and without prejudice to any special provisions contained therein'. This is changed in the final version of Article 13 into 'without prejudice to the other provisions of this Treaty and within the limits of powers conferred upon the Community'. The meaning of both parts of this opening sentence of Article 13 has been subject to considerable discussion in the literature (Allen 1999: point 4; Chopin 1999: 120–1; Flynn 1999: 1132–4; Waddington 1999: 136–7; Bell 2000: 88–95; Guild 2000b: 66-9; Bryan 2002: 226–7). The first part, 'without prejudice to the other provisions of this Treaty', appears to indicate that Article 13 'cannot be applied in a way that would limit the scope of pre-existing clauses of the Treaty' (Chopin 1999: 121) or, in Bell's words, that 'nothing within Article 13 should be taken as constraining the scope or effects of any other provision of the Treaty. In other words, Article 13 shall not act to the detriment of other Treaty articles' (Bell 2000: 87). Guild (2000b: 67) writes that the second part 'within the limits of powers conferred by it' is ambiguous. She discerns two possible legal positions:

> Article 13 can only be used to give specificity to the duty not to discriminate in areas which are already regulated by Community law or so closely attached to such areas as to make it necessary to regulate them; or
>
> Article 13 provides a new and autonomous power for Community action in the field of non-discrimination but that, in exercising that power, the Community must act in accordance with the procedural powers at its disposal.

Guild does not indicate which of these positions she supports. Bell concludes, based on an examination of other EC Treaty provisions, of case law and of non-English Treaty versions, that 'powers' in Article 13 EC means 'competences', which implies that Article 13 may only be relied upon to prohibit discrimination within those areas for which the Community already has competence (Bell 2000: 94–5). This, according to Waddington (1999: 137), suggests that Article 13 can only provide a legal basis for measures to combat discrimination in those areas. Bell and Waddington thus both suggest that the first legal position distinguished by Guild is the correct interpretation of Article 13. This appears to be the view of most writers. As Bryan (2002: 227) writes, 'the view taken by leading commentators is that the power … is subject to the limits of the existing Community competencies'. The Starting Line Group is of a different opinion, as are Chopin and Niessen (Chopin 1999: 121; Chopin and Niessen 1998: 21–2). Chopin and Niessen point to the use of the word 'powers' in Article 308 EC and argue that 'powers' in Article 13 should be explained in the same way; both refer to the manner of taking decisions. Article 13 does not confer a power to widen the scope of the Treaty, but it provides the necessary powers, where these are lacking, for measures to be taken. Authors distinguish the word 'powers' from the word 'scope' in Article 12. The opening sentence of Article 12, 'within the scope of application of this Treaty' means that Article 12 cannot be extended beyond the existing boundaries of Community law. They write:

> By contrast, no such limitation applies to the new Article 13. The intention of the drafters of Article 13 is clearly to provide a wider protection against discrimination than is provided on the basis of nationality in Article 12. For this reason, Article 13 is not limited to the scope of the Treaty.

Chopin and Niessen thus opt for the second legal position distinguished above. This uncertainty about the meaning of Article 13 EC has, however, not stopped the EU from adopting measures based on this Article.

Apart from the ambiguity in its opening sentence, Article 13 has been criticized for a number of other reasons (Duncan 1997a; Chopin and Niessen 1998; Allen 1999; Chopin 1999; Flynn 1999; Hervey 1999; Waddington 1999; Bell 2000: Guild 2000b; O'Hare 2001; Bell 2002a: 121–44; Brown 2002; Bryan 2002; McInerney 2003; Allen 2007: 38–72). First, many writers point to the fact that Article 13 does not establish a general principle of equality or non-discrimination and lacks direct effect, which means that individuals cannot invoke this article in their national courts. In contrast, Article 12 EC is held to have direct effect. Guild mentions that the Conference Secretariat proposed to change the opening words of the Article from those initially proposed by the Irish Presidency, partly to avoid giving Article 13 EC direct effect (Guild 2000b: 66).

Second, Article 13 requires unanimity in the Council, which means that any one Member State can block any action being taken. Furthermore, the Article determines that the Council 'may take appropriate action' and it therefore permits the Council to take action, but it does not contain any obligation to do so, nor does it contain a time limit within which such action would have to be taken.

Third, the European Parliament is given a very limited role: it needs to be consulted, but there is no obligation on the Council to accept any of its suggestions or recommendations for amendments. This is especially unfortunate as the European Parliament has been, and is, the most active of the Community institutions in calling for action against racism and discrimination.

The fourth point of criticism is that Article 13 contains a closed list of grounds for discrimination rather than an open-ended, non-exhaustive list like many international instruments. This reflects 'the current level of political consensus amongst the Member States' (O'Hare 2001: 142).

However, despite these criticisms, most authors agree that the addition of Article 13 to the EC Treaty, by allowing legislative measures to be taken, was a monumentally important step in the fight against racism and (racial) discrimination within the EU. Allen calls the adoption of Article 13 'a significant political fact. *It has created an expectation that action will be taken* [his italics]. Despite the need for unanimity it will surely be impossible for no action to be taken under this provision' (Allen 1999: point 7).

The Treaty of Amsterdam did not come into force until 1 May 1999. In the meantime, there were some other noteworthy developments in the EU. The first results of Eurobarometer Opinion Poll 47.1, on Racism and Xenophobia in Europe, were presented at the Closing Conference of the European Year against Racism in December 1997. This Europe-wide survey was commissioned as part of the European Year against Racism and was carried out in early 1997. The results showed 'a worrying level of racism and xenophobia in the Member States', with nearly one third of all people interviewed describing themselves as 'quite racist' or 'very racist', about one third seeing themselves as 'a little racist' and the remaining third considering themselves 'not at all racist'.

In its 1998 Resolution, the European Parliament welcomed the fact that the new Article 29 TEU 'expressly states for the first time that the fight against racism and xenophobia makes a vital contribution to creating an area of freedom, security and justice' (1998: para 1). The Parliament regretted that Article 13 did not enshrine a non-discrimination principle with immediate effect, but that it required implementing measures unanimously adopted by the Council (Ibid: para 4). It called on the Commission to propose 'appropriate action' as soon as the new article came into force (Ibid: para 5) because it believed that directives prohibiting discrimination 'could make a major contribution to curbing racism and xenophobia in the European Union'. Again, it is the Parliament that is pressing for action (Ibid: para 8).

On 28 February 1998, the Charter of European Parties for a Non-Racist Society was signed in Utrecht. In this Charter, the democratic political parties of Europe stated their conviction that 'free use of one's political rights can and must go hand in hand with firmly upholding the principle of non-discrimination'; and that representation of ethnic minority groups in the political process is 'an integral part of the democratic process'. The parties committed themselves to adhere to a number of principles of good practice mentioned in the Charter. Although most of the larger European Political Parties signed this Charter, it is not clear what, if any, effect this Charter has had in practice. Niessen (2001a: 83) looks at the results of a survey done amongst political parties at the end of 1999 and concludes that 'the Charter is not very well known, or does not play an important role in the life of the party'.

The Starting Line Group brought out the 'New Starting Line', a revised version of their 1993 draft directive, incorporating the changes which the Treaty of Amsterdam would bring (Chopin and Niessen 1998: 23–32). The Group opted to cover racial or ethnic origin and religion or belief in one directive because they had been mentioned together in a number of Declarations made at Community level and because they might arise from overlapping causes (Ibid: 19–20). This 'New Starting Line' would apply to 'any person, regardless of nationality, status or country of origin or residence' (Chopin 1999: 123).

The Commission launched an Action Plan (COM (1998) 183) 'for combating racism across the European Union in the period leading up to the new millennium'. The Commission proposed 'practical and procedural measures to prepare for future and more ambitious action to combat racism at European level'. The plan stressed the importance of partnership with everyone involved in the fight against racism and the need to promote the value of diversity and pluralism. It consisted of four strands: paving the way for legislative initiatives; mainstreaming the fight against racism in all relevant Community programmes and policies; developing and exchanging new models for combating racism; and, strengthening information and communication work. The Commission planned to publish a report on the progress made in the fight against racism at European level by the end of 1999.

Commissioner Flynn (Closing Address 1998) called the Treaty of Amsterdam 'a huge step in the fight against discrimination'. According to him, Article 13 made clear the Community's intention to act as well as establishing its competence to do so. Building an inclusive society, achieving equality and fighting discrimination were things the Union must do, not only because they were right, but also because they made economic sense. This makes clear that there were also economic reasons for action against discrimination at EU level. The Commissioner announced that, when the Treaty of Amsterdam came into force, he would propose 'an Article 13 anti-discrimination package' containing a framework directive that would deal on a general basis with all grounds of discrimination in employment; a directive dealing specifically with racial discrimination, which would go beyond the workplace; and an action programme. He also mentioned that there is 'undeniable political momentum' for a directive against racial discrimination that goes beyond the workplace.

The Commission's report on the results of the European Year against Racism (COM (1999) 268) stated that the Year had boosted the fight against racism. The report described a number of activities that had taken place and mentioned that the Year had contributed to a number of major political advances: first, the insertion of a general non-discrimination clause into the EC Treaty by the Treaty of Amsterdam; second, the creation of a European Monitoring Centre for Racism and Xenophobia; third, the creation of a European network of NGOs active in the fight against racism; and fourth, the launch of an Action Plan Against Racism, aiming to place the fight against racism at the heart of a number of European policies, in other words, aiming to mainstream racial equality. The Commission concluded that the European Year was a step towards greater collaboration in the fight against racism. The year succeeded in mobilizing people and organizations across Europe and created a favourable climate for political progress. It confirmed 'the role of the European Institutions in the fight against racism' and created a 'consensus on action in the longer term. It also contributed to building a Europe which is true to its values and guarantees equality and respect for all'.

1.2.4 Commission uses the competence given by Article 13 EC

The Treaty of Amsterdam came into force on 1 May 1999 and in November of that same year, after wide consultations, the Commission launched a Communication (COM (1999) 564) introducing three proposals based on Article 13 EC. These were intended to supplement and reinforce national legislative measures implementing the principle of equality (Ibid: 7). The Communication proposed a directive to combat discrimination in the labour market on all grounds referred to in Article 13, except sex, which had already been covered by other EC legislation; a directive to combat discrimination on grounds of racial and ethnic origin which went beyond the labour market; and an action programme to combat discrimination for the years 2001–2006. The latter was designed to complement and support the two legislative proposals, as a combination of legislative and practical action, each reinforcing the other, was considered the most effective way of combating discrimination. The Commission made it clear, therefore, that it considered legislative measures necessary, but that these needed to be underpinned by practical action. In the Commission's own words:

> Together these three proposals will constitute a comprehensive basis for action, providing a minimum level of legal rights not to be discriminated against, supported by practical action to promote the effective application of those rights on the ground.
>
> (Ibid: 8)

In a Press Release (IP/99/895), the Commissioner for Employment and Social Affairs, Anna Diamantopoulou, explained that the proposals aimed to establish a common level of protection against discrimination across the EU and to provide victims with a clear remedy against discrimination.

The proposal for the Race Directive (COM (1999) 566: Explanatory Memorandum: III) stated:

> The adoption of a Directive at Community level will constitute an unequivocal statement of public policy towards discrimination. It will lay down common protections against racial discrimination to be enjoyed by citizens all over the Union. … It will reinforce the fundamental values on which the Union is founded – liberty, democracy, the respect for human rights and fundamental freedoms and the rule of law – and contribute to the development of the Union as an area of freedom, security and justice. And it will help strengthen economic and social cohesion by ensuring that people in all Member States enjoy a basic level of protection against discrimination.

The Commission also pointed out that 'the Directive will provide a solid basis for the enlargement of the Union' and that 'to create a common Community of respect and tolerance for racial and ethnic diversity, it is essential to put in place a common European framework for the fight against racism'. The Commission explained that it had chosen a broad scope for the Race Directive because 'a comprehensive coverage is necessary to make a serious contribution to curbing racism and xenophobia in Europe' (Ibid: IV).

However, the choice of two separate Directives, one dealing with racial and ethnic origin and one dealing with the other grounds of Article 13 EC, has been criticized for creating a hierarchy of discrimination grounds,[7] because the EU protection against sex and racial or ethnic origin discrimination is stronger than the protection against discrimination on the other grounds. The omission of religion or belief as a discrimination ground in the Race Directive is seen as especially problematic[8] because religion is often closely related to racial and ethnic origin, so it can be difficult to distinguish between the two. Racial discrimination may be interwoven with discrimination on grounds of a person's adherence to a (minority) religion or ethnicity.

7 For more on this see: Waddington 1999: 142; Bell 2000: 80; Waddington 2000: 176–7; Fredman 2001b: 151–2; O'Hare 2001: 144 and 158; Waddington and Bell 2001; Bell 2002a: 32–3 and 52–3; Brown 2002: 222–3; Schiek 2002: 308–9; Bell and Waddington 2003: 349–69; Waddington 2003b: 47–9; Liegl *et al.* 2004: 9; Howard 2006; and Bell 2007: 178–201.

8 See, for example, Guild 2000a: 418; Bell 2001: 25; Fredman 2001b: 158–9; Niessen 2001b: 9; O'Hare 2001: 145; Bell 2002b: 12; Brown 2002: 204–5; Sierra 2002a: 16–7; McInerney 2003: 12; Liegl *et al.* 2004: 9; Vickers 2006: 34–5; Howard 2007a: 463–4; and Schiek *et al.* 2007: 60–1.

Returning to the proposals, the opinions of the Committee of the Regions (Opinion 2000), the Economic and Social Committee (Opinion 2000) and the European Parliament (Opinion 2000) were received and an amended proposal came out on 31 May 2000 (COM (2000) 328). The Race Directive itself was accepted by the Council on 29 June 2000 and came into force on 19 July 2000, the day of its publication in the Official Journal.[9] It should be kept in mind that the final text was the product of negotiations between the Member States (Tyson 2001).

So, after the initial reluctance to enact Community laws against racial discrimination, the Race Directive was adopted very quickly, just over a year after the Community competence was established, and within seven months of the proposal being published. This is, as Tyson (2001: 201) writes, 'a record for the adoption of a piece of Community law requiring substantial legislative changes at national level'. And Moraes (2000), writing about the new Directive the day after it was adopted, mentioned that 'even the most optimistic Euro-MPs have been surprised at how fast the European Union turned aspiration into reality'. It is suggested that the speedy adoption is linked to the strong political will present at that time. In its Communication accompanying the Proposals, the Commission explains that the proposal for the Race Directive has a scope that extends beyond the labour market, while the scope of the Framework Directive is limited to employment and occupation. This takes account of the 'strong political will which exists to take action to combat as many aspects as possible of racial discrimination' (COM (1999) 564: 8).

Why was the political will to act against racial discrimination so strong at that time? The results of the elections in Austria in February 2000 are mentioned as influential by a number of authors (Guild 2000a: 416; Goldston 2001: 127; Barnard 2001: 966–7; and Bell 2002a: 74). Goldston, for example, writes that the Race Directive was 'given renewed political impetus by the electoral developments in Austria … which prompted a number of EU member governments to offer tangible evidence of their commitment to combating racism'. And Bell explains that, in February 2000, Jorg Haider's Freedom Party, an extreme right-wing party, became part of the government of Austria. The other Member States protested against this and imposed bilateral diplomatic sanctions. This led the Portuguese Presidency to fast-track the Race Directive as a sign of the Union's commitment to combating racism. It also pressurized the individual Member States to be more flexible in their negotiating positions – 'with presumably no state wishing to be regarded as blocking new laws combating racism'. Bell (Ibid: 180) reports that evidence from his study of existing race and sexual orientation discrimination laws in the EU Member States shows a favourable environment for anti

9 The differences between the original proposal, the amended proposal and the final text will be discussed in the following Chapters where relevant.

discrimination law at that time, which also helps to explain the relative ease with which the Article 13 Directives were adopted. The Framework Directive and the Action Programme took slightly longer but they were both adopted in November 2000, a year after they had been proposed. Ellis (2002: 293–4) also mentions the rise to power of the Freedom Party in Austria. She adds that:

> there was a perception among the Member States that some of the aspiring entrant states in central and eastern Europe posed serious problems in relation to racial, ethnic and religious tolerance, especially as far as the Roma were concerned. The Commission and the Member States took the view that it was vital to ensure that the 'acquis communautaire' contained strong anti-discrimination legislation in good time before those states became members of the Union.

As we saw, the importance of the Race Directive in relation to the enlargement of the EU was also mentioned by the Commission in the Explanatory Memorandum. Another factor that might have played a role in the quick adoption, again because the Member States wanted to show their genuine commitment to the fight against racism and racial discrimination, is the United Nations World Conference against Racism, Racial Discrimination, Xenophobia and Related Intolerance (WCAR), which took place in Durban in August/September 2001. Preparations for this Conference were well under way when the Race Directive was negotiated, with regional Conferences taking place in 2000. In April 2000, the European Commission prepared its contribution to the regional European Conference (Contribution from the Commission Services 2000). It is interesting that the EU contributed to this Conference, organized by the Council of Europe, in its own capacity, which shows the links between the two and the influence of the Council of Europe in the EU. The European Regional Conference itself took place after the adoption of the Race Directive, in October 2000. It ended with a Political Declaration of the Member States of the Council of Europe (2000) in which they reaffirmed that Europe is a community of shared values, multicultural in its past, present and future; that all humans are born free and equal in dignity; that all persons are equal before the law and entitled to the equal protection of the law; and that racism and racial discrimination are serious violations of human rights and threaten democratic societies and their fundamental values. The Member States of the Council of Europe committed themselves to take further steps to prevent and eliminate racism, racial discrimination, xenophobia, anti-Semitism and related intolerance and to monitor and evaluate such action. The action should encompass legal, policy, educational and training measures and the legal measures should include adopting and implementing national legislation.

Whatever the reasons for the quick adoption, the Race Directive entered into force on 19 July 2000 and put a duty on Member States to implement its provisions by 19 July 2003. The Framework Directive entered into force on 2 December 2000, so the Member States had until 2 December 2003 to implement this.

1.2.5 *After adoption of the Race Directive*

For the sake of clarity, this part will be divided in two sub-parts: first, the further developments at EU level in relation the fight against racism and xenophobia will be discussed. A separate part will deal with the implementation of the Race Directive in the Member States.

1.2.5.1 *Developments at EU level*

Apart from the adoption of the Race and Framework Directives, another major development in the EU in 2000 was the official proclamation of the European Charter of Fundamental Rights at the Council in Nice in December (Charter 2000). This Charter contains a chapter on equality, which states that everyone is equal before the law and which provides a prohibition of discrimination. This is the first time that the general principle of equality before the law and non-discrimination is expressly laid down in EU legislation. Although the Charter was officially proclaimed, it was not included in the Treaty of Nice in December 2000. It became Part II of the Draft Constitution for Europe, adopted in 2004. This Constitution was, however, never ratified. It was replaced by the Reform Treaty, signed in Lisbon in December 2007, which will confer legally binding status on the Charter when it comes into force (Article 6(2) Consolidated Version TEU). It was envisaged that this Treaty of Lisbon would come into force before the next European Parliament elections in June 2009, but because it needs ratification by all Member States and it was rejected in a Referendum in Ireland in June 2008, the Treaty cannot come into force yet. However, at the Brussels summit in December 2008, Ireland agreed to hold a second ballot on the Reform Treaty next year (before November 2009), once the concerns of the Irish voters are addressed.[10] Therefore, the Charter has as yet no legal force.

The European Council in Nice also agreed the Treaty of Nice, which entered into force on 1 February 2003 and left paragraph 1 of Article 13 EC as it is, but added a second paragraph:

> By way of derogation from paragraph 1, when the Council adopts Community incentive measures, excluding any harmonisation of the laws and regulations of the Member States, to support action taken by the Member States in order to contribute to the achievement of the

10 http://ec.europa.eu/news/economy/081212_1_en.htm (accessed 1 April 2009).

> objectives referred to in paragraph 1, it shall act in accordance with the procedure referred to in Article 251.

Decisions under Article 251 EC can be made by qualified majority voting rather than requiring unanimity and the European Parliament has a co-decision role rather than just a consultative role. However, this applies only to 'incentive measures', and thus excludes binding legislative instruments (Bell 2002a: 126). Where legislative measures are concerned, this change does not remove two of the points of criticism raised against Article 13 – the requirement of unanimity and the limited role of the European Parliament.

The WCAR took place in Durban, South Africa, from 31 August to 7 September 2001. The focus of this conference was on action-oriented and practical steps to eradicate racism, including measures of prevention, education, protection and the provision of effective remedies (WCAR 2001). The European Commission brought out its contribution to this Conference, summing up what had been done and what was being done to combat racism within the EU. It ended with the same recommendations the Commission had made to the Strasbourg Conference (COM (2001) 291). The WCAR Declaration (para 107) underscored:

> the need to design, promote and implement at the national, regional and international levels strategies, programmes and policies, and adequate legislation, which may include special and positive measures, for furthering equal social development and the realization of the civil and political, economic, social and cultural rights of all victims of racism, racial discrimination, xenophobia and related intolerance including through more effective access to the political, judicial and administrative institutions, as well as the need to promote effective access to justice,...

Therefore, the Declaration mentioned legislation against racism and racial discrimination as one of a number of measures; it recognized positive action measures; it emphasized equal enjoyment of all human rights; it stressed participation in society's institutions; and it stressed that victims should have adequate access to justice. The WCAR Action Programme urged, requested or encouraged states to do a number of things, among which is establishing and implementing 'national policies and action plans to combat racism, racial discrimination, xenophobia and related intolerance'; designing, reinforcing, promoting and implementing 'effective legislative and administrative policies'; adopting or strengthening national legislation; and ratifying and effectively implementing international human rights instruments, especially the ICERD (paras 66–8 and 75). However, both Declaration and Action Programmes have been described as disappointing (Sierra 2002b: 260: Banton 2002b: 359–60). Banton criticizes the Declaration for not being 'forward looking' and the Action Programme for not being what its title says, a programme for action, and for not saying 'who is to do what, when and how'.

He calls the whole WCAR a 'calamity that has damaged the reputation of the UN and attitudes towards international co-operation'. Both Banton and Sierra stress the importance of regional efforts to fight racism and racial discrimination (Sierra 2002b: 260; Banton 2002b: 366).

At the end of 2001, the Commission brought out a proposal for a Framework Decision to combat racism and xenophobia (COM (2001) 664). The Proposal had a twofold purpose: first, to ensure that racism and xenophobia are punishable in all Member States by effective, proportionate and dissuasive criminal penalties, which can give rise to extradition and surrender (approximation); and, second, to improve and encourage judicial cooperation by removing potential obstacles (cooperation). The proposal gave minimum standards for approximation in criminal laws, leaving the Member States free to go further (Ibid: 6).

The Equal Treatment (Amendment) Directive,[11] adopted in 2002, amended the Equal Treatment Directive 1976[12] to bring it more in line with the Race and Framework Directives. The European Commission brought out a number of publications in the latter part of 2003 (European Commission 2003a, b and c). In the same year, a Directive to extend the protection against gender discrimination to the area of goods and services was proposed (COM (2003) 657) and a Directive on the legal status of long-term resident third-country nationals was adopted (Council Directive 2003/109/EC). At the Brussels European Council in December 2003, the representatives of the Member States decided to extend the remit of the European Monitoring Centre on Racism and Xenophobia to make it into a Human Rights Agency (Presidency Conclusions 2003).

In May 2004, the Commission published its Annual report (European Commission 2004a) and a Green Paper on equality and non-discrimination in an enlarged European Union (COM (2004) 379). According to its introduction, the aim of the latter was to analyze the progress made so far and to help decide how to continue and reinforce this. The Green Paper was a consultation exercise which would help shape the Commission's future policy strategy with regards to non-discrimination and equal treatment. The Paper mentioned the Commission's concern about delays in the transposition of the Race and Framework Directives in many Member States, although there had been some positive signs of progress in recent months. The Commission was taking the necessary legal action with a view to ensuring that the Directives were transposed in all Member States. It expressed its approval of the fact that some Member States had gone beyond the minimum standards set out in Community legislation: some had extended the protection beyond employment to discrimination on the grounds of religion or

11 Council Directive 2002/73/EC. Hereafter referred to as the Equal Treatment (Amendment) Directive.

12 Council Directive 76/207/EC. Hereafter referred to as the Equal Treatment Directive.

belief, disability, age and sexual orientation; some had opted for a single framework addressing all grounds; and many had established single equality bodies dealing with all the grounds of discrimination covered by the Directives (Ibid: 7).

According to the Paper, the immediate challenge was to ensure the full and effective implementation of the framework against discrimination. The Commission noted that demands had emerged to further extend and reinforce the scope of protection offered by Community law in respect of some of the grounds covered by Article 13 (Ibid: 14–15). In the Conclusion of the Green Paper the Commission stated that much had been achieved, but that much remained to be done. It was important to acknowledge that legislation is but one tool in the fight against discrimination. Changes to attitudes and behaviour required sustained effort and action to back up legislation with concrete measures (Ibid: 20).

Waddington (2004: 369) criticizes the Green Paper, because the Commission mentions a number of positive developments in the Member States in implementing the Directives, but:

> The Commission clearly regards such developments as positive yet, in spite of having the legal competence to propose (new) legislation … it has not yet done so, and has no plans to do so in the immediate future. The reason for this reluctance is arguably the poor response of some Member States to the current Article 13 Directives and the anticipated difficulties of securing the adoption of future such Directives.

In October 2004, the Commission launched a Consultation paper on the Fundamental Rights Agency (COM (2004) 693). This paper built upon the decision to extend the mandate of the European Monitoring Centre on Racism and Xenophobia and to convert it into a Fundamental Rights Agency. The paper requested contributions so consultations could take place with all those involved in the development of fundamental rights in the EU, which should then lead to a Commission proposal for a regulation in 2005.

In the same month, the (then) President-Designate of the European Commission, Barroso, announced that he intended to create a Group of Commissioners responsible for fundamental rights, anti discrimination and equal opportunities (Barroso 2004: 3). Two points to note here: first, anti discrimination and equal opportunities are, again, firmly linked with fundamental human rights; and, second, the term 'equal opportunities' is used rather than equality and non-discrimination, which were most commonly used until then.

In November, at the Dutch Presidency Conference on Anti Discrimination, Spidla, Commissioner for Employment, Social Affairs and Equal Opportunities, announced that the Commission would conduct a feasibility study to see whether there was a need to extend the scope of the Framework Directive to combat discrimination outside employment. This study would lead to a

Communication presenting a framework for the development of Europe's anti discrimination policy by the end of 2005 (Spidla 2004).

Also in November 2004, a Press Release (IP/04/1408) gave some of the responses to the Green Paper on equality and non-discrimination and announced that 'one of the Commission's first steps will be to issue a Communication on anti-discrimination before the end of 2005'. 88% of respondents said that the EU should step up its efforts to combat discrimination following enlargement. Opinions were divided as to the impact of the new Equality Directives so far, with national authorities, equality bodies and employers feeling that they have had some impact, but individuals and NGOs generally disagreeing. Nearly half of all respondents felt that they had had no or little impact. This may have been 'due to certain Member States' delays in implementing the new rules'. The answer to the question whether existing legislation was sufficient saw a similar split: some – mostly NGOs and individuals – wanted to bring the level of protection against discrimination on all Article 13 EC grounds up to the level of the Race Directive, while others – mainly national authorities and employers – thought that further legislative action would be premature. Another interesting finding was that 'respondents felt that legislation is the most effective tool in addressing discrimination (34.2%), more than awareness raising (31.8%) and affirmative action (22.6%)'.

In December 2004, the Equal Treatment (Goods) Directive[13] was adopted on the basis of Article 13 EC. This Directive prohibits gender discrimination in the access to and the supply of goods and services, and thus extends the protection against gender discrimination outside the employment sphere. One of the points of criticism against the Equal Treatment (Amendment) Directive was that it did not go beyond that sphere, while the Race Directive's protection did. However, the 2004 Directive did not extend the protection to all areas covered by the Race Directive, only to the area of the provision of goods and services.

In June 2005, the Commission issued a Communication containing a framework strategy for non-discrimination and equal opportunities for all (COM (2005) 224), accompanied by a Proposal to designate 2007 as the European Year of Equal Opportunities for All (COM (2005) 225). The introduction to the Communication describes the EU legislation against discrimination as 'some of the most comprehensive and far-reaching anti-discrimination legislation to be found anywhere in the world'. The Commission emphasizes that full and effective implementation and enforcement of this legal framework must be ensured. However, this is followed by the consideration that individual implementation of anti discrimination is

13 Council Directive 2004/113/EC. Hereafter this Directive will be referred to as the Equal Treatment (Goods) Directive.

not enough 'to tackle the multifaceted and deep-rooted patterns of inequality experienced by some groups'. The EU must increase its efforts to promote equal opportunities for all in order to tackle the structural barriers faced by migrants, ethnic minorities, the disabled, older and younger workers and other vulnerable groups (COM (2005) 224: 2).

Later in the Communication, the Commission states that the experience in the gender discrimination field has shown 'that protection of individual rights must be backed up by accompanying measures in order to bring about lasting change and to promote genuine equal opportunities for all' (Ibid: 6). One of the accompanying measures the Commission suggests is the promotion of mainstreaming of non-discrimination and equal opportunities for all in relevant EU policies.

The Communication then announces that it proposes to designate 2007 as the European Year of Equal Opportunities for All. The aims of the Year are to:

> inform people of their rights to protection against discrimination under European and national law; celebrate diversity as an asset for the EU; and to promote equal opportunities for all in economic, social, political and cultural life.
>
> (Ibid: 8–9)

The conclusion reiterates that 'in addition to the legal protection of individual rights, this Communication sets out a strategy for the positive and active promotion of non-discrimination and equal opportunities for all' (Ibid: 12). However, 'the Commission is not proposing to come forward at this stage with further legislative proposals based on Article 13 of the Treaty', but it 'will undertake an in-depth study into the relevance and feasibility of possible new measures to complement the current legal framework' (Ibid: 6).

According to the Communication, the Commission will aim to ensure that a range of EU funding instruments contribute to the promotion of non-discrimination and equal opportunities for all. The Commission also proposes an annual high-level Equality Summit to bring together key stakeholders (Ibid: 7–9). And, to support policy development to tackle discrimination and social exclusion faced by disadvantaged ethnic minorities, the Commission plans to establish a high-level advisory group on social and labour market integration of these disadvantaged ethnic minorities (Ibid: 10).

The Explanatory Memorandum to the Proposal for the Year of Equal Opportunities for All (COM (2005) 225: 2) states:

> The global objective of the Year will be to raise awareness of the benefits of a just, cohesive society where there is equality of opportunity for all. This will require tackling barriers to participation in society and promoting a climate in which Europe's diversity is seen as a source of socio-economic vitality.

The Year 'will provide an opportunity to promote a more cohesive society that celebrates differences within the framework of EU core values ...' (Ibid: 4). The four specific objectives of the Year, which can be found in Article 2, are rights, representation, recognition and respect and tolerance (Ibid: 20–5 and Article 2). 'Rights' refers to the raising of awareness on the right to equality and non-discrimination and of the existing anti discrimination legislation. 'Representation' means the promotion of full and equal participation of all groups in society. 'Recognition' indicates the celebration and accommodation of diversity. 'Respect and tolerance' relates to the promotion of a more cohesive society.

The Communication proposes the development of tools to promote mainstreaming of non-discrimination and equal opportunities for all in relevant EU policies, not only in relation to gender discrimination, but also in relation to discrimination on the other grounds of Article 13 EC.

All this suggests a shift in the language used in the EU from about 2004 onwards from anti discrimination and equal treatment towards equal opportunities. We will come back to this shift in language in Chapter 6.

In 2006, the Recast Directive[14] was adopted. This Directive aimed to bring together in a single text a number of Directives on gender discrimination in employment and occupation (including the Equal Treatment Directive and its amending Directive and the Burden of Proof Directive (Council Directive 97/80/EC)). However, it does not replace the 2004 Equal Treatment (Goods) Directive. It follows the definitions of direct and indirect discrimination and harassment in the Race and Framework Directives.

The EU Agency for Fundamental Rights, established by Council Regulation No 168/2007, opened in Vienna on 1 March 2007 and built upon the mandate of the European Monitoring Centre on Racism and Xenophobia. According to Article 2, its objective is to provide the relevant institutions, bodies, offices and agencies of the Community and its Member States when implementing Community law with assistance and expertise relating to fundamental rights by providing information and data on fundamental rights matters. There will be a Multi-Annual Framework for the Agency, adopted by the Council on a proposal from the Commission and after consulting the European Parliament. This Framework will 'determine the thematic areas of the Agency's activity, which must include the fight against racism, xenophobia and related intolerance' (Article 5(2)(b) Regulation 168/2007).

Five reports commissioned by the European Commission came out in 2007, on non-discrimination mainstreaming (Centre for Strategy and Evaluation Services 2007); on equal rights versus special rights (Henrard 2007); on going beyond formal equality and positive action (de Vos 2007); on the development of anti-discrimination law in the Member States (Bell *et al.* 2007); and, on multiple discrimination (European Commission 2007).

14 Council Directive 2006/54/EC. Hereafter referred to as the Recast Directive.

These studies all show not only the Commission's interest in the subject of discrimination but also a shift in emphasis towards going beyond equal treatment. The Council Resolution on the follow-up of the European Year of Equal Opportunities for All reflects this shift as well where it mentions that 'realising a full equality of opportunities is essential for the growth, cohesion, prosperity and well–being of Europe and its people' (Council Resolution 2007: 3) The Resolution also notes that 'equal opportunities need to be mainstreamed' (idem: 6), and that 'improving participation in society of groups at risk of discrimination' is a key issue (ibid: 7). A report commissioned by the European Commission in 2008 on indirect discrimination is also an illustration of this shift (Tobler 2008).

On 2 July 2008, the European Commission issued a Communication on Non-Discrimination and Equal Opportunities (COM (2008) 420) and a Proposal for a Council Directive which would extend the protection against discrimination on the grounds of religion or belief, disability, age and sexual orientation beyond the employment field to all areas covered by the Race Directive (COM (2008) 426). The Proposal puts a duty on Member States to designate a body for the promotion of equal treatment, irrespective of their religion or belief, disability, age or sexual orientation, a duty which already existed in relation to racial and ethnic origin and gender. The Communication uses the term equal opportunities coupled to non-discrimination and mentions the need to strengthen policy tools for the active promotion of equal opportunities. Amongst these are non-discrimination mainstreaming for all grounds covered by Article 13 EC; positive action measures and social inclusion (COM (2008) 426: 6–10).

Negotiations on the 2001 Proposal for a Framework Decision on Racism and Xenophobia (COM (2001) 664) took place at intervals between 2001 and 2007. During these negotiations, the Decision was amended considerably and the text agreed upon in April 2007 was a much weakened version of the original (DROIPEN 34, 8544/07). Since important amendments had been made to the original proposal, the European Parliament had to be consulted again. The Decision was then formally adopted on 28 November 2008 (Council Framework Decision 2008).

1.2.5.2 *Implementation of the Race Directive in the Member States*

As the deadline for implementation of the Race Directive – 19 July 2003 – approached it became clear that many Member States had not done enough. The Commission expressed its concern that many Member States were set to miss the deadline (Press Release IP/03/1047).

It appears that only Belgium, Sweden and the UK did comply fully with the Race Directive by 19 July 2003 (Chopin *et al.* 2004). And even though these countries had implemented the Directive, the Belgian law did not cover the whole of the territory of the Belgian state; the Swedish report points to two areas that need further investigation; and the UK report criticizes the way the amendments have been made (by regulation rather than by primary legislation) and its content, which creates even more complexities in an already overly complex area of law. On the date the Race Directive should have been implemented, the situation in the other Member States was thus: Austria, Finland, the Netherlands and Spain hoped to have legislation in place by the end of 2003. France had transposed the Directive partially, but there appeared to be no draft legislation to transpose the rest. Denmark had transposed the Directive for all spheres apart from the employment sphere and had a draft bill to cover the employment sphere as well, although this bill's progress seemed to have stalled. Portugal, Italy, Greece and, possibly Luxembourg, had draft legislation. (The report on Luxembourg stated that the intention of the legislator was unknown; that there was a law in preparation, but that there was no indication as to its content). Germany appeared to have no draft legislation yet, but foresaw implementation by May 2004. Ireland did not seem to have any plans for any legislation to cover the gaps that existed between the legislation already in place and the Race Directive (Ibid).

What happens when a Member State does not comply with Community law? Articles 226 and 228 EC provide a procedure for the situation where a Member State has failed to fulfil an obligation under the Treaty, which includes violating or not implementing binding legislation like a directive. There are two types of 'infringement procedure'. The first is when a Member State does not communicate to the Commission the measures it has taken to implement a directive into its national law. The second is when a Member State has transposed a directive into its national law but has not done so completely or correctly. In both procedures, the Commission first sends a letter of formal notice. If the Member State does not reply to this letter within two months, the Commission will issue a reasoned opinion. Again, if no reply is received within two months, the Commission can refer the Member State to the ECJ. If the ECJ finds that the Member State has failed to fulfil its obligations, the State must take the necessary measures to comply with the Court's judgment. If the Commission then finds that the Member State does not do so, it issues another reasoned opinion dealing with the points with which the Member State has not complied and giving it a limited time to do so. If the Member State still does not comply, the Commission can refer it back to the ECJ and specify the amount the Commission thinks the Member State should pay. If the ECJ then finds that the Member State has not complied with its judgment, it can impose a lump sum or penalty payment.[15]

It appears that the Commission sent a letter of formal notice concerning the non-communication in relation to transposition of the Race Directive into national law on 6 October 2003 to Belgium, Germany, Greece, Spain,

15 See further on Article 226–228 EC: Steiner *et al.* (2006): 225–39.

Ireland, Luxembourg, the Netherlands, Austria, Portugal, Finland and the UK. This was followed on 5 February 2004 by a 'reasoned opinion' to the same Member States except Spain and Portugal ((2005) 3, Equal Rights in Practice: 4).

On 1 May 2004, ten new Member States joined the EU: Cyprus, Czech Republic, Estonia, Hungary, Latvia, Lithuania, Malta, Poland, Slovakia and Slovenia, bringing the number of Member States to 25. The Race and Framework Directives are part of the *Acquis Communautiare*, the body of law that a state needs to adopt before it accedes to the EU and thus both Directives should have been transposed into the national laws of these new Member States by that date. The Commission's policy is to take action against the new Member States separately from the old Member States, because of the later deadline and because action will always be taken against several states at the same time. All new states, except the Czech Republic, have notified the Commission that they have implemented both the Race and Framework Directives ((2005) 1, European Anti-Discrimination Law Review: 31–2).

June 2004 saw the publication of another set of expert reports on the implementation of the EU anti-discrimination laws regarding race, religion, sexual orientation and disability in the 15 old Member States (European Commission 2004b).

On 19 July 2004, exactly one year after the expiry of the deadline for the transposition of the Race Directive, the Commission announced that it would refer five Member States – Austria, Germany, Finland, Greece and Luxembourg – to the ECJ for failure to pass all the necessary national measures to introduce, amend or up-date their equality legislation in relation to the Race Directive (Press Release IP/04/947 and Memo 04/189). The Memo explained that this action is the first type of infringement procedure against failure to communicate to the Commission. The Press Release mentioned that the Commission was in the process of examining the national laws of the Member States which had already adopted legislation transposing the Directive.

On 24 February 2005, the ECJ ruled that Finland and Luxembourg had breached EU law by failing to transpose fully the Race Directive. The same ruling was made against Germany on 28 April 2005 and against Austria on 4 May 2005.[16] All four Member States were ordered by the ECJ to pay costs. In Finland and Austria, the legislation did not cover the whole of the territory, while Luxembourg and Germany both had draft legislation, but this had not yet been adopted. The case against Greece was dropped when a law was enacted in January 2005. But Greece was ordered to pay costs as the law was

16 Finland and Luxembourg: *Commission v Luxembourg* and *Commission v Finland;* and *Finland and Luxembourg are found guilty of failing to implement EU race anti-discrimination law*. Germany: *Commission v Germany;* and *Germany has failed to implement EU race anti-discrimination law*. Austria: *Commission v Austria;* and *Austria fails to implement EU race anti-discrimination law*.

adopted after the Commission had initiated infringement proceedings.[17] So four Member States were fined for not communicating that the Race Directive had been transposed, while Greece was fined for doing this too late.

According to the European Commission's Annual Report (2005b: 11–2), a letter of formal notice has been sent to the Czech Republic for non-communication.

In December 2006, the European Commission published its report on the application of the Race Directive (COM (2006) 643), as obliged by Article 17 of the Directive. Rather than giving a detailed account of the transposition of the provisions of the Directive, the report aimed to flag up certain particularly problematic aspects and to identify good practice (Ibid: 2). The Report mentioned problems with the definitions of direct and indirect discrimination and harassment; too broad exceptions to the principles of non-discrimination; incorrect transposition of the burden of proof provisions; enforcement by individual victims; and sanctions and remedies (Ibid: 3–4). The Commission wrote that it is examining national legislative measures in order to assess their conformity with the Directive. Under Article 13 of the Directive, the Member States were under an obligation to designate a body or bodies for the promotion of equal treatment of all persons without discrimination on the ground of racial or ethnic origin. The Commission reported that several Member States have taken the 'very positive step' of extending the remit of their equality bodies, so that they could deal with discrimination on all the grounds of discrimination covered by EU anti discrimination law and/or more general human rights instruments (Ibid: 3 and 5). The Commission concluded that it was too early to come forward with proposals for updating and revising the Race Directive (Ibid: 8).

On 27 June 2007, the Commission sent reasoned opinions for lack of complete and correct transposition of the Race Directive to the following 14 Member States: Czech Republic, Estonia, France, Greece, Ireland, Italy, Latvia, Poland, Portugal, Slovakia, Slovenia, Spain, Sweden and the UK. According to the latest issue of the European Anti-Discrimination Law Review (6/7), 'the Commission is in contact with all these Member States on these issues and – in a number of cases – it is clear that changes to national laws are already in the pipeline'.[18] To date, no Member State has been referred to the ECJ. In the Explanatory Memorandum to the Proposal to extend the fields covered by the Framework Directive outside the employment area, it is

17 (2005) 1 and 2, *European Anti-Discrimination Law Review*. For more detailed information on the implementation of the Race and Framework Directives in the 25 EU Member States see European Commission 2005a.

18 (2007) 6/7, *European Anti-Discrimination Law Review*: 54. The reasoned opinion on the UK, for example, concluded that the UK had failed to implement the definition of indirect discrimination correctly. In its response the UK Government agreed to make further amendments. This was done in the Race Relations Act (Amendment) Regulations 2008, SI 2008/3008.

stated that 'all except one Member State have transposed these directives [the Race and Framework Directives]' but there is no indication of how many have transposed them incorrectly or incompletely or of any action taken by the Commission (COM (2008) 426: 3).

1.3 Conclusion

In this Chapter, we described the development of the fight against race discrimination within the EU because this has been instrumental in shaping the Race Directive. Up to the early 1990s, there was, except in the European Parliament and within NGOs, little interest in taking any legislative action against racial and ethnic origin discrimination at EU level. The following reasons were suggested for this: Member States might have seen this as a matter for national law or they might have considered national and international legislative measures sufficient. However, the reluctance could also have been caused by a failure to acknowledge that the problem of racism existed within the Member State or by the lack of political capital that could be made out of supporting such measures. Whatever the reasons, the reluctance started to disappear in the early 1990s as the Member States realized that the development of cross-border racism might influence the functioning of the internal market and that the effects of the growing cooperation on immigration and asylum policies needed to be balanced by anti discrimination measures.

It was not clear, however, whether the EU had the competence to adopt legislative measures against racial discrimination. This was addressed in the Treaty of Amsterdam, which established this competence and just over a year after this Treaty came into force the Race Directive was adopted. The Race Directive's speedy adoption, despite it's wide scope – going well beyond the employment sphere – was the result of the fact that Member States wanted to show their firm commitment to combating racial and ethnic origin discrimination towards Austria, towards the then Candidate Countries and towards the rest of the world. When it came to implementation of the Directive, however, the Member States were less quick. A number of reasons can be put forward for this. First, the political will, which existed in 2000, appears to have dwindled. The political climate in Europe has changed and, in many Member States, support for extreme right-wing parties was and is on the increase. Proclaiming opposition to racism and the fight against discrimination no longer appears to be such good publicity or a vote winner. MacEwen writes that 'much of the history of race relations has been bound up in ideas about electoral tolerance' (MacEwen 1995: 25). This 'electoral tolerance' appears to have diminished in most EU Member States. Second, other, more pressing, matters – like the 2004 enlargement, the Constitution, and later the Treaty of Lisbon, and economic measures – appear to have pushed the fight against racial discrimination further down the EU agenda.

A number of points can be made in relation to the history of the adoption of the Directive. First, there was, from quite early on, an emphasis on tolerance and respect for individual dignity, and the importance of education as a means of teaching tolerance and understanding, as, for example, the Joint Declaration of 1986 shows. Second, the right to equality and non discrimination appears to have been considered as a fundamental human right from the early discussions onwards. This can be gleaned from the stress on combating every form of discrimination in the Charter of Fundamental Social Rights (COM (1989) 471) and the stress on the importance of cooperation between the Community and the Council of Europe in the 1990 Council Resolution. Again, the European Parliament was the most vociferous here, with its 1990 proposal to add the right of everyone to equality before the law and a general prohibition of discrimination to the EC Treaty (European Parliament Resolution 1990c). Third, the Commission's Action Plan of 1998 (COM (1998) 183) mentions the importance of partnership with everyone involved and of mainstreaming the fight against racism in all relevant Community programmes and policies. And, fourth, the negotiations on the Race Directive showed clearly that, for many people in Europe, race and racism are sensitive subjects and still strongly associated with the events of World War II.

But the fight against racism and racial discrimination did not end with the speedy adoption of the Race Directive. Non-discrimination and equal treatment, and more recently, equal opportunities, have stayed on the agenda. A number of legislative and non-legislative measures have been taken or are proposed. The Commission is also monitoring the correct transposition of the Race and Framework Directives.

2 International human rights instruments to combat racial discrimination

2.1 Introduction

Legal measures against discrimination can be taken at international, regional or national level. In the international and regional sphere, there are a number of human rights treaties and conventions that contain rights to equality and non-discrimination. In this Chapter, global measures and measures taken at the level of greater Europe (this includes other states beyond the EU Member States) are examined. For a proper analysis and evaluation of the anti race discrimination legislation in the EU, it needs to be placed within this wider European and international context.

The examination starts with a discussion on why the international context is important and then proceeds with giving an overview of equality and/or anti discrimination clauses in the main global human rights instruments. This will be followed by a more extensive discussion of the ICERD, which is a United Nations Convention; and two instruments of the Council of Europe: the anti discrimination article (Article 14) of the ECHR and Additional Protocol 12 to the ECHR. As will become clear, these three are especially important in the EU.

For a proper understanding of the equality clauses in international human rights instruments, it is important to keep in mind why they were adopted in the first place, especially those that were adopted just after the end of World War II. There was a general feeling at that time that such a disastrous event should never be allowed to happen again and that future generations should be saved from the ravages and sorrows of war. The world reacted against the use of theories of race to declare some races inferior, which justified their exclusion, subordination and extermination. This was to be avoided in future and, therefore, the United Nations was established, with its peoples determined 'to practise tolerance and live together in peace with one another as good neighbours, and to unite our strength to maintain international peace and security' (Preamble of the Charter of the United Nations, 1945). A number of international treaties and declarations followed, proclaiming the equality of every person. Boyle and Baldaccini (2001: 141) point out that 'it was largely the search for an effective international response to racism that produced the main components of the United Nations human rights regime'.

In the analysis of the international instruments, attention will be given to the following questions which are relevant for subsequent chapters: whether a measure prohibits both direct and indirect discrimination; whether it allows for positive action measures; whether it is more sensitive to group aspects of discrimination and allows for actions by groups as well as by individuals; and whether it puts a positive duty on public authorities to eliminate discrimination.

2.2 Why are international instruments important?

It is important to place the EU measures against racial and ethnic discrimination in their international context because this context has been, and still is, influencing the EU instruments. This is for a number of reasons, the first of which is that all Member States of the EU have signed and ratified most of the international conventions and treaties, and, by doing so, have accepted certain obligations. But, even if they have not signed and/or ratified some of the Conventions, there is still the fact that 'it is now established in international law that the prohibition of racial discrimination ... is part of *ius cogens*' (Goldston 1999: 480; O'Hare 2000: 10; Boyle and Baldaccini 2001: 144) which means that it is part of the peremptory norms or overriding principles of international law.[1]

Second, from the very first discussions on the fight against racism and racial discrimination, the EU institutions have placed the right to equality and non-discrimination firmly within the wider human rights context. In their earliest coordinated joint declaration against racism and xenophobia (1986) the European Institutions stressed the importance of respect for fundamental rights and considered that 'respect for human dignity and the elimination of forms of racial discrimination were part of the common cultural and legal heritage of all the Member States'. The Race Directive also places the right to equality and non-discrimination clearly on a human rights basis. Recital 2 to the Directive mentions Article 6 TEU, which determines that the Union shall respect fundamental rights as guaranteed by the ECHR and as they result from the constitutional traditions common to the Member States, as general principles of Community law. Note that the Lisbon Treaty will change Article 6 TEU and Article 6(1) will read: 'the Union recognises the rights, freedoms and principles set out in the Charter of Fundamental Rights of the European Union ... which shall have the same legal value as the Treaties'. And, Article 6 (3) will determine: 'Fundamental rights, as guaranteed by the European Convention for the Protection of Human Rights and Fundamental Freedoms and as they result from the constitutional traditions common to the Member States, shall constitute general principles of the Union's law'.

1 The Vienna Convention on the Law of Treaties gives a definition of *ius cogens* in Article 53 http://members.yline.com/~waltergehr/trea/wvkengl.html (accessed 1 April 2009).

Recital 3 of the Race Directive reads:

> The right to equality before the law and protection against discrimination for all persons constitutes a universal right recognised by the Universal Declaration of Human Rights, the United Nations Convention on the Elimination of all Forms of Discrimination against Women, the International Convention on the Elimination of all Forms of Racial Discrimination and the United Nations Covenants on Civil and Political Rights and on Economic, Social and Cultural Rights and by the European Convention for the Protection of Human Rights and Fundamental Freedoms, to which all Member States are signatories.

Therefore, the Race Directive itself refers to most of the international instruments discussed in this Chapter.

Third, the ECJ has considered the principle of equality to be a fundamental principle of Community law. For example, in *Frilli v Belgium* (para 19), the ECJ stated that equality of treatment is 'one of the fundamental principles of Community law'. In *Ruckdeschel* (para 7), the ECJ held that the prohibition of discrimination was 'merely a specific enunciation of the general principle of equality which is one of the fundamental principles of Community law'. In *Defrenne v Sabena No. 3* (paras 26–7), the ECJ repeated what it had said in earlier cases 'that respect for fundamental personal human rights is one of the principles of Community law, the observance of which it has a duty to ensure'. It concluded that 'the elimination of discrimination based on sex forms part of those fundamental rights'. In *Karlsson* (paras 37–9), the ECJ held that the fundamental rights in the Community legal order 'include a general principle of equality and the obligation not to discriminate'. And, in two recent cases concerning the Framework Directive – *Mangold* (para 75) and *Chacon Navas* (para 56) – the ECJ again mentioned the principle of non-discrimination as a general, fundamental principle of Community law. The general principles of Community law are binding on the Community institutions and the primary source of guidance on which principles are to be considered as general principles of Community law is Article 6 TEU, mentioned above. The ECJ also uses as guidelines 'international treaties for the protection of human rights on which the Member States have collaborated or of which they are signatories' (*Nold*: para 13). The ECJ 'has consistently held that all sources of fundamental rights support the existence of a strong principle of equality and non-discrimination' (Bell 2002a: 20).[2]

The fourth reason why the international human rights instruments are important for the EU anti discrimination measures is that the European

2 For more information on the development of equality as a fundamental principle of Community law see also: Bernard, N. 1996: 77–99; de Burca 1997; Barnard 1998; More 1999; O'Hare 2000; McCrudden 2003: 9–11; and Waddington 2003a.

Union Charter of Fundamental Rights refers to the ECHR and its case law and other international human rights instruments. In its Preamble, the Charter reaffirms:

> the rights as they result, in particular, from the constitutional traditions and international obligations common to the Member States, the Treaty on European Union, the Community Treaties, the European Convention for the Protection of Human Rights and Fundamental Freedoms, the Social Charters adopted by the Community and by the Council of Europe and the case-law of the Court of Justice of the European Communities and of the European Court of Human Rights.

The text of the Charter itself also refers to the ECHR, in Article 52(3), where it states that where the Charter contains rights that correspond to rights guaranteed by the ECHR 'the meaning and scope of those rights shall be the same as those laid down by the said Convention'. This is followed by Article 53, which determines that:

> Nothing in this Charter shall be interpreted as restricting or adversely affecting human rights and fundamental freedoms, as recognised … by Union law and international law and by international agreements to which the Union, the Community and all the Member States are party, including the European Convention for the Protection of Human Rights and Fundamental Freedoms, and by the Member States' Constitutions.

The Updated Explanatory Memorandum to the Charter (CONV 828/1/03: 49) states, in relation to Article 52, that the reference to the ECHR covers not only the text of the Convention and the Protocols to it, but also the case law of the European Court of Human Rights and of the ECJ. And, in relation to Article 53, it states that 'owing to its importance, mention is made of the ECHR' (Ibid: 52). Therefore, the Charter, which will become legally binding once the Treaty of Lisbon comes into force, stresses the importance of the ECHR within the EU legal order.

The influence of international and regional human rights instruments, especially the ECHR, in the EU is, for all these reasons, considerable. Accession of the EU as a Contracting Party to the ECHR has also been suggested and the Treaty of Lisbon determines that the Union shall do so (Article 6(2) Consolidated version TEU). This again shows the importance of the ECHR and the Council of Europe within the EU. Accession to the ECHR would bring the EU Institutions under the scrutiny of the European Court of Human Rights in Strasbourg.[3]

3 Discussion of this falls outside the subject of this book. For more information see: Kruger and Polakiewicz 2001; Drzemczewski 2001; Jacobs 2002: 289–90; Mahoney 2002. See also

2.3 International equality and anti discrimination clauses, an overview

According to the Preamble to the Charter of the United Nations of 1945, the peoples of the UN were determined 'to save succeeding generations from the scourge of war' and, 'to reaffirm faith in fundamental human rights, in the dignity and worth of the human person, in the equal rights of men and women and of nations large and small'. The Universal Declaration of Human Rights (UDHR), adopted by the United Nations in 1948, starts in Article 1 with 'all human beings are born free and equal in dignity and rights'. This is followed by Article 2 which declares that:

> Everyone is entitled to all the rights and freedoms set forth in this Declaration, without distinction of any kind such as race, colour, sex, language, religion, political or other opinion, national or social origin, property, birth or other status.

Article 7 then proclaims that 'all are equal before the law and entitled without any discrimination to equal protection of the law'. The UDHR thus declares everyone's equality before the law as a basic human right.

Article 2(1) of the International Covenant on Civil and Political Rights (ICCPR) and Article 2(2) of the International Covenant on Economic, Social and Cultural Rights (ICESCR), which are both UN instruments, determine that States parties

> … undertake to guarantee that the rights enunciated in the present Covenant will be exercised without discrimination of any kind as to race, colour, sex, language, religion, political or other opinion, national or social origin, property, birth or other status.

The ICCPR, however, also declares in Article 26:

> All persons are equal before the law and are entitled without any discrimination to the equal protection of the law. In this respect, the law shall prohibit any discrimination and guarantee to all persons equal and effective protection against discrimination on any ground such as race, colour, sex, language, religion, political or other opinion, national or social origin, property, birth or other status.

Opinion 2/94, paras 20–2, in which the ECJ held that, as Community law then stood, the Community had no competence to accede to the ECHR. When the Treaty of Lisbon comes into force this competence is established.

Article 26 ICCPR gives a much broader right to non-discrimination than Article 2 UDHR, Article 2(1) ICCPR or Article 2(2) ICESCR. While the latter provisions only prohibit discrimination in relation to the rights and freedoms set forth in the Declaration/Covenants, Article 26 ICCPR gives a freestanding right to non-discrimination. The Human Rights Committee (HRC), established under Article 28 ICCPR, discusses in paragraph 12 of its General Comment No. 18 that Article 26 provides an autonomous right. And Liegl *et al.* (2004: 21–2) write that:

> Article 26 of the Covenant provides one of the strongest antidiscrimination rights that can be found in legally binding international treaties. ... Article 26 does not only prohibit discrimination in regard to the rights guaranteed by the Covenant itself but includes a freestanding prohibition of discrimination. This means that in whatever case a signatory state guarantees rights it has to do so without discrimination on the grounds of ...

All three instruments contain the same, non-exhaustive list of grounds for discrimination: 'or other status' indicates that other grounds can be recognized by the courts as a prohibited ground.

These instruments are very important because together they make up the International Bill of Human Rights. As Boyle and Baldaccini (2001: 138–40) write:

> It was on these foundations, entrenching the norms of equality and non-discrimination, that all other international human rights instruments created through the United Nations and the regional systems have been built.

All Member States of the EU are members of the United Nations and all have signed and ratified or acceded to the two Covenants and are, therefore, bound by the obligations imposed.

Both Covenants appear to include protection against indirect discrimination. The HRC's General Comment No. 18 (para 7) gives the following definition of discrimination – taking into account the ICERD and the CEDAW:

> the Committee believes that the term 'discrimination' as used in the Covenant should be understood to imply any distinction, exclusion, restriction or preference which is based on any ground such as ... and which has the *purpose or effect* [our italics] of nullifying or impairing the recognition, enjoyment or exercise by all persons, on an equal footing, of all rights and freedoms.

The use of the words 'purpose or effect' indicates that both direct and indirect discrimination are included. We will discuss this in more detail when we discuss the ICERD, as this definition, given by the HRC, is the same as that of Article 2 ICERD, apart from the grounds mentioned. The ICESCR also appears to include indirect discrimination in its prohibitions.[4]

Both Covenants allow for positive measures to be taken in order to eliminate conditions which cause or help to perpetuate discrimination prohibited by the Covenant. However, these measures are seen as exceptions from equal treatment and are limited in time (HRC General Comment 18: para 10; CESCR 1999: para. 32).

As far as allowing action by groups is concerned, the ICESCR has no individual or state complaints procedure. Optional Protocol No. 1 of the ICCPR provides that individuals can complain to the HRC. All EU Member states, except the UK, have ratified the Protocol. The Rules of Procedure for the HRC (Rule 96) state, as one of the conditions for admissibility, that it emanates from an '*individual or individuals*' [our italics], which indicates that more than one individual victim can complain and it is thus arguable that the ICCPR allows for group actions.

Do these instruments impose any positive duties on states and public authorities to eliminate discrimination and/or to promote tolerance and respect for diversity? First of all, international treaties bind the contracting parties, i.e. the states that sign up to it. It is the States Parties that are under an obligation to do what they agree to by signing. So, international instruments could impose a duty on States Parties to eliminate discrimination and to promote diversity and tolerance and/or a duty to mainstream equality in all state policies. But only the States Parties can be bound by the treaty/convention.

There are, however, two problems with international treaties imposing duties. The first problem is that international treaties are usually not easy to enforce, even if they do contain some enforcement mechanisms and, if they do, sanctions for non-compliance are not particularly effective. It is submitted that most international treaties are not strictly legally enforceable but have a more political and persuasive force. States Parties might sign and ratify them because not doing so would make them look 'bad', would harm their public image, both at home and at the international stage. If an international measure contains a reporting procedure and the body receiving the report can remark on or criticize the failure of a State Party to follow and implement the measure, then this could have persuasive influence, especially if these comments are made public, because a Government would not like to be publicly 'named and shamed'. A report criticizing a government could also assist organizations lobbying for implementing legislation. In this way, international measures can exert influence on a State Party. The problem with

4 Committee on Economic, Social and Cultural Rights, (CESCR) 1994: para 12, where the Committee mentions that direct and indirect discrimination of gypsies appears to continue; Ibid. 2000: para 22, where the Committee mentions that a rule has 'indirectly discriminatory impact on women'.

enforcement is made worse by the fact that States Parties can, and often do, make reservations to some of the articles, i.e. opt out of some of the duties imposed by the Convention, or do not recognize the enforcement procedures provided.

The second problem with international treaties imposing duties is that these measures are limited in the obligations they can impose because they have to respect the States Parties sovereignty and independence.

The UDHR, the ICCPR and the ICESCR do not appear to impose a positive duty on States to eliminate discrimination, to promote tolerance and diversity or to mainstream non-discrimination. They only prohibit discrimination in guaranteeing rights and freedoms. However, both the UDHR and the ICCPR state that 'all are equal before the law and are entitled to equal protection of the law'. According to Liegl *et al.* (2004: 22), this involves a two-fold obligation: 'states must refrain from adopting discriminatory laws and ... public authorities have to apply laws in a non-discriminatory way'. They continue: 'furthermore, Article 26 obliges Member States to prohibit discrimination by enacting special laws and to afford effective protection against discrimination'. This suggests that at least the ICCPR contains a positive duty on states to eliminate discrimination.

The last instrument to discuss is the International Labour Organization's Convention C111 on Equality in Employment and Occupation of 1958, signed and ratified by all EU Member States. This Convention prohibits discrimination in the field of employment. Article 1 defines discrimination as:

> ... any distinction, exclusion or preference made on the basis of race, colour, sex, religion, political opinion, national extraction or social origin, which has the effect of nullifying or impairing equality of opportunity or treatment in employment or occupation.

This definition covers both direct and indirect discrimination (ILO Reports 1988: 23 and 1996: 12; Cox 2002: 5). The Convention 'requires special measures to be taken by state parties where necessary to eliminate discrimination in employment' (MacEwen 1995: 55). Cox mentions that positive action is specifically required (Cox 2002: 6). In this, C111 actually goes further than most national and international anti discrimination laws, which usually only permit, but do not require positive action.

Cox (2002: 5) also points out that Article 1:

> ... requires that each ratifying State must adhere to the basic goal of promoting equality of opportunity and treatment by means of a national policy which aims to end all forms of discrimination.

C111 thus imposes an obligation on States to eliminate discrimination and to promote equal opportunity. But it must be remembered that its scope is confined to the area of employment and occupation.

2.4 International Convention for the elimination of all forms of racial discrimination

This Convention was adopted in 1966 with a unanimous vote and deals, as its name suggests, specifically with racial discrimination and will therefore be discussed in more detail. Its adoption was considered necessary because of the 'manifestations of racial discrimination still in evidence in some areas of the world' and the existence of 'government policies based on racial superiority or hatred, such as policies of *apartheid,* segregation or separation' (Preamble). The Convention was in part a reaction against the devastating effect of Nazism, but it was also a reaction against colonialism and all the practices of segregation and discrimination associated with it. Furedi (1998) argues that, after World War II, public attitudes to racism changed quickly and the principle of racial equality was rapidly accepted. This was a defensive and pragmatic reaction of the Western world which feared revenge of non-white people for the domination by the West. World War II brought out the inconsistency and the conflict between the denouncing of the prevailing Nazi ethos and the practice of discrimination and feelings of racial superiority. Therefore, Furedi concludes, the principle of race equality had to be conceded to ensure a stable world order. World War II had helped to discredit racism and to make the question of race an international issue.

Banton (1996: 50 and 2002a: 42) mentions the rise of fascism and the revulsion felt against *apartheid* as spurs for international action which led, among others, to the ICERD. He argues that the Convention obtained the support of the international community and was adopted unanimously because it was based on a 'lie': that racial discrimination as defined by Article 1(1) ICERD could be eliminated by political action. He distinguishes two ways to view racial discrimination: it can be viewed either as a pathological illness or as a normal part of everyday society. Without the political myth that it was a social sickness that could be eliminated, and be eliminated quickly, states would surely not have invested so much energy in the Convention (Ibid. 1996: 67–74 and 2002a: 65–7). The title of the Convention confirms that the view that racial discrimination could be eliminated was the prevailing one, as does the Preamble, which:

> ... solemnly affirms the necessity of speedily eliminating racial discrimination throughout the world, in all its forms and manifestations and of securing understanding of and respect for the dignity of the human person.

Banton (2002a: 44–5) concludes that this dubious assumption served a noble purpose: the axiom that racial discrimination as defined by the Convention can be eliminated is a lie, but, because it made possible agreement on a Treaty that now restrains racial discrimination in most of the world's states, it was a 'noble lie'.

Banton (1996: 305) also mentions that states regarded racial discrimination as a social pathology which afflicted other states than their own and was thus a matter for foreign policy. Therefore, signing the Convention brought a state credit on the international stage without many domestic demands.[5]

The ICERD came into force in 1969 after it had been ratified by 27 states and is now one of the most widely ratified UN human rights treaties. However, many states have made reservations, especially to Article 4 and to the enforcement mechanism adopted (McColgan 2003: 165). All Member States of the EU have signed and ratified this Convention, although some of them have made reservations.

In its Preamble, the Convention expresses the conviction:

> … that any doctrine of superiority based on racial differentiation is scientifically false, morally condemnable, socially unjust and dangerous, and that there is no justification for racial discrimination, in theory or in practice, anywhere.

Article 1(1) ICERD defines 'racial discrimination' as:

> any distinction, exclusion, restriction or preference based on race, colour, descent or national or ethnic origin which has the purpose or effect of nullifying or impairing the recognition, enjoyment or exercise, on an equal footing, of human rights and fundamental freedoms in the political, economic, social, cultural or any other field of public life.

A number of observations can be made about this definition. First, the definition clearly shows that racial discrimination is considered to be a violation of fundamental human rights. This is also very clear from the 1993 United Nations Declaration on the Elimination of All Forms of Racial Discrimination, which preceded the ICERD and which states that the UN Charter 'is based on the principles of dignity and equality of all human beings'. Article 1 of the Declaration then states that:

> Discrimination between human beings on the ground of race, colour or ethnic origin is an offence to human dignity and shall be condemned as a denial of the principles of the Charter of the United Nations, as a violation of the human rights and fundamental freedoms proclaimed in the Universal Declaration of Human Rights …

5 The notion that racism and racial discrimination were seen as an issue of foreign policy and foreign relations is also mentioned by van Boven 2001: 111–13.

This is the established view within international law. See, for example, Petrova (2001: 61) who writes: 'racial discrimination is understood in human rights law as a violation of human rights'.

Second, the definition in Article 1(1) ICERD covers race, colour, descent, or national and ethnic origin. This is wider than, for example, the EU Race Directive, which only covers racial and ethnic origin.

Third, it covers a wide range of protected fields (see Article 5): those of human rights and fundamental freedoms, including equality before the law, the right to security, political and civil rights and economic, social and cultural rights (Banton 2002a: 64). This corresponds with the rights guaranteed in the International Bill of Rights.

Fourth, according to the Committee on the Elimination of All Forms of Racial Discrimination (CERD), the words 'purpose or effect' indicate that both direct and indirect discrimination are covered. In its General Recommendation No. 14 the Committee has stated:

> In seeking to determine whether an action has an effect contrary to the Convention, it will look to see whether that action has an unjustifiable disparate impact upon a group distinguished by race, colour, descent, or national or ethnic origin.

'Disparate impact' is a term often used, especially in the US, instead of 'indirect discrimination' but denoting the same. On the other hand, MacEwen (1995: 51) expresses doubt whether the definition covers indirect discrimination, although he writes that 'a number of international lawyers are of the view that the Convention does cover indirect discrimination'.

Lastly, the definition refers to 'public life'. Does this mean that the ICERD is not applicable where non-governmental or private actors are involved? According to Boyle and Baldaccini (2001: 159–60) there are two opinions; the first one holds that private acts are excluded from the scope of the Convention. The second opinion interprets 'public life' as being opposed to private life rather than just referring to government actions. The latter is supported by provisions such as those laid down in Article 5(e) and (f) ICERD. Authors point out that the distinction between the public sphere, which is subject to government regulation and the private sphere, which is not, is becoming more blurred with the extension by many governments of programmes of privatization and with the ever more prominent role of private actors at the global level. The issue is important because the scope of the ICERD would be wider, and thus it would be preferable if the second opinion was followed because it would put a duty on States Parties to prohibit, for example, a private employer or landlord discriminating against a person on the grounds of race, colour, descent, or national or ethnic origin. National legislation prohibiting discrimination often covers parts of the private sphere: purely private relationships, like who a person wants to marry, fall outside the scope of the legislation – although many States do intervene when a party is subject to immigration control (for an example see Sections 19–25 of the British Asylum and Immigration (Treatment of Claimants, etc.) Act 2004) – but relationships between, for example, a private landlord and tenant or a private employer and employee are covered by the prohibition. The EU anti discrimination legislation explicitly mentions that it covers both the public and private sectors, including public bodies (Articles 3(1) of the Race, Framework, Equal Treatment (Amendment) and Equal Treatment (Goods) Directives and Article 14(1) of the Recast Directive).

The ICERD provides expressly for positive action measures: Article 1(4) determines that:

> Special measures taken for the sole purpose of securing adequate advancement of certain racial or ethnic groups or individuals requiring such protection as may be necessary in order to ensure such groups equal enjoyment or exercise of human rights and fundamental freedoms shall not be deemed racial discrimination, provided, however, that such measures do not, as a consequence, lead to the maintenance of separate rights for different racial groups and that they shall not be continued after the objectives for which they were taken have been achieved.

Article 2(2) is even stronger in its formulation in that it actually prescribes that States Parties shall take 'special and concrete measures to ensure the adequate development and protection of certain racial groups or individuals belonging to them …'. Here again, the measures should not lead to the maintenance of unequal or separate rights and should not be continued after their objective has been achieved. Like Convention C111 above, the ICERD thus imposes a duty on States Parties to take positive measures, but these measures should be for a limited time only.

Article 14 ICERD provides for an individual right to petition to the CERD, if the State Party makes a declaration

> that it recognizes the competence of the Committee to receive and consider communications from *individuals or groups of individuals* [our italics] within its jurisdiction claiming to be victims of a violation by that State Party of any of the rights set forth in this Convention.

This Convention thus allows for actions by groups of individuals as well. Of the EU Member States, Estonia, Greece, Latvia, Lithuania and the UK have not made such a declaration, the others have all recognized the individual right to petition.

Two more problems in relation to the ICERD need to be pointed out because they affect its practical value. First, Article 1(2) allows for distinctions between citizens and non-citizens. Article 1(3) recognizes a State's sovereignty in matters of nationality, citizenship or naturalization, but does put a proviso on this: such provisions should not discriminate against any particular nationality. CERD has brought out a General Recommendation on discrimination against non-citizens (No 30) in which it affirms, first (point 1, 2), that Article 1(2) should not be interpreted to detract in any way from the rights and freedoms recognized in particular in the UDHR, the ICECSR and the ICCPR. Second (point 1, 3), that Article 5 ICERD incorporates the obligation of States Parties to prohibit and eliminate discrimination in the enjoyment of a number of human rights, which are, in principle, to be enjoyed by all persons. States Parties are under an obligation to guarantee equality between citizens and non-citizens in the enjoyment of these rights to the extent recognized in international law. And, third (point 1, 4), and most importantly, that:

> Under the Convention, differential treatment based on citizenship or immigration status will constitute discrimination if the criteria for such differentiation, judged in the light of the objectives and purposes of the Convention, are not applied pursuant to a legitimate aim, and are not proportional to the achievement of this aim. Differentiation within the scope of Article 1, paragraph 4, of the Convention relating to special measures is not considered discriminatory.

The CERD follows this with an enumeration of measures that it recommends the States Parties to adopt. Therefore, Article 1(2) must be construed narrowly and differential treatment of non-citizens will be considered to be discrimination unless it is objectively justified.

Like with other international instruments, there are also problems with the enforcement of the ICERD. Despite Article 6 providing that States Parties shall assure 'effective protection and remedies through the competent national tribunals and other state institutions' and that such tribunals should give 'just and adequate reparation or satisfaction', in practice, as MacEwen (1995: 51) writes, 'the sanctions for non-compliance are largely ineffective' and there is no specific obligation for signatories 'to demonstrate that individuals are provided with appropriate remedies for acts of discrimination, or that there are effective state systems for monitoring and review'.

What are the obligations of the signatories? According to Article 9, States Parties undertake to submit periodic reports on the legislative, judicial, administrative or other measures they have adopted following the Convention for the consideration of the CERD. The CERD reports annually to the General Assembly of the UN on its activities and it may make suggestions and general recommendations based on the examination of the reports from the States Parties. The provisions on reporting are therefore rather vague.[6] Article 11 determines that if a State Party considers that another State Party

6 For more information on the reporting procedure see Banton 1996 and 2002a: 67–87.

is not giving effect to the provisions of the Convention, it may bring this to the attention of the Committee. However, this procedure has never been utilized. This could be because of the possible adverse diplomatic consequences or of the awareness that the Committee has 'no power to legally adjudicate on a state's complaint. The Committee may only recommend a friendly settlement and has no enforcement powers' (Boyle and Baldaccini 2001: 173).

There is also the, already mentioned, individual complaint procedure of Article 14. However, this can only be used if a State Party has recognized the competence of the Committee to do so. This procedure also has the same problem that, as O'Flaherty notes, the CERD 'is not a court, does not issue "judgements" and has no means to enforce any views it might adopt' (O'Flaherty 1997: 221). The problem with enforcement is compounded by the fact that many States Parties have made reservations to the ICERD and/or have not recognized its individual complaints procedure.

We can conclude that the ICERD, despite these limitations, can be a very useful convention in the fight against racial discrimination, first, because it is the only UN instrument specifically aimed at the elimination of such discrimination; second, because it contains a clear and wide definition of race discrimination which encompasses both direct and indirect discrimination; third, because it puts a duty on States to take positive action measures; and, fourth, because it provides for an individual complaints procedure as long as States Parties have agreed to be subject to it.

2.5 Council of Europe and the fight against racial discrimination

The instruments discussed so far are global instruments adopted through the UN. In contrast, Article 14 ECHR and Protocol 12 to the ECHR are European measures adopted by the Council of Europe. The ECHR was agreed in 1950 and Protocol 12 was adopted in 2000.

The Council of Europe, with its seat in Strasbourg, is an international organization established in 1949 in order to promote greater unity between its members. At present (April 2009), the Council has 47 Member States among which are all EU Member States. Any European State can become a member provided it accepts the principle of the rule of law and guarantees human rights and fundamental freedoms to everyone under its jurisdiction. The Council of Europe is thus an organization specifically focusing on human rights in greater Europe. The Council has no legislative powers.

In 1993, the Council established the European Commission against Racism and Intolerance (ECRI). This monitoring body has been given the task to 'combat racism, xenophobia, antisemitism and intolerance at the level of greater Europe and from the perspective of the protection of human rights in the light of the European Convention on Human Rights, its additional protocols and related case law' (Council Of Europe, Statute: Article 1).

ECRI's action covers 'all necessary measures to combat violence, discrimination and prejudice faced by persons or groups of persons, notably on grounds of "race" [*sic*] colour, language, religion, nationality and national or ethnic origin'.[7] Therefore, ECRI is a body specifically focusing on the fight against racism and racial discrimination in greater Europe. It is important to note that religious discrimination is included in its mandate.

ECRI's programme, according to Article 10 of its Statute, shall include three aspects: country-by-country approach; work on general themes; and activities in relation to civil society. Under the first aspect, ECRI produces periodic (every four/five years) country reports in which it reviews a Member State's legislation, policies and other measures to combat racism, xenophobia, anti-Semitism and intolerance and its effectiveness, and proposes further action. These reports are published unless the Member State expressly opposes such publication (Article 11). Under the second aspect of its programme, ECRI adopts General Policy Recommendations and collects and disseminates examples of 'good practices' (Article 12).[8] General Policy Recommendation 7, on national legislation to combat racism and racial discrimination, is of some interest for the subject of this book. Adopted in December 2002, it recommends that the Governments of the Member States enact legislation against racism and racial discrimination if such legislation does not already exist or is incomplete, and that they ensure that the key components set out in the Recommendation are included in such legislation. ECRI has taken account of, among other instruments, the EU Race Directive and many of the key components set out in the Recommendation are similar to the provisions of the Directive. However, the Recommendation has no legally binding force, whereas the Directive is binding on the EU Member States, who are obliged to implement the Directive in their national legislation (Howard 2005). Under the third aspect of its programme, ECRI aims to promote dialogue and mutual respect among the general public and it organizes awareness raising and information activities (Article 13).

The ECHR was adopted in Rome in 1950. Article 19 of the Convention established a European Court of Human Rights to ensure that contracting states observe their obligations under the Convention. Article 14 contains a prohibition of discrimination on an extensive number of grounds:

> The enjoyment of the rights and freedoms set forth in this Convention shall be secured without discrimination on any ground such as sex, race, colour, language, religion, political or other opinion, national or social origin, association with a national minority, property, birth or other status.

7 See www.coe.int/t/dghl/monitoring/ecri/default_en.asp (accessed 27 April 2009)

8 To date, ECRI has adopted 12 General Policy Recommendations, see European Commission against Racism and Intolerance 2007 and 2009.

The terms 'any ground such as' and 'or other status' indicate that the list is open-ended and can be extended through the case law. Feldman (2002: 145) calls the list 'illustrative, not exhaustive' and writes:

> The open-ended nature of the list of improper grounds for differentiation enables changing *mores* [his italics] to be fed into the protection available under Article 14 without the need for further treaties or legislation, unlike the approach taken in UK and EC law.

This implies that UK and EC laws contain closed lists of grounds, which can only be added to via new legislation. For EC law this can be seen in Article 13 EC which allows 'action to combat discrimination based on sex, racial or ethnic origin, religion or belief, disability, age and sexual orientation'. This leaves no room for any other grounds to be recognized except via a Treaty revision.

Despite the extensive and open-ended list of prohibited grounds, Article 14 has one major drawback: it does not give an independent, freestanding right to non-discrimination. It only secures 'the enjoyment of the rights and freedoms set forth in this Convention' without discrimination. Therefore, the right to non-discrimination is accessory or parasitic and discrimination can only be challenged in relation to the other Convention rights. This situation has been criticized for falling short of the standard of protection provided in other international human rights instruments (O'Hare 2001: 133 and 135; Grief 2002: HR/4). ECRI itself noted that the Convention was 'lagging behind other international instruments in the matter of non-discrimination' (Schokkenbroek 2000: 31). O'Hare even called it a 'prominent failure of the Convention system' (2001: 135). To overcome this problem, the Council of Europe's Committee of Ministers approved, following a proposal from ECRI, an additional Protocol 12 to the ECHR. This Protocol, which opened for signature on 4 November 2000, provides an independent, freestanding right to non-discrimination in Article 1(1): 'The enjoyment of any right set forth by law shall be secured without discrimination on any grounds such as …' and then it mentions the same grounds as Article 14 ECHR. Protocol 12 uses the same terms 'any grounds such as' and 'or other status' and thus the list of grounds is also open-ended. Many Member States appear reluctant to ratify the Protocol because, on the one hand, it is said to be too broad and to give too much discretion to the European Court of Human Rights to determine the obligations of States, and, on the other hand, it is criticized for not providing for positive measures. However, the Preamble makes it clear that positive measures are allowed. It states:

> Reaffirming that the principle of non-discrimination does not prevent States Parties from taking measures in order to promote full and effective equality, provided that there is an objective and reasonable justification for those measures.

We will come back to this statement later.

Another criticism of the ECHR, related to the criticism about its accessory character, is that it does not give a guarantee of equality before the law or a right to protection against discrimination like Article 26 ICCPR does. Both Article 24 of the American Convention on Human Rights and Article 3 of the African Charter on Human and Peoples' Rights contain such a guarantee. Protocol 12 does extend Article 14 ECHR beyond the rights and freedoms of the Convention to 'any right set forth by law,' but it still does not contain a guarantee of equality before the law, although its Preamble mentions that the Member States are 'having regard to the fundamental principle according to which all persons are equal before the law and entitled to equal protection of the law'. However, the principle is not explicitly stated in the operative part of the Protocol itself. Therefore, Protocol 12 can be seen as an improvement on Article 14 ECHR by creating a freestanding right, but it would have been better if it had expressly stated the principle of equality before the law.[9] The Protocol entered into force on 1 April 2005.[10] As the Protocol has only been in force for a very short time and has been ratified only by a small number of States, there is no case law on it yet.

The Court[11] has stated clearly that the right under Article 14 not to be discriminated against was violated 'when States treat differently persons in analogous situations without providing an objective and reasonable justification' but also 'when States without an objective and reasonable justification fail to treat differently persons whose situations are significantly different' (*Thlimmenos v Greece*: para 44). Therefore, the ECHR prohibits direct discrimination. Note that a difference in treatment is not considered to be discrimination if it is objectively and reasonably justified, as the Court has frequently expressed.[12]

Does Article 14 cover indirect discrimination as well? In the *Belgian Linguistics* case, the Court referred to the 'aim and effects' of the measures under consideration in the case. The use of the term 'effects' appears to imply that indirect discrimination is covered as well as direct discrimination. However, in the *Abdulaziz* case, the Court seemed to implicitly reject the concept of indirect discrimination. In that case, the applicants argued that British immigration rules were discriminatory on the grounds of race because

9 Whether an equality clause and a clause expressly allowing for positive action measures should be added to the provision of Protocol 12 or whether a mention in the Preamble was sufficient, was part of the discussions on the text of Protocol 12, see Schokkenbroek 2004: 70–2.

10 Of the EU Member States, Cyprus, Finland, Luxembourg, the Netherlands, Romania and Spain have signed and ratified the Protocol: http://conventions.coe.int/Treaty/Commun/ChercheSig.asp?NT=177&CM=8&DF=2/8/2009&CL=ENG (accessed 1 April 2009).

11 In this section of the Chapter, reference to 'the Court' will mean the European Court of Human Rights in Strasbourg.

12 See for example: *Case relating to Certain Aspects of the Laws on the Use of Languages in Education in Belgium v Belgium* (*Belgian Linguistics* case): para 10; *Marckx v Belgium*: para 33; *Rasmussen v Denmark*: para 36; *Abdulaziz, Cabales and Balkandali v UK*: para 72.

their effect was to prevent substantially more men from the New Commonwealth and Pakistan than from elsewhere from entering Britain. The Court did not accept this argument and did not find the rules racially discriminatory, although it did find them directly discriminatory on the grounds of sex. Small (2003: 60) discusses this case and writes:

> ... it was precisely because the generally applicable rules disproportionately affected these men that they should have been reviewed as indirectly discriminatory on the test in *Belgian Linguistics*.

In the *Thlimmenos* case, the Court accepted that indirect discrimination was covered by Article 14 ECHR, as will be clear from the second part of the statement quoted above. As Small writes, that case 'has finally settled the issue in favour of indirect discrimination under Article 14' (ibid: 60–1). Mr Thlimmenos, a Jehova's Witness, was convicted and served a prison sentence for refusing, on religious grounds, to wear a military uniform while performing his military service. About nine years later he was refused access to the chartered accountancy profession because he had a previous conviction for a serious criminal offence and this barred him from access. He argued that this was a violation of Article 14 ECHR taken together with Article 9 (freedom of religion). The Court decided that the Greek Government had failed to treat Thlimmenos differently from other people convicted of a serious crime without an objective or reasonable justification. It considered that 'a conviction for refusing on religious or philosophical grounds to wear the military uniform cannot imply any dishonesty or moral turpitude likely to undermine the offender's ability to exercise this profession' (para 47). The State should have provided for appropriate exceptions to the rule barring persons convicted of a serious crime from the profession of chartered accountant. So, the Greek Government was held to be in violation of Article 14, because it had not taken into account that the rule for access to the chartered accountancy profession could have disproportionate adverse effects for people like Thlimmenos. The following passage of the *Jordan v UK* case[13] also indicates that the Court has accepted that Article 14 ECHR covers both direct and indirect discrimination:

> Where a general policy or measure has disproportionately prejudicial effects on a particular group, it is not excluded that this may be considered as discriminatory notwithstanding that it is not specifically aimed or directed at that group.

13 Para 154. This case was conducted together with three other cases, in each of which the same passage was quoted. Judgment in all four cases was given on 4 May 2001. See *McKerr v UK*: para 165; *Kelly and others v UK*: para 148; *Shanaghan v UK*: para 129.

Gerards (2004a: 13) writes that the Court in the *Thlimmenos* case 'explicitly accepted that not only formal discrimination (unequal treatment of equal cases), but also substantive discrimination falls within the scope of Article 14 ECHR'. The Court has mentioned repeatedly that 'the Convention is intended to guarantee not rights that are theoretical or illusory but rights that are practical and effective' (*Artico v Italy*: para 33; *Loizidou v Turkey*: para 72) which also suggests that both direct and indirect discrimination are covered.

The interpretation of Protocol 12 will, very likely, follow the interpretation of Article 14 ECHR in this, and we can thus conclude that both prohibit direct and indirect discrimination.

Do these instruments allow for positive action? As mentioned, the Court allows justification for discrimination under Article 14 ECHR. This enables positive measures to be accepted as a justified form of differential treatment provided that the justification is objective and reasonable, has a legitimate aim, and there is a reasonable relationship of proportionality between the means employed and the aims sought. The latter is the test for justification used by the Court.[14] Feldman (2002: 145–6) points to the *Belgian Linguistics* case to support this, as it mentions that 'certain legal inequalities tend only to correct factual inequalities' (para 10). In the case of *Lindsay v UK* (p. 559), it was found 'that the difference in treatment in the present case has an objective and reasonable justification in the aim of providing positive discrimination in favour of married women who work'. Small explains that the Court held that the failure to treat Mr. Thlimmenos differently from others convicted of a felony was without objective and reasonable justification. The specific failure in this case was the failure of the Greek law to provide for appropriate exceptions to the rule barring persons convicted of a felony from the profession of chartered accountant. In other words, Greek law should have provided for exceptions. From this, she then concludes that 'it is implicit in the reasoning of *Thlimmenos* that positive discrimination may sometimes be required' (Small 2003: 61–2).

This indicates that Article 14 ECHR allows for positive measures. As we have seen, Protocol 12 does not explicitly allow for positive measures in the Protocol itself, but the Preamble states that they are allowed if there is an objective and reasonable justification. This confirms what has been said about Article 14. So both measures allow for positive measures, but neither of them put a duty on states to take such measures.

Article 32 ECHR determines that the jurisdiction of the Court extends to all matters concerning the interpretation and application of the Convention and the Protocols thereto. Under Article 33, any State Party may refer another State Party for any alleged breach of the provisions of the Convention and the Protocols. Article 34 gives 'any person, non-governmental organization or

14 See cases op. cit. n. 12.

group of individuals' who claim to be the victim of a violation by a State Party of the rights of the Convention or its Protocols, the right to apply to the Court. These enforcement mechanisms are also available for Protocol 12 as the Articles mention both the Convention and its Protocols. So both Article 14 and Protocol 12 allow for actions by groups as well as by individuals.

Do Article 14 ECHR and Protocol 12 put positive duties on states to eliminate discrimination? Article 14 ECHR obliges States Parties to secure the enjoyment of the rights and freedoms set forth in the Convention without discrimination, while Article 1 obliges them 'to secure to everyone within their jurisdiction the rights and freedoms defined in Section 1 of this Convention'. Section 1 includes Article 14. This appears to put a positive duty on states to protect a person against discrimination in relation to his or her Convention rights. This is supported by the Report from the Commission in the *Belgian Linguistics* case. The Commission expressed its opinion that the word 'secured' implies the placing of an obligation which is not simply negative on the Contracting States (para 10 and Feldman 2002: 143 and 145–6). Article 1 of Protocol 12 has two paragraphs; according to the first one, the enjoyment of any right set forth by law shall be secured without discrimination, while the second paragraph states that no one shall be discriminated against by any public authority on any of the grounds mentioned in paragraph 1. The duty imposed on States by the first paragraph is formulated in the same way as Article 14 ECHR, although it covers 'any right set forth by law', so the same reasoning can be used here: the state has a duty to protect a person against discrimination in any rights set forth by law. The second paragraph puts a (negative) duty on any public authority not to discriminate. However, neither instrument seems to require States to enact new legislation to guarantee non-discrimination. The Explanatory Report to Protocol 12 (Council of Europe ETS No. 177: para 24) states that 'while such positive obligations cannot be excluded altogether, the prime objective of Article 1 is to embody a negative obligation for the Parties: the obligation not to discriminate against individuals'. It continues:

> On the other hand, it cannot be totally excluded that the duty to 'secure' under the first paragraph of Article 1 might entail positive obligations. For example, this question could arise if there is a clear lacuna in domestic law protection from discrimination.
>
> (Ibid: para 26)

The latter infers that a failure to act could be a violation of the Protocol. According to O'Hare (2001: 140), 'this approach is supported by the case law of the Court in the context of other Convention rights'. This therefore suggests that both Article 14 ECHR and Article 1 Protocol 12 contain a very tentative positive duty to protect from and to prevent or remedy discrimination (Schokkenbroek 2004: 75–9).

The ECHR has been in force for more than 50 years but, because of the accessory character of Article 14, the Court has not often made a decision on that article. Article 14 can only be invoked together with one or more of the other rights in the Convention. Often, if the Court has decided that there is a breach of the other article(s), it will find it unnecessary to consider if there was also a breach of Article 14. In fact, until 2004, the Court has never found a violation of Article 14 on the grounds of racial discrimination. *Nachova and others v Bulgaria*[15] was the first case concerning racial discrimination in which a violation of Article 14 (in conjunction with Article 2) was found. This case involved the treatment of people of Roma origin. It was followed by other cases in which racial discrimination was held to be a violation of Article 14: *Moldovan and others v Romania (No 2), Cobzaru v Romania, Secic v Croatia,* and *Stoica v Romania,* all concerning Roma People, and *Timishev v Russia*, involving a Russian national of Chechen origin. In *D.H. and others v Czech Republic*, the second Chamber of the Court found no breach of Article 14 (in conjunction with Article 2, Protocol 1, which states the right to education). However, the Grand Chamber decided, by thirteen votes against four, that there had been a violation. In this case, 18 children of Roma origin complained that the decision to place them in special schools was discriminatory. The judgment of the Grand Chamber also contains a clear and explicit recognition that indirect discrimination is covered by Article 14 ECHR (in para 40). A violation of Article 14 was also found in relation to the segregation of Roma children in education in *Sampanis and others v Greece*.

There is another area of the Court's case law where racism and racial discrimination have played a role and that is in cases where the issue has been whether prohibitions on, and limitations to, the expression of racism and racial hatred are compatible with the rights of the Convention. In these cases there is often a clash between different human rights, like the right to freedom of expression (Article 10) or freedom of association (Article 11) and the right to be free from discrimination.

The views in Europe with regard to interference with freedom of expression or association to ban expressions of racist hatred are in marked contrast to those in the US, where freedom of expression and the right to voice political dissent is afforded greater protection under the First Amendment of the US Constitution. In the US, racist propaganda is seen as part of the legitimate political discourse.[16] Here we will concentrate on the position taken by the

15 In this judgment a violation was found both concerning the lack of investigation into whether discriminatory attitudes played a role in the shootings of Roma people by police officers and concerning the shootings themselves. The Grand Chamber, in its judgment of 6 July 2005, [2005] ECHR 465, also found a violation of Article 14, but only concerning the lack of investigation, not concerning the shootings themselves.

16 For more information on the situation in the US see, for example: Coliver 1992; Jacobs and Potter 1998; Hepple 2000; Iganski 2001, 2002; Gelber 2002; Nathwani 2002.

European Court of Human Rights, as this is relevant for the EU Member States. The Convention gives the right to freedom of expression in Article 10:

> Everyone has the right to freedom of expression. This right shall include freedom to hold opinions and to receive and impart information and ideas without interference by public authority and regardless of frontiers. …

However, the Convention itself states clearly that this right carries duties and responsibilities and is not absolute. Paragraph 2 of Article 10 states when interference is justified:

> The exercise of these freedoms, since it carries with it duties and responsibilities, may be subject to such formalities, conditions, restrictions or penalties as are prescribed by law and are necessary in a democratic society, in the interests of national security, territorial integrity or public safety, for the prevention of disorder or crime, for the protection of health or morals, for the protection of the reputation or rights of others, for preventing disclosure of information received in confidence, or for maintaining the authority and impartiality of the judiciary.

This right to freedom of expression as a fundamental human right, which carries with it duties and responsibilities, can also be found in the UDHR (Articles 19 and 29) and in the ICCPR (Article 19).

In many of the cases someone has been convicted for defamation or incitement to racial hatred for what s/he has said or written. The person convicted then applied to the Strasbourg Court, claiming that this was a violation of Article 10, a breach of his/her right to free expression. There are a number of points that can be made about the decisions of the Court. First, the Court has often stressed that freedom of expression constitutes one of the basic conditions of a democratic society and is essential for its progress and for the development of every man (*Handyside v UK:* para 49). Second, the Court has stressed the importance of freedom of the press and freedom of political debate for a democratic society and that the limits of acceptable criticism are wider with regard to a politician acting in his official capacity than in relation to a private individual. The protection of the reputation of a politician, acting in his public capacity, has to be weighed against the interests of open discussion of political issues (*Oberschlick v Austria*: para 59). Third, the Court has held that freedom of expression under Article 10 may not be invoked in a sense contrary to Article 17. The latter article prohibits abuse of the rights of the Convention. Therefore, Article 10 cannot be invoked contrary to the text and the spirit of the Convention which would contribute to the destruction of the rights and freedoms set forth in the Convention.[17] Fourth, the Court

17 See Cases *Glimmerveen and Haagenbeek v the Netherlands* and *Kuhnen v Federal Republic of Germany*. Glimmerveen and Haagenbeek were convicted for distributing leaflets

will take into account the medium and manner of the communication. For example, in the *Jersild* case, the Court considered that television would have more impact than an article in a paper (para 31). It also considered that the programme in that case was broadcast as part of a serious news programme and was intended for well-informed people (para 34). In *Lopez Gomes da Silva v Portugal*, the Court considered that the applicant acted in accordance with the rules governing the journalistic profession by placing the editorial in question, which described a politician as being fascist and anti-Semitic, alongside the declarations of that politician (para 35).

We can conclude that the Court will allow for interference with freedom of expression in case of racist expressions or incitement to acts of violence, but that these exceptions have to fulfil strict conditions: they have to be prescribed by law, be necessary in a democratic society to achieve a legitimate aim, which means that they have to fulfil a pressing social need, that the means used must be proportionate to the aim pursued and that the reasons given for the justification must be relevant and sufficient. The Court will thus accept (criminal or other) laws against hate speech and racist expressions, as does Article 4 ICERD. However, some States Parties see these laws as an infringement of freedom of expression rights and have, therefore, made reservations against Article 4 when they signed the Convention.

Within the EU it appears to be accepted that such laws are justified restrictions on a person's freedom of expression. For example, the European Council Consultative Commission on Racism and Xenophobia (the Kahn Commission) (1995: 49) wrote in its report:

> The legal systems of all EU Member States as well as the international human rights instruments to which the Member States are parties allow for such restrictions ... [i.e. criminal laws prohibiting incitement to racial hatred] of the freedom of expression and association, provided these are lawful and necessary to protect the rights of others. Moreover, various international human rights instruments to which most EU Member States are parties prohibit by law the advocacy of national, racial or religious hatred that constitutes incitement to discrimination, hostility and violence.

In the Charter of European Parties for a Non-Racist Society, the democratic political parties of Europe express their awareness of the fact that, according

advocating racial discrimination and repatriation of all non-whites from Holland. Kuhnen had a leading position in an organization attempting to reinstitute the National Socialist Party in Germany. They were all considered to invoke freedom of expression against the spirit of the Convention and therefore the interference with their right was considered justified.

to the international human rights instruments signed and ratified by the EU Member States:

> one's political freedoms are not absolute in view of the equally fundamental right to be protected against racial discrimination and that therefore political freedoms cannot be allowed to be abused to exploit, cause or initiate prejudice on the grounds of race, colour, ethnic origin or nationality or for the purpose of seeking to gain the sympathy of the electorate for prejudice on such grounds.

Another example is a Resolution in which the European Parliament mentions freedom of speech where it welcomes Member States' equality laws which are 'protective of the rule of law in setting the limit to freedom of speech at the point where it incites to racial hatred or violence' (European Parliament 1999: QQ). The Parliament goes on to call for, amongst other things, 'adequate checks and balances on the role of the media, including the Internet, while avoiding the infringement of truthful reporting, free speech, and ability to counter extremist opinions' (Ibid: RR). Further on in the Resolution, the Parliament 'calls on the Member States and the Community institutions to ensure that rules restricting freedom of opinion and expression are not contrary or disproportionate to national, European and international rules on the subject' (Ibid: 25).

These examples all suggest that, within the EU, restrictions on free expression to protect against racist speech and incitement to racial hatred are accepted. The general opinion appears to be that a balance needs to be found between the protection of freedom of expression on the one hand, and the right not to be discriminated against on the other hand. States have a margin of appreciation in balancing these rights, but the Court will be the ultimate judge on whether the state has come to the right conclusion.

Two more articles of the ECHR could be important to racial discrimination. First, in the *East African Asians* Case (paras 207–8), the Commission found that racial discrimination could amount to degrading treatment and thus be in violation of Article 3 of the Convention. Second, the Court has held that racial prejudice expressed by jurors in jury trials impedes the right of the accused to a fair trial under Article 6 ECHR. The Court held that the Convention imposes an obligation on national courts to check whether it is an impartial tribunal under Article 6(1) when there are serious allegations about racist expressions by a juror (*Remli v France*: para 48; *Gregory v UK*: para 45; *Sander v UK*: para 34).

2.6 The EU agency for fundamental rights and international cooperation

The EU Agency for Fundamental Rights (FRA), which started operating in 2007, merits a mention here, as the Council Regulation (168/2007) establishing this Agency prescribes cooperation with 'the Organisation for Security and Cooperation in Europe (OSCE), especially the office for Democratic Institutions and Human Rights (ODIHR), the United Nations and other organisations' (Article 8(2)(b)). And Article 9 determines that: 'in order to avoid duplication and in order to ensure complementarity and added value, the Agency shall coordinate its activities with those of the Council of Europe …'. The Community shall, therefore, 'enter into an agreement with the Council of Europe for the purpose of establishing close cooperation between the latter and the Agency'. The Council of Europe will appoint an independent person to sit on the Agency's Management Board and on its Executive Board. This Agreement was concluded between the EU and the Council of Europe in July 2008 (Agreement 2008). It establishes a 'cooperation framework' (Article 2) and 'regular contact' (Article 3) between the Agency and the Council of Europe and determines that this 'cooperation shall cover the whole range of the Agency's activities, both present and future' (Article 6). It also contains rules on the exchange of information and data (Article 7) and determines that:

> The Agency shall take due account of the judgments and decisions of the European Court of Human rights concerning the areas of activity of the Agency and, where relevant, of findings, reports and activities in the human rights field of the Council of Europe's human rights monitoring and intergovernmental committees, as well as those of the Council of Europe's Commissioner for Human Rights.
>
> (Article 8)

Some examples of this cooperation can be found in the Joint Statement of the FRA and the Council of Europe against Racism (Joint Statement 2008); in the Joint Statement on the Occasion of the International Day for the Elimination of Racial Discrimination made by the ODIHR, the ECRI and the FRA (Joint Statement 2009a); and in the Joint Statement on the Occasion of the International Roma Day (8 April 2009), made by the FRA, the Council of Europe Commissioner for Human Rights, the ODIHR and the OSCE High Commissioner on National Minorities (Joint Statement 2009b).

2.7 Conclusion

In this Chapter, we have discussed the anti discrimination clauses of the international human rights instruments which are influential in the EU. One reason for this influence is that all EU Member States have signed and ratified most of the international measures, and protection against racial discrimination is part of the general principles of international law, or *ius cogens*. Another reason is that all institutions of the EU have put the fight against racial and ethnic discrimination firmly within an international human rights context, as is clear from, for example, the texts of Article 6(2) TEU, the Preamble of the Race Directive and the European Charter of Fundamental Rights. The ECJ has also stressed the importance of the principle of equality and non-discrimination as a general principle of Community law. Within the EU, the ECHR and the case law of the European Court of Human Rights are the most important and influential. These have, therefore, been discussed in more detail, together with Protocol 12, as that widens the protection against discrimination given in Article 14 ECHR to cover 'any right set forth by law'. The other instrument discussed in detail is the ICERD because it is the only international measure specifically aimed at the elimination of racial discrimination and because it is one of the most widely ratified UN Conventions. The ICERD is also useful because it gives a clear definition of racial discrimination.

The aim of this Chapter has been to provide the international human rights context for the anti race discrimination legislation of the EU. Boyle and Baldaccini end with a mixed verdict on the achievement of the international human rights approaches, but conclude:

> The most important achievement of the international human rights approach to the elimination of racial discrimination has been to establish in international law a prohibition on racism as a state ideology and on the practice of all forms of racial and ethnic discrimination. Not only are these prohibitions part of international customary law but the majority of the world states that have ratified ICERD have embraced a range of duties obligating them to eliminate any such discrimination by legislative, educational and other means.
>
> (Boyle and Baldaccini 2001: 191)

It is with this in mind that we will examine the EU measures against racial or ethnic origin discrimination in the following chapters.

3 Definitions of race, racism and racial discrimination

3.1 Introduction

In this Chapter, the concepts of race, racism and racial discrimination are explored and defined and the possible pitfalls in using these terms are highlighted. This is followed, in the next chapter, by an analysis of these terms in relation to the Race Directive.

The first concept to be explored is race and this is followed by racism. In some ways, which will be touched upon in the discussion, it is difficult to define race without also mentioning racism. However, the opposite, defining racism without touching on race would be even more difficult. The two concepts are linked in many ways, although they can also be seen, as Benedict (1983, preface) does, as being 'poles apart'.

After the discussion of race and racism, the concept of discrimination, and especially racial discrimination, is explored. Although the emphasis is on racial discrimination, other forms of discrimination will also be mentioned. It is difficult to discuss racial discrimination without looking at discrimination in a wider context, as the demarcation between the different grounds for discrimination is not always clear and people are often discriminated against on more than one ground.

3.2 Race

3.2.1 Historically specific

Perhaps the simplest way to find a definition of race or a good first step would be to look up the term in the dictionary. The *Collins Concise Dictionary* 1990 defines race as: 'A group of people of common ancestry, distinguished from others by physical characteristics such as hair-type, colour of skin, stature, etc. …'. But does this definition help us in explaining what race is, how it has been understood in the past and how it is understood now?

The literature on the subject suggests that it is not as simple as this, that defining race is much more complicated because the term appears to be changing over time; it is not a static concept with a single meaning. It has had different meanings in different historical settings and we will therefore have to trace the meaning of the term over time. Goldberg (1999: 371) suggests looking at race 'as a fluid, transforming, historically specific concept parasitic on theoretic and social discourses for the meaning it assumes at given historical moments …'. Race, in other words, is a fluid concept that takes its meaning in a historically specific context. We therefore have to look briefly at this history.[1]

The term race was hardly used before the eighteenth century, but when it was used it denoted nothing more than lineage or line of descent; therefore, race was a group of people with a common line of descent, a common ancestry. When people came into contact with other people, race was used as a term to relate to these other people and to define themselves in relation to these other people. Race denoted observed variations between people, what Banton (1983: 34–8) describes as 'phenotypical variations', for example variations in complexion, hair type, and physique.

Not until the eighteenth century did race become a biological term, a subject of the biological sciences. The world was seen as populated by distinct races, each with different biological and cultural characteristics. This biological distinction became linked to a hierarchy between the races, with some races being considered superior to others. This inferiority/superiority was used to justify exclusion, subordination and even extermination of certain groups considered to be inferior. Many people argue that race was used or 'reinvented' with this ranking attached to it to explain events in the eighteenth and nineteenth centuries like white domination, colonization, slavery and other forms of exploitation (Miles 1989; Furedi 1998). Even in the twentieth century, race is used for political goals. The International Council on Human Rights Policy states that: 'in many cases race is made use of, or even invented, to justify discrimination. Race or a myth of race serves political ends' (International Council on Human Rights Policy 2000: 4).

Scientists in the 1930s disproved the theories about biological differences and most writers, writing after World War II, acknowledge that there is no scientific evidence to support any theory that there are different, separate, biological races. However, biological notions of race do still appear to be present in political discourse and popular thinking. The term is still used in everyday language to label differences between people, especially differences in skin colour (Miles 1989: 37–8; Banton 1992: 78; Solomos 1993: 8; Mason 1995: 7; Guillaumin 1999: 355–62).

1 Because we are only defining race and racism for the purpose and in the context of this book, this look at the history is necessarily short and does not go into details. For more information on the history of these two terms the reader is referred to Benedict 1983; Miles 1989; Furedi 1998; Bulmer and Solomos 1999; and Banton 2002a.

3.2.2 Hierarchy of races

Race, therefore, has been and still is connected to the idea of a hierarchy between races. The hierarchy meant that some races were considered to be inferior and this has led to inferior treatment of people of certain races. This is where race and racism are so closely linked that one cannot describe one without touching on the other. Because the term race has this 'negative' link, some writers suggest that it should be dropped altogether. See, for example, the quote from Montagu that 'it were better that the term "race", being so weighed down with false meaning, be dropped altogether from the vocabulary' (Miles 1989: 45). Other writers clearly state that they reject any link. Benedict, writing in 1942, expresses emphatically in her preface that using the category race does not entail supporting or authorizing racism. According to her, race is a matter of scientific study, while racism is an unproven assumption of the biological and perpetual superiority of one human group over another. Race and racism are therefore 'poles apart' (Benedict 1983: preface).

That theories of the superiority of some races over others still exert their influence and that the negative connotation of the term race still exists can be seen in the Third UNESCO *Statement on Race* of 1964, which declared that 'all men living today belong to a single species, homo sapiens, and are derived from common stock' (UNESCO 1969: 44). Further on it states that 'it is not possible from the biological point of view to speak in any way whatsoever of a general inferiority or superiority of this or that race' (Ibid: 45).

Another example can be found in the Preamble of the ICERD, the 1966 United Nations Convention, where the conviction is stated:

> That any doctrine of superiority based on racial differentiation is scientifically false, morally condemnable, socially unjust and dangerous, and that there is no justification for racial discrimination, in theory or in practice, anywhere.

Even at the beginning of the twenty-first century, the link between the use of the term race and support for racist theories is still present, as is clear from Tyson's article on the negotiations of the Race Directive which took place in the EU in 1999–2000 (Tyson 2001: 201–2). During these negotiations there was controversy about using race or racial origin as, for some Member States, this denoted accepting racist theories that alleged the existence of separate human races. Other Member States wanted to use the word race, rather than solely relying on ethnic origin, in order to make clear that the Directive was combating racism. The compromise that was reached was the addition of a Recital 6 to the Preamble of the Race Directive, which states:

> The European Union rejects theories which attempt to determine the existence of separate human races. The use of the term 'racial origin' in this Directive does not imply an acceptance of such theories.

3.2.3 Social construct

Connected to the fact that race is historically specific and should therefore be studied within the society in which it is used, is the view, often expressed by modern writers, that race is a social relationship and a social construct. Race is created in a particular society to justify differences in treatment or in position. Miles (1989: 37) writes that people have continued to use race to label difference and as a result certain types of social relations are defined as race relations, as relations between people of different races. He also writes that the use of the word race to label groups is 'an aspect of the social construction of reality: races are socially imagined rather than biological realities' (Ibid: 72).

Mason (1995: 1) starts his book with the assumption that there are no races in the biological sense of distinct divisions of the human species. Rather there are sociological interactions which are constituted by their participants as a particular kind of social relationship: race. In his words, race 'was always more than just a way of thinking about and describing human differences. It was a social relationship characterized by an unequal distribution of power and resources' (Ibid: 8). Mason therefore sees race as:

> a social relationship in which structural positions and social actions are ordered, justified, and explained by reference to systems of symbols and beliefs which emphasise the social and cultural relevance of biologically rooted characteristics. In other words, the social relationship race presumes the existence of racism.
>
> (Ibid: 9)

Fredman (2001a: 2 and 9–10) argues that 'race is itself a social construct, reflecting ideological attempts to legitimate domination, and heavily based on social and historical context'.

3.2.4 Concluding remarks

Summarizing, it will be clear that there is little agreement about what the concept of race means, especially when looking at the use of the term at different points in history. What needs to be kept in mind is that it is a fluid concept, changing over time and, indeed, changing with the use a person makes of it. It is suggested that there are no superior or inferior races, but that large numbers of people behave as if there are. In this sense, it is not relevant whether races exist or not, but it is important to observe that social actors treat races as real and organize their lives and exclusionary practices by reference to this. When studying race as a ground for discrimination, the perception in the minds of people is important; they discriminate against another person because they perceive him or her to be different and therefore inferior or threatening.

Race in everyday meaning is still often based on a difference between races, although not necessarily based on biological differences. It is also, and sometimes exclusively, based on cultural differences. It must also be kept in mind that the term race has been and is often used in political contexts, to support all kinds of policies, from right wing to left wing.

One more point needs discussing under this heading. The terms ethnicity or ethnic origin are often used together with, or as an alternative to, race or racial origin. An example of the former is the title the Race Directive. How closely the two concepts are related can be seen from the description of ethnic (with the noun ethnicity) in the *Collins Concise Dictionary* 1990:

1 of or relating to a human group having *racial*, linguistic and other traits in common (our italics).
2 relating to the classification of mankind in groups especially on the basis of *racial* characteristics (our italics).
3 denoting or deriving from the cultural traditions of a group of people.
4 characteristics of another culture.

From this dictionary definition it will be clear that it is difficult to draw a boundary between the concepts of ethnicity and race, as they overlap in many aspects. As the European Court of Human Rights mentioned in the *Timishev v Russia* case:

> Ethnicity and race are related and overlapping concepts. Whereas the notion of race is rooted in the idea of biological classification of human beings into subspecies according to morphological features such as skin colour or facial characteristics, ethnicity has its origin in the idea of societal groups marked by common nationality, tribal affiliation, religious faith, shared language, or cultural and traditional origins and backgrounds.
>
> (Para 55)

Therefore, the terms ethnic and ethnicity are seen as relating to cultural characteristics. It is suggested that the terms, when coupled with race in anti discrimination measures, are used to clarify that cultural traits are also included, while, when used instead of race, it is often as a euphemism, to avoid the negative implications that the word race has. Ethnic and ethnicity are less negatively loaded. Ethnic minority is also an often-encountered term. In this book it will be understood as meaning a group differentiated by racial origin or cultural background. But we should keep in mind that, as Bell (2008a: 16) writes: 'within the EU official documents, the term "ethnic minorities" is often adopted as a catch-all label for those groups in society which experience inequality arising from racism'.

3.3 Racism

3.3.1 Ideology/actions

The concept of racism is, just like race, a contested concept. Starting from the same basis as race, we find the following definition of racism in the *Collins Concise Dictionary* 1990:

1 The belief that races have distinctive cultural characteristics determined by hereditary factors and that this endows some races with intrinsic superiority.
2 Abusive or aggressive behaviour towards members of another race on the basis of such a belief.

This definition uses the term race, like most definitions of racism do. This shows the strong link between the two concepts, and also the reason why race was defined first.

The definition includes in the concept of racism not only beliefs, but also behaviour. Not all definitions given in the literature include both views and behaviour. Some writers define racism as beliefs, doctrines, views or ideologies and specifically exclude the actions or behaviour based on those doctrines. The reasons they give for this exclusion is that an inclusive definition is too wide, covers too much and is therefore of limited analytical use. Such a concept often obscures more than it reveals (Mason 1995: 11). Miles especially is very clear on this; he rejects what he calls 'an inflated concept of racism' and uses racism to denote only ideologies and beliefs (Miles 1989: 41–61).

Banton (1992: 69–72) writes that, at the United Nations, the word racism is taken to mean almost the same as racial discrimination. The two terms are often coupled together in the same sentence because some people do not regard the two terms as synonymous. Many writers use medical metaphors when writing about racism, it is seen as something pathological like an illness or a cancer. Racial discrimination is seen as something more normal and general, in the sense that crime is a normal feature of any human society. Banton writes that on a general level the two terms offer distinct and possibly competing conceptions, but that their differences often dissolve when it comes to practical applications. For some then, racism is a doctrine while racial discrimination is a practice (Solomos 1993: 79; Furedi 1998: 14). In that view, racism only covers ideologies and doctrines, while actions based on those views are called racial discrimination.

It is suggested that it is important to keep this distinction in mind when discussing legislative measures because laws against racism and racial discrimination aim at the practical occurrences of racism, at prohibiting the behaviour based on racist beliefs rather than at views and ideas. Prohibiting racist beliefs and views in legislation is problematic because it would be a breach of the fundamental human right to freedom of thought.

It can also be seen as problematic because it is contested whether legislation against race discrimination can change views and beliefs. Some people argue that providing against racist behaviour and racial discrimination can, in the long term, change the views and ideas on which the behaviour is based. Legislation against race discrimination can reduce prejudice by prohibiting behaviour in which prejudice is expressed; it can have an important educational and persuasive function, teaching people that discrimination is wrong. It can thus help create conditions in society which favour the growth of tolerance. The 1967 UNESCO *Statement on Race and Racial Prejudice* (1969: 54–5) states:

> Law is among the most important means of ensuring equality between individuals and one of the most effective means of fighting racism. ... It is not claimed that legislation can immediately eliminate prejudice. Nevertheless, by being a means of protecting the victims of acts based upon prejudice, and by setting a moral example backed by the dignity of the courts, it can, in the long run, even change attitudes.

This view – that laws can help to reduce prejudice and change attitudes and behaviour – has been expressed within Europe as well. The European Commission considers that the experience of the Community in combating gender discrimination has shown that 'legislation to outlaw discrimination is an essential part of an effective strategy to change attitudes and behaviour ...' (COM (1999) 564: 7). And the Explanatory Memorandum to the Proposal for the Race Directive states that 'the enforcement of anti-racist laws can have a significant effect on the shaping of attitudes' (COM (1999) 566: 1).

As mentioned, this argument is contested and the opposite opinion, that laws cannot change attitudes at all, that they cannot change the way people think, has been voiced as well. It can be argued that anti race discrimination laws ultimately aim to transform society; because their aim is to stop people discriminating, this aim is, by its nature, to change behaviour and attitudes and ultimately to transform society into a discrimination free society. However, many writers are doubtful about such laws being able to do so (e.g. Hepple 1992: 19–34; Lustgarten 1986; Allott 1980). They consider anti race discrimination legislation of limited impact because law is not suited to changing attitudes and reducing or removing prejudice. Hepple (1992: 19–21) discusses the lack of social change that the British Race Relations Acts have brought. He writes that law is more likely to be effective in facilitating action which people want to take than in creating new rights to protect weaker parties. That is why law, especially where the long-term aim is to alter entrenched attitudes and behaviour, is not often effective as an instrument of social change.

Another writer who argues that laws, including anti discrimination laws, cannot change inner attitudes or transform society is Allott (1980). He writes that the legislator becomes a social engineer who tries to bring about an immediate and major change in human relationships. The problem is that the legislator cannot change the inner man; he must direct his action to external behaviour. According to Allott, social transformation through law contains the seeds of resistance against itself. The social transformer has no time, is unwilling to resort to persuasion, displays no responsiveness to people's feelings and desires and is not prepared to make any accommodations. All of these are essential ingredients of a successful attempt to cause people to change voluntarily and effectively. Because of this, such laws can actually create strong resentment, especially if they are using criminal sanctions. Such legislation can only touch on the exterior behaviour, but repression of undesired action by (criminal) law does not necessarily change the inner attitude. The resentment that such laws can create could even harden people's feelings against certain groups.

Therefore, laws against discrimination can have a deterrent effect in that they can stop people discriminating or behaving in a discriminatory way, but they might not touch people's inner feelings and prejudices. They could actually make these prejudices go underground and strengthen them. It appears that Allott argues that laws that aim to transform society try to push this change through too quickly and with too much force. To persuade people to comply with such laws, strong sanctions are needed. But if the legislator tries to change attitudes and prejudices in society too quickly by heavy-handed measures, people will react against this. Resentment and bad feelings against certain groups which the law is trying to protect would result.

However, Allott (Ibid: 236) does admit that there can be change over time, but suggests that in such cases 'it is not the law which changes attitudes so much as the accompanying education and persuasion'. He also expresses as his personal view 'that the elaborate structure of anti discrimination legislation is misconceived and self-defeating. Much simpler and less ambitious laws would in the long run stand a greater chance of success' (Ibid). This does suggest that Allott does not rule out the possibility that law against discrimination could be effective.

It is submitted that anti race discrimination laws can help in changing people's attitudes, but this cannot and will not be done overnight. It is a slow and long-term process. Laws may, in the short term, change people's behaviour. In the longer term, however, this changed behaviour may become a habit and may be seen as the normal behaviour in society. This will then lead to changes in the attitudes behind the behaviour. As the quote from the UNESCO *Statement on Race and Racial Prejudice*, above states, 'it is not claimed that legislation can immediately eliminate prejudice. Nevertheless … it can, *in the long run, even change attitudes*' (our italics). Banton (1985: 130) expresses the same:

> It is sometimes said that the suppression of discrimination does not eradicate sentiments of prejudice in the minds of the discriminators, but there is good reason to believe that much expressed prejudice is to be

> understood as stemming from the pressure individuals feel to conform to what they believe to be the social norms prevailing in the groups to which they belong or seek to belong. If actual patterns of behaviour are changed by legal regulation, this gradually changes group norms and the pressures of conformity then operate so as to induce people to conform to the new norms.

The fact that laws against race discrimination can create resentment should not be overlooked and neither should the fact that sometimes there will be initial resentment, but that this will dissipate over time. And, as Cohen writes: 'the experience in countries like the UK or the USA is that, over time, even unwelcome laws begin to change behaviour' (Cohen 2005: 1). Ultimately, though, it will be a political decision: how much does the legislator want to change beliefs and attitudes and how much (initial) resentment is he/she able and willing to put up with to reach that goal.

It is submitted that, even if laws against race discrimination cannot change beliefs and reduce prejudice overnight, they can have a more immediate effect by prohibiting the behaviour in which prejudice finds its expression. Dr. Martin Luther King Jr replied to the argument that laws cannot make people love each other and treat each other with dignity and respect: 'Law can not make a man love me, but it can keep him from lynching me, and I think that is pretty important' (Quoted in the *Wall Street Journal*, 13 November 1962). By doing so, these laws might, in the longer term, reduce the prejudices that lie behind the behaviour.

3.3.2 Historically specific

An aspect that the concept of racism has in common with the concept of race is that racism is not a static phenomenon but is historically specific: it has to be studied in its historical and geographical setting. Banton (1992: 70) writes that racism is usually assumed as 'historically specific, something that originated in a particular time to rationalise an economic interest'. And Solomos (1993: 4) writes that debates about racism 'do not make sense outside particular social, political and economic contexts'.

Although the history of notions about race can be traced back to ancient times, most writers place the emergence of what we now call racism at the end of the eighteenth century. That is when racial doctrines and ideologies began to develop. Most writers link this emergence to processes of European expansion, slavery, colonization and domination, which could all be seen as institutions of white supremacy. Racist theories, doctrines that some races, i.e. the white race, were superior, were used to rationalize why white people should exploit black people or why black people should be slaves. The development of racism was linked with processes of economic expansion and capitalist development, which were happening at the same time (Benedict 1983; Miles 1989; Furedi 1998; Bulmer and Solomos 1999: 57–120).

Although racism emerged at the end of the eighteenth century, the term itself did not gain common currency until much later. The usage of the term racism is linked to the rise of Nazism in the 1930s. Prior to that decade the concept of racism was not used to identify theories about the superiority of certain races and the inferiority of others.

3.3.3 Hierarchy of races

Racism, whether used to denote only ideologies or also actions, is grounded in a hierarchy of races, and is based on the belief that some races are superior to others. If it can be said that race has a negative link to such a hierarchy, it will be clear that this link is very much stronger with racism. The concept is, in Miles' words, 'heavily negatively loaded. To claim someone has expressed a racist opinion is to denounce them as immoral or unworthy' (Miles 1989: 1). Banton (1992: 71–2) writes:

> By 1971 the word 'racism' had become a sufficiently accepted designation for indefensible attitudes and practices. It had enormous rhetorical power. ... To join in the condemnation of racism was one way a person, or a state, could assert it was not racist.

Furedi (1998: 14) also points out that, after the World War II, 'racism as a theory and discrimination as a practice acquired negative connotations'. Racism, therefore, has a strong negative connotation and is often seen as socially unacceptable. In today's language: racism is not 'politically correct'.

3.3.4 Social construct

Connected with its historically specific character is the fact that racism, just like race, has been described as a social construct, as something that has been created within a society to justify inequality and to protect the political and economic interests of those who discriminate. The International Council on Human Rights Policy (2000: 4) expresses it thus:

> Racism created and sustained the relevant distinctions of race on which social and economic discrimination in these societies depend. It is a social construct that created and then justified patterns of inequality and discrimination.

Because of the fact that racism can be seen as historically specific and as constructed in different ways within the societies in which it appears, some writers are of the opinion that it is more correct to speak about multiple racisms. Miles (1989: 82–3), for example, writes that there have been many significantly different racisms, although they are not necessarily independent of each other: one form of racism will take on some new elements and so develop into a new form. Bulmer and Solomos (1999: 15) write, 'there is no single monolithic racism ... Rather there are quite distinct racisms that are constructed and reconstructed through time and space by social action'. Fredman also writes about multiple racisms, and continues: 'colour racism must be examined together with cultural racism, which include ethnicity, religion, and language' (Fredman 2001a: 2).

Sometimes the term 'new racism' is used to refer to racism in modern times, which is based on cultural and social differences rather than on biological differences. But if racism is seen as historically specific, a term like new racism is not needed because it is racism in its specific present day form. Mason (1995: 10) even argues that the term is actually just a 'rhetorical smokescreen behind which lurk old beliefs about race'. Social and cultural differences are used to differentiate between people because biological differences have been rejected by science. But ideas about biological differences are still widespread and are often at the basis of ideas about cultural and social differences.

3.3.5 Acknowledgement and denial

Some writers have pointed out that, to combat racism effectively, we first have to acknowledge that it exists. Denial of racism occurs frequently and is seen as an obstacle to any progress in addressing it effectively. Petrova (2001: 45) sums this up in four assumptions: first, all societies are racist to some degree; second, racism is ubiquitous; third, the existence of racism is widely denied; and, fourth, the acknowledgement of racism is a prerequisite (but not at all a guarantee) to overcoming it.

Petrova concludes that the discussion of denial of racism should be accompanied by a discussion of acknowledgement. Van Boven (2001: 111–15) writes that the denial of the existence of racism, racial discrimination and related phenomena is still widespread, although awareness is slowly growing that no society is free from racism. Acknowledgement that these phenomena exist is needed if a strategy to combat racism and racial discrimination is to be effective.

3.3.6 Institutional racism

The term 'institutional racism' is used regularly in Britain since it was defined in the MacPherson Report (*Stephen Lawrence Inquiry* 1999: para. 6.34). This report was the conclusion of an inquiry into the death, in 1993, of black teenager Stephen Lawrence. The Report gave the following definition of institutional racism:

> the collective failure of an organisation to provide an appropriate and professional service to people because of their colour, culture or ethnic origin.

> It can be seen or detected in processes, attitudes and behaviour which amount to discrimination through unwitting prejudice, ignorance, thoughtlessness and racist stereotyping which disadvantage minority ethnic people.

The Report contained a harsh verdict of institutional racism within the London Metropolitan Police. Three points need to be made; first, the use of the term 'unwitting' indicates that the people within the organization (the police in the Lawrence case) are not aware of the prejudices and the racist stereotyping, they do not disadvantage minority ethnic people intentionally. They do so because it is the normal thing to do, because it is the 'culture' of the organization. It is seen like normal to act like that within the organization.

Second, this definition uses racism to include both attitudes and behaviour. And, third, since the report, the term institutional racism has become common currency in Britain and both the Crown Prosecution Service and the Prison Service have been accused of institutional racism. The term has also been mentioned in relation to other services, including the National Health Service and the mental health service. However, the term does not appear to have played a role in discussions on anti discrimination law within the EU at the time the Race Directive was negotiated.

3.3.7 Xenophobia

The term xenophobia is often used coupled together with racism, especially within the EU.[2] The dictionary definition of xenophobia is a dislike or fear of foreigners and all things foreign. The term xenophobia is also often used as a euphemism for racism because of the negative connotation of racism and the links between racism and fascism and the holocaust. As Spencer (1995: 127) writes:

> Xenophobia … implies an irrational but more excusable sentiment, capable of being expressed as much by jokes about foreigners as by violent expressions of hatred. … In practice the two words express aspects of the same thing: a mistrust and fear of any person whose language, culture or appearance is different to that of the majority, allied with a conviction that one's own 'race', nation or culture is superior to any other.

2 See for example: Joint Declaration 1986; COM (1988) 318; Declaration 1998; and, European Monitoring Centre for Racism and Xenophobia (EUMC), the European Institution set up to monitor racism, now changed into the European Fundamental Rights Agency.

3.3.8 Concluding remarks

Racism thus appears to be an even more contested concept than race. Because it is closely related to the concept of race, the problems with the latter are equally problematic in relation to the concept of racism. First of all, racism is used in two distinct ways, either to denote beliefs and ideologies or to denote these ideologies and the attitudes and actions based on these views. What has to be kept in mind when studying racism is that the term is used by some for both ideologies and attitudes and that others distinguish the two, often calling the ideologies, theories, views, beliefs or doctrines racism and the practices, attitudes, behaviour or actions based on them racial discrimination.

Just like race, the concept of racism must be seen as a fluid concept that should be studied in its historic, geographical, economic, political and social context. And, again just like race but to a much greater degree, racism has a negative connotation, although its history suggests that this connotation is a product of the post World War II era. This negative connotation has led to widespread denial of the existence of racism and racial discrimination and the need for acknowledgement before these can be overcome effectively.

In this book, the concept of racism will be used to indicate the belief that races have distinctive hereditary characteristics, which can be biological or cultural, and that this endows some races with intrinsic superiority, while the term racial discrimination is used for the behaviour based on such a belief. However, the concepts are often used in the same way or will run over into one another when it comes to their practical applications. Therefore, the following must be kept in mind. First, it is often difficult to distinguish between beliefs and views on the one hand and attitudes and behaviour on the other. When talking about an ideology or doctrine of racism, one usually visualizes a clear, well-formulated theory but, in practice, in most people's minds the racist feelings will not be so clearly formulated and separated from racist attitudes and behaviour. Second, racist views and beliefs often only show themselves or become manifest through racist behaviour or action. And, third, legislation will prohibit the practical occurrences of racism, such as (incitement to) racist violence, racist hate speech and discrimination in employment and other areas of life, rather than views and ideas.

It is submitted that racism is negative and that it is a phenomenon that needs to be combated. This raises the central question: can racism ever be fully overcome; can there be a world without racism? On the one hand, it is suggested that much has already been achieved in the last two centuries in the sense that slavery, Nazism and *apartheid* have been prohibited and firmly condemned in international law and in many national laws. Banton (1992: 83) remarks on the rapid development of international human rights law and states that:

> jurists can now confidently testify that freedom from slavery, from genocide, from racial discrimination, and from torture, are protected by

> international law. These developments force the view that moral progress in human affairs is possible, and furnish a standard against which other changes may be judged.

On the other hand, as Bulmer and Solomos (1999: 3) summarize:

> ... there is clear evidence that existing initiatives are severely limited in their impact, given the socially entrenched character of much racist behaviour. A number of commentators have pointed to the limitations of legislation and public policy interventions in bringing about a major improvement in the socio-political position of minorities.

Therefore, can racism be eradicated or is it a natural part of any society? It is natural for people to identify themselves by reference to the group to which they belong. This might be any group, large or small, like a family, a social or sports club, a political party, a religious, ethnic or linguistic community or a region or nation. In this sense, humans have a natural tendency to see themselves as part of a group, as 'us' and others outside their group as 'them'. Thus, in any society, groups will be formed which identify themselves because of differences with others and the 'us' and 'them' division can be seen as a natural condition of every society. Race, which is often a clearly observable difference in skin colour or other physical characteristics, is just one of many reference points that people use to set themselves apart from others. But will race as a criterion become less important in future because races appear to become increasingly mixed? Bulmer and Solomos (1999: 389) write:

> What are treated as socially defined racial groups are likely to become less sharply delineated in future, and an increasing number of people will identify with more than one racial group or some kind of mixed group.

So the line between races, often referred to as the colour line, will become more blurred. But will it ever be completely erased? It is suggested that complete eradication of racism is unlikely to be achieved in the near future, as it is a phenomenon that is deeply entrenched in every society. It might well never be fully eliminated. But, in the words of Winant (1998: 765) 'nor can we expect that it [i.e. racism] will ever be fully overcome. That does not mean, however, that we are free to desist from trying'.

3.4 Racial discrimination

3.4.1 Negative connotations

Racial discrimination is, especially where legislative texts are concerned, a different concept from race and racism. The latter two are usually not defined at all and racism is seldom mentioned, while legislation often provides a definition of discrimination. However, as already mentioned, racism and racial discrimination are sometimes taken to be almost synonymous and the possible differences between the two often dissolve when it comes to practical applications. Solomos (1993: 79) writes that the two concepts – racism and racial discrimination – become merged in practice, so that they have little apparent difference. If a difference is to be made, then racism is more often seen as an ideology or doctrine, as a theory about the existence of different races and a hierarchy between these races, while racial discrimination is more often seen as a practice, as behaviour or acts.

The *Collins Concise Dictionary* 1990 defines discrimination as:

1 Unfair treatment of a person, racial group, minority etc.; action based on prejudice;
2 Subtle appreciation in matters of taste;
3 The ability to see fine distinctions and differences.

The descriptions under point two and three are referring to discrimination as discriminating between people or things, as making a distinction, while the description under point one refers to discrimination as discriminating against. The latter has a negative connotation.

Feldman (2002: 135) writes that 'discrimination, when it consists of the ability to differentiate right from wrong and good from bad, is an everyday part of life'. He continues that it 'becomes morally unacceptable only when it takes a particular form, namely treating a person less favourably than others on account of a consideration that is morally irrelevant'. So, according to Feldman, differentiating between people is not wrong as long as the criteria used for the different treatments are morally acceptable.

Discrimination can mean discernment or differentiation but in everyday use the negative meaning of the term appears to have gained ground over the other meaning and the term discrimination is thus more often tied up with a moral judgment that discriminating is unfair or bad. Sunstein provides an example of the use of the term in this negative sense, where he writes that discrimination includes any decision to treat a black person, a woman or a disabled person less favourably than a white, able-bodied male; and that 'the term tends to connote irrational differentiation' (Sunstein 1991: 753 and 770). Townshend-Smith (1998: 65) also mentions that a stigma is implied in the term discrimination.

In his book on discrimination, Banton (1994: 1) distinguishes between the objective definition of discrimination as differential treatment of people supposed to belong to a particular class of persons and the moral judgment about whether the differential treatment is morally justified and lawful. He suggests splitting these two up because discrimination is more difficult to define if it is coupled with a moral judgment, as morality is a difficult concept. As suggested above, in practice this split is not often made and the term discrimination is usually used with the judgment that it is bad or immoral implicit in the term.

3.4.2 Discrimination: A normal part of society

It was contended above that it is natural for people to form groups. Groups exist because they maintain criteria of membership and because they distinguish between members and non-members. Non-members do not receive the benefits of group membership; they are treated less favourably and thus one could say that they are discriminated against. As Goldschmidt (1999: 441) writes, 'awareness of one's specific position as a group, identification with that specific group, involves a certain urge to distinguish that group, to exclude outsiders'. In this sense, everyone discriminates and discrimination is therefore socially normal and a characteristic of every society. People identify with those with whom they have shared experiences and define others as outsiders, which is a normal process of human socialization. But not all discrimination is unlawful. Anti discrimination laws do not prohibit discrimination in protected spheres of private life. If a person wants to marry only someone from his/her own race, religion or culture, anti discrimination laws will not prohibit this. They will only prohibit discrimination in the sphere of public life. As Banton (1992: 79) writes: 'anti-discrimination legislation is designed, among other things, to restrain the tendency to extend such patterns of behaviour from the private to the public sphere'. However, the difference between the two spheres is not always clear-cut and in the economic sphere (in employment and in access to goods and services) anti discrimination legislation is spreading from the public sphere to the private sphere. This will be mentioned in more detail later.

So it is natural for people to discriminate against people who are different from them, who are not part of their group. The motivation for this can be manifold: prejudice, hostility, (economic) self-interest, taste, habit or custom, stereotyping, fear of the unknown, ignorance, etc. It will not always be clear, even for the discriminator, which motive is behind the decision. Often more than one motive will be present. According to Banton (1994: 8), 'motives are often mixed and people may be unaware of some of the forces that stimulate their behaviours'.

Both Sunstein (1991: 752–3)[3] and Townshend-Smith (1998: 63) point out that the most obvious meaning of discrimination puts emphasis on hostility and prejudice, and both writers criticize this. They do this, first, because disadvantageous differential treatment frequently occurs in the absence of prejudice and hostility, and, second, because hostility or prejudice is not always easy to define or prove.

3 Sunstein argues that civil rights law has often identified discrimination with prejudice, irrationality and hostility and that this is a fallacy.

3.4.3 Points for analysis and evaluation of anti discrimination law

As mentioned, discrimination is not always bad or unlawful. It is not wrong when the criteria used to justify differential treatment are morally acceptable or when it takes place in certain spheres. And, even if distinctions between people are made on grounds that are unacceptable or in prohibited areas, exceptions or justifications to the prohibition could mean that the distinctions are not considered unlawful. The following qualifications are used in the analysis and evaluation of anti discrimination provisions.

3.4.3.1 Grounds for discrimination

Just like the motives for discrimination can be many and varied, there are also many grounds for discriminatory behaviour. This book is mainly concerned with race as a ground for discrimination. But legal instruments prohibiting race discrimination often mention race with a number of other grounds or as including other grounds. For example, Article 1 of the ICERD, mentioned in Chapter 2, refers to race, colour, descent or national or ethnic origin, while the British Race Relations Act 1976 prohibits discrimination on racial grounds, which means 'any of the following grounds, namely, colour, race, nationality or ethnic or national origins' (S 3(1)). However, these can all be seen as being connected with race, as is clear from the first part of this Chapter.

There are numerous other grounds for discrimination. For example, Article 14 of the ECHR mentions discrimination on any such grounds as sex, race, colour, language, religion, political or other opinion, national or social origin, association with a national minority, property, birth or other status, while Article 13 EC gives the following grounds: sex, racial or ethnic origin, religion or belief, disability, age or sexual orientation.

There are two problems that can occur in relation to the grounds of discrimination: first, it will not always be easy to distinguish between the different grounds because some of them are very close to each other or even overlap. For example, if a person is discriminated against because he/she is Jewish, is this on racial or ethnic or religious grounds? If gypsies are treated less favourably, is this on the ground of their race or ethnicity, their national or social origin, or their association with a national minority? (Schiek 2002: 311–2). Second, there is the problem of multiple discrimination: a person could be discriminated against on more than one ground. For example, a black woman could be discriminated against because she is black and because she is a woman (Fredman and Szyszczak 1992: 221–2). These problems arise especially where protection against discrimination is provided in different ways for different grounds. The problems with multiple discrimination will be discussed later in this book.

3.4.3.2 Protected fields of discrimination

Legislative provisions against discrimination describe the areas in which they are applicable. Sometimes these descriptions are in broad terms, but they can also be more specific. For example, Article 1(1) of the ICERD gives its field of application in broad terms; it is applicable 'in the political, economic, social, cultural or any other field of public life'. The Race Directive is much more specific: Article 3 (1) determines that it is applicable as regards both public and private sectors in relation to employment, self-employment and occupation; education and vocational training; social protection, including social security and healthcare; social advantages; and access to and supply of goods and services available to the public, including housing. Because most anti discrimination legislation determines its own field of application, the problems encountered here are mainly with interpretation. However, what has to be kept in mind is, as Banton (1994: 40) points out: 'The failure to appreciate that anti-discrimination provisions are restricted to particular fields has been one of the prime sources of opposition to legislation against discrimination'.

3.4.3.3 Exceptions and justification

Most laws against discrimination allow certain exceptions to the prohibition of discrimination. International instruments often exclude distinctions made between citizens and non-citizens and decisions on nationality and naturalization (e.g. Articles 1(2) and (3) ICERD and Article 3(2) of the Race Directive).

Another exception to be found in both national and international laws is the exception based on inherent requirements of a particular job. This is usually subject to a proportionality test, either via the legislation itself or via the case law of the appropriate court. This requires that the means used to achieve the given end must be no more than that which is appropriate and necessary to achieve that end. For example, Article 4 of the Race Directive determines that a difference in treatment shall not constitute discrimination where there is a genuine and determining occupational requirement, providing that the objective is legitimate and the requirement is proportionate.

A third exception found in both national and international legislation against discrimination is the possibility of taking positive measures to correct or redress factual inequalities. Positive measures can include special protection of or assistance to disadvantaged groups and are based on the principle that action needs to be taken to overcome the effects of past discrimination (e.g. Article 5 International Labour Organisation's Discrimination (Employment and Occupation) Convention C111, 1958; Article 5 Race Directive).

Frequently, anti discrimination laws will allow for justification of discrimination. In other words, discrimination is not considered to be against the law if it can be objectively justified by a legitimate aim and the means of achieving that aim are appropriate and necessary (Article 2(2)(b) Race Directive). So, here again, a proportionality test must be fulfilled.

The reasons for mentioning exceptions and justifications in anti discrimination law is that these have to be studied carefully because they could severely limit the effect of such laws as instruments against discrimination. Therefore, exceptions should be clearly specified and be able to be challenged in a court.

3.4.3.4 Direct and indirect discrimination

The distinction between direct and indirect discrimination needs to be mentioned here as well. Banton (1994: 45) describes direct discrimination as disparate treatment and indirect discrimination as disparate impact. Indirect racial discrimination takes place when someone imposes a condition which has a disparate and unfavourable impact on a racial group and which cannot be shown to be justifiable on other grounds. In other words, direct discrimination consists of difference in treatment, of treating a person less favourably because of his or her race, while indirect discrimination consists of apparently equal treatment which has an unequal impact on persons of a certain racial group (e.g. Article 2(2)(b) Race Directive). The concepts are here described for racial discrimination but can be used for discrimination on other grounds as well.

3.4.4 Concluding remarks

Summarizing, it can be seen that the term discrimination is more often than not used with a negative connotation, with the implication that it is morally wrong, although the term is still also used as a synonym for the words distinction and differentiation without any negative connotation at all. Discrimination in both these meanings is part of everyday life and a normal process in any society. Discrimination does not have to be motivated by prejudice or hostility and there can be many and mixed motives.

When studying anti discrimination measures, a number of questions need to be asked: what are the grounds on which discrimination is prohibited? In what fields is the legislation applicable? Does the provision allow for exceptions and can these be challenged in law? Does the measure prohibit both direct and indirect discrimination?

Finally, some writers have made the point that discrimination should be distinguished from disadvantage. These writers argue that some groups in society are disadvantaged because of past and present discrimination and the transmission of these disadvantages from one generation to the next. As Banton (1994: 19) writes:

> It is essential to distinguish discrimination from the larger phenomenon of disadvantage, as this can be seen in patterns of gender and racial inequality. These patterns are the products of a great variety of causes, of which discrimination is but one.

Sunstein (1991: 770) writes that the problem is not discrimination, but 'second-class citizenship' and that legal and social structures should not turn differences between groups that are morally irrelevant into social disadvantage, especially not when the disadvantage is systemic.

3.5 Conclusion

None of the terms discussed in this Chapter are easy to define or uncontested in their meaning. All have been and are used in different ways. The terms race and racism are fluid concepts which are both historically specific. The term race in its common meaning is still based on a difference between races, although these differences can be biological as well as cultural. For the purpose of this book, the term race will mean a group of people with a common descent or common ancestry and the term will be used without any link with biological or cultural ideas of inferiority and superiority. The term ethnic minority will be understood as meaning a group differentiated by racial origin or cultural background.

The term racism is even more contested than the term race and is linked to ideas of superiority/inferiority of certain races. It must be kept in mind that the term racism is often understood as indicating ideologies and doctrines that races have distinctive hereditary characteristics and that this endows some races with intrinsic superiority, while the term racial discrimination is then used for the behaviour and attitudes based on these ideologies. Whether this distinction is made or not, it must be kept in mind that legislation against racism and racial discrimination prohibits the behaviour based on racist beliefs rather than the beliefs itself. Prohibiting racist views in legislation is problematic because it would be a breach of the fundamental human right to freedom of thought; and, because laws cannot, in the eyes of some, change beliefs and attitudes. It was suggested that such legislation can bring about a change in racist views but that this cannot and will not be done overnight. Instead, it is a slow and long-term process.

Racism in this book is considered as a negative phenomenon which is part of society and which needs to be fought, although it can probably never be fully eradicated. Denial that racism exists within a society is widespread, although an acknowledgement that no society is free from racism is slowly starting to develop. This acknowledgement is seen as a prerequisite to overcoming racism. The term xenophobia is less negatively loaded and is, therefore, sometimes used as a euphemism.

Racial discrimination shall be taken to mean distinguishing or differentiating in a negative way between people because they are assigned to a certain racial or ethnic group. In relation to anti (race) discrimination legislation, a number of points are important: the grounds covered by the legislation; the areas in which the legislation is applicable; the provision of exceptions to any prohibitions of discrimination and whether the discriminatory behaviour can be justified under the law; and what forms of discrimination are covered by the prohibition.

4 The Race Directive and definitions of race, racism and racial discrimination

4.1 Introduction

In the previous Chapter, the concepts of race, racism and racial discrimination were explored and defined. This Chapter contains an analysis of these theoretical concepts in relation to the Race Directive. This analysis must be placed within the context of the historical development of the measures against racial discrimination in the EU in Chapter 1 and the international human rights context in Chapter 2.

The first part of this Chapter contains a discussion of the way the EU has dealt with the concepts of race, racism and racial discrimination in legislation specifically aimed at combating racism and xenophobia. From previous Chapters, it will already be clear that measures against racism and racial discrimination vary in what exactly they cover under these terms. For example, the ICERD includes race, colour, descent and national or ethnic origin in its definitions of racial discrimination, while the British Race Relations Act 1976 covers colour, race, nationality and ethnic or national origin. Many national anti discrimination measures include race and ethnic origin as one of a number of grounds on which discrimination is prohibited in a general equality law. For example, Article 3(2) of the Irish Equal Status Act 2000 covers gender, marital status, family status, sexual orientation, religion, age, disability, race, colour, nationality, national or ethnic origin and membership of the Traveller community, while the Belgian Act against discrimination covers sex, a so-called race, colour, descent, national or ethnic origin, sexual orientation, marital status, birth, fortune, age, religion or belief, current or future state of health, a disability or physical characteristic (Article 2 Act of 23 February 2003 pertaining to the Combat of Discrimination and to the Amendment of the Act of 15 February 1993 pertaining to the Foundation of a Centre for Equal Opportunities and Opposition to Racism).

The Race Directive prohibits discrimination between persons 'irrespective of racial or ethnic origin'. The second part of this Chapter will analyze what 'racial or ethnic origin' means. Does the Directive also protect a person against discrimination on the ground of his/her colour, descent or nationality? The question whether nationality as a ground for discrimination is covered by the Race Directive will be given special attention, together with the question, linked to this, whether all persons who find themselves in the EU are protected against racial or ethnic origin discrimination or only those who have the nationality of one of the Member States. We also discuss whether racial or ethnic origin should cover any other related concepts, like religion or belief.

4.2 Definitions

4.2.1 Race and racism

In Chapter 3, we concluded that the terms race, racism and (racial) discrimination are far from easy to define and that their meaning is by no means uncontested. We also concluded that these terms are both historically specific and socially constructed, or, in other words, they have different meanings in different historical and societal settings. As mentioned, all three terms carry a negative connotation, but this is strongest for the term racism. This negative connotation is linked to the fact that theories of race and racism were used to justify suppression, persecution and extermination of people considered to be of inferior races. The memory of the Holocaust and the abuse of theories about race made under Nazism in Germany cast long shadows over the debates in the EU and wider Europe and the use of the terms race and racism were and still are very sensitive for many Member States. The European Parliament even advocated in a Resolution in 1996 (para K) that the term race 'should be avoided in all official texts'. The negotiations on the Race Directive show clearly that some Member States saw the use of the term race as 'tantamount to accepting racist theories that alleged the existence of separate human races' (Tyson 2001: 201). As we saw in Chapter 3, Recital 6 states that the EU rejects theories which attempt to determine the existence of separate human races and that the use of the term racial origin does not imply acceptance of such theories. The Recital was added as a compromise between those Member States who had problems with the use of the term race and others who did not want to rely solely on the term ethnic origin. The problematic nature of these terms also shows itself in the fact that the collection of data on racial or ethnic origin is prohibited in many Member States. According to Johansson (2004: 162), legislation which prohibits the collection and processing of data that refers to an individual's race or religion without that person's consent, exists in Bulgaria, the Czech Republic, Denmark, France, Greece, Italy, Latvia, Poland, Portugal, Slovakia and Sweden.

The problems about the wording during the negotiations might explain why there is no definition of the key terms race, racism and racial or ethnic origin. Article 13 EC requires unanimity in the Council and it appears unlikely that agreement about definitions of these terms could have been reached. The Directive has, however, been widely criticized in the literature for this omission.[1] According to Brown (2002: 204), the marked lack of key definitions 'may create uncertainty and generate a fair amount of litigation'.

However, other documents within the EU appear to show the same lack of definitions of key terms. In many of the Resolutions and Declarations issued by the EU which were mentioned in Chapter 1, the term racism can be found together with the term xenophobia, while the European Parliament also often used anti-Semitism. The terms racism and xenophobia are also used together in Article 29 TEU, where 'preventing and combating racism and xenophobia' is mentioned as one of the means by which the Union shall provide citizens with a high level of safety within an area of freedom, security and justice. But no definitions of these terms are given in any these documents.

As the Race Directive contains minimum requirements only, Member States could define race, racism, racial origin or ethnic origin in their national laws. In some language versions, the Directive uses 'race or ethnic origin' rather than 'racial or ethnic origin' which would suggest that race and racial origin have the same meaning. Are there any definitions of race/racial or ethnic origin which the Member States could follow if they want to define these concepts in their national law? An example can be found in S 3 of the British Race Relations Act 1976, which defines 'racial grounds' as meaning 'colour, race, nationality or ethnic or national origins'. However, the Regulations transposing the Race Directive into British law refer only to race, ethnic or national origin, which suggests that the Government held 'racial or ethnic origin' in the Directive to mean race, ethnic or national origin, and not colour or nationality.[2] The exclusion of 'nationality' is most likely the result of Article 3(2) of the Directive, which we will look at in the next section of this Chapter. Why the British Government also excluded colour is less easy to understand, although colour discrimination would likely qualify as race or ethnic or national origin discrimination. We will come back to colour as a ground for discrimination in the next section as well.

1 See for example: Guild 2000a: 418; Barnard 2001: 968; Brown 2002: 204; Brennan 2002/2003: 320–4; Jones 2003: 517; Parmar 2004: 137; and Liegl *et al.* 2004: 9.

2 See Race Relations Act 1976 (Amendment) Regulations 2003, SI 2003/1626, Section 3. Note that this means that the amended Race Relations Act 1976 applies to discrimination based on race, ethnic or national origin, but that the un-amended 1976 Act applies to discrimination based on colour or nationality. The British Government is working on a new Equality Bill, expected to be published in late April 2009, which should cover all prohibited grounds of discrimination and which aims to replace the large number of statutes and regulations in the discrimination field. The anomaly mentioned should thus disappear.

Other Member States could follow the definition from the British Act or, alternatively, they could omit any definition of racial or ethnic origin and leave the interpretation to the ECJ. The ECJ might well look at the same British Race Relations Act 1976 and the case law relating to this Act for guidance, as this Act has been in place for thirty years. The leading decision which could help the interpretation of the term 'ethnic origin' is the *Mandla v Dowell Lee* case, where the House of Lords had to decide whether Sikhs were protected under the 1976 Act. As Sikhs could not be identified by colour, race, nationality or national origin, the question was whether Sikhs were covered by the term 'ethnic group'. Lord Fraser set out two essential and five other relevant characteristics of an ethnic group. The essential characteristics are:

(a) a long shared history of which the group is conscious as distinguishing it from other groups and the memory of which it keeps alive;
(b) a cultural tradition of its own, including family and social customs and manners, often but not necessarily associated with religious observance;

The other relevant characteristics are:

(c) either a common geographical origin, or descent from a small number of common ancestors;
(d) a common language, not necessarily peculiar to the group;
(e) a common literature, peculiar to the group;
(f) a common religion different from that of neighbouring groups or from the general community surrounding it;
(g) being a minority or being an oppressed or a dominant group within a larger community.

Using these criteria, Sikhs were held to be an ethnic group. By applying the same test, gypsies or travellers were also held to be an ethnic group, but Muslims and Rastafarians were not.[3] The ECJ might well use this case as guidance in its interpretation of race/racial or ethnic origin.

3 Jews had been held to be an ethnic group in an earlier case: *Seide v Gillette* [1980] IRLR 427. Gypsies: *CRE v Dutton* [1989] QB 783; Muslims: *Nyazi v Rymans Ltd* EAT 6/88 (unreported); Rastafarians: *Dawkins v Department of the Environment* [1993] ICR 517. See further McColgan 2005: 534-48. Therefore, Muslims and Rastafarians were not protected against discrimination. However, now there is protection against discrimination on the grounds of religion and belief in the employment field under the Employment Equality (Religion or Belief) Regulations 2003, which implemented the Framework Directive. And the Equality Act 2006, which came into force in April 2007, has extended this protection to the provision of goods, facilities, services, the disposal and management of premises, education and the exercise of public functions.

The Race Directive does not provide a definition of racism either, but, again, there are examples which the Member States could follow. Within the EU, 'racism and xenophobia' was defined in the 2001 Proposal for a Framework Decision to combat racism and xenophobia (COM (2001) 664). Article 3(a) of the Proposal stated:

> 'racism and xenophobia' shall mean the belief in race, colour, descent, religion or belief, national or ethnic origin as a factor determining aversion to individuals or groups.

However, the Framework Decision as adopted in November 2008 (Council Framework Decision 2008), no longer contains the definition, although the measure still covers race, colour, religion, descent or national or ethnic origin (Article 1(a), (c) and (d)). As the Race Directive only mentions racial and ethnic origin, it appears rather inconsistent that the two EU measures aimed at combating racism differ in what they cover.

Another example of a definition of racism can be found in General Policy Recommendation 7 of the Council of Europe's European Commission against Racism and Intolerance (ECRI), which defines racism as:

> the belief that a ground such as race, colour, language, religion, nationality or national or ethnic origin justifies contempt for a person or a group of persons, or the notion of superiority of a person or a group of persons (para 1(a)).[4]

Note that this definition contains a non-exhaustive, open-ended list of grounds as it mentions 'any ground such as', which leaves room for changes in the concept of racism. According to the Explanatory Memorandum (para 7), ECRI's definition is provided for the purposes of the Recommendation and it is up to the States Parties to decide whether they want to include it in their national law. In contrast to this, the definition of racial discrimination of the Recommendation has to be included. Coomber (2003: 23) makes an interesting point in relation to this ECRI definition where she writes that, in the drafting of other international instruments, such as the ICERD and the Race Directive, the drafters avoided defining racism. She continues:

> ECRI's attempt at a definition indicates why it is perhaps wiser to define unlawful conduct rather than ambiguous concepts such as 'racism'. Moreover, by linking such activities to an ambiguous standard based on

4 The footnote added after race in this paragraph is interesting, as it states: 'since all human beings belong to the same species, ECRI rejects theories based on the existence of different "races"'. Therefore, like the EU Member States, ECRI also found it necessary to state this explicitly. It also placed 'races' in quotation marks.

the 'belief' of the person, Recommendation No. 7 introduces a concept that is difficult for any legal system to prosecute.

This suggests that it might be better for the legislator not to give a definition of racism but to define racial discrimination only. It is submitted that prosecuting a person for his/her beliefs is problematic not only because it might be difficult to prove such beliefs, but, more importantly, because, as mentioned in Chapter 3, this would violate the fundamental human right to freedom of thought. Legislation aims at the practical occurrences of racism, at the behaviour based on racist beliefs rather than at views and ideas, and the Race Directive, although it does not define racism, defines both direct and indirect discrimination on the grounds of racial or ethnic origin in its Article 2. We discuss these definitions in the next Chapter.

4.2.2 What is included under racial or ethnic origin?

Can racial or ethnic origin be interpreted as including other grounds of discrimination? As mentioned, the ICERD includes race, colour, descent and national or ethnic origin in its definitions of racial discrimination. Neither the Proposal for the Directive (COM (1999) 566) nor the Directive itself or its Preamble give any indication as to whether colour and descent are included, but all three mention discrimination based on nationality. In the following, we first discuss these grounds and then consider whether any of the other grounds mentioned in Article 13 EC should be included in the Race Directive.

4.2.2.1 Colour and descent

Because 'racial or ethnic origin' is not defined in the Directive, the exact grounds the Directive covers are not clear. Can 'racial or ethnic origin' be taken to include colour, nationality or descent? Brennan (2002/2003: 320–1) mentions that 'a series of reports on Northern Ireland consider that characteristically the principal trigger for racially discriminatory behaviour is "skin colour racism"'. The reports show that 'in Northern Ireland discriminators do not generally know the ethnic or national background of victims' but they tend to 'discriminate on the basis of "visible" characteristics'. It could be argued that skin colour is included as a ground in the Race Directive, as it is used as an indication of a person's racial or ethnic origin, and it is hoped that the ECJ will decide that this is so. The same can be said about descent: race/racial or ethnic origin appear to include descent. According to Recital 7 of the Council Framework Decision 2008, descent 'should be understood as referring mainly to persons or groups of persons who descent from persons who could be identified by certain characteristics (such as race and colour) ...'. However, it would have been clearer if the Directive itself had mentioned both colour and descent as grounds on which discrimination is prohibited.

4.2.2.2 Nationality

The personal scope of the Race Directive, in other words, which persons are covered, can be found in Article 3. However, this Article is not very clear. On the one hand, Article 3(1) states that the Directive 'shall apply to all persons' and Recital 3 explicitly mentions that 'the right to equality before the law and protection against discrimination for all persons constitutes a universal right'. The words 'shall apply to all persons' were not present in the Proposal (COM (1999) 566) or in any of the Proceedings of the Social Questions working Party (Council of the European Union 2000a,b and c). The words suggest that, as Liegl *et al.* (2004: 10) write, 'the protection against discrimination conferred by the [Race and Framework] directives applies to all persons that are on the territory of one of the EU Member States irrespective of their nationality'. The European Parliament,[5] the Starting Line Group[6] and the Kahn Commission[7] all expressed the opinion that all people within the EU, whether citizens of the EU or not, should be protected against racial discrimination.

On the other hand, however, the Race Directive makes an explicit exception for nationality in Article 3(2) and also adds a further proviso:

> This Directive does not cover difference of treatment based on nationality and is without prejudice to provisions and conditions relating to the entry into and residence of third-country nationals and stateless persons on the territory of the Member States, and to any treatment which arises from the legal status of the third-country nationals and stateless persons concerned.

Article 3(2) was not present in either the original or the amended proposals, but was added, together with Recital 13, after much discussion during the negotiations of the Directive (Tyson 2001: 209–10; Council of the European Union 2000a: 3 and Recital 10; and Council of the European Union 2000b and c: both Recital 10). Recital 13 determines that discrimination under the Directive 'should be prohibited throughout the Community'. It then adds:

> This prohibition of discrimination should also apply to nationals of third countries, but does not cover differences of treatment based on nationality and is without prejudice to provisions governing the entry and

5 E.g. the European Parliament Report (1990a) recommended that a Community Directive cover all Community residents.

6 See on the Starting Line: Dummett 1994: 533; on the New Starting Line: Chopin and Niessen 1998: 23–32. Chopin (1999: 123) writes that the New Starting Line would apply to 'any person, regardless of nationality, status or country of origin or residence'.

7 European Council 1995: 39: 'all individuals' and 59: 'whether citizens of the European Union or not'.

residence of third-country nationals and their access to employment and to occupation.

Therefore, the first part of Article 3(2) makes an exception for discrimination on grounds of nationality. According to the Explanatory Memorandum of the Proposal for the Race Directive:

> the Directive does not prohibit differences in treatment based on nationality, which is dealt with by separate Articles of the Treaty (in particular Articles 12 and 39) and by existing secondary legislation.
>
> (COM (1999) 566: 4)

However, there are two problems with the exclusion of nationality discrimination from the Directive. First, it is not always easy to distinguish discrimination on grounds of racial or ethnic origin from nationality discrimination. And, second, Article 12 does not apply to third-country nationals so they are not protected against nationality discrimination. The second part of Article 3(2) of the Race Directive appears to limit the protection afforded to third-country nationals against racial discrimination even further.

During the negotiations on the Directive, some Member States were concerned about preserving their immigration and asylum systems. The Commission argued that admission policies were not included in the material scope of the Directive, but this did not satisfy all Member States and, in the end, it was agreed that Article 3(2) and Recital 13 would be added (Tyson 2001: 209–10). The exception in Article 3(2) reflects the fact that it is up to a state to decide on whether to admit a person to its territory and whether to give him/her a residence or work permit as this is a power of the Member State and not of the Community. The same reason lies behind Article 1(2) and 1(3) ICERD, discussed in Chapter 2. Article 3(2) has been severely criticized in the literature and many writers have called for a narrow interpretation of this paragraph because a broad interpretation would greatly reduce the effectiveness of the Directive for third-country nationals who are often the main target of discrimination.[8] According to Lord Lester (2000: 565), for example:

> The blanket exclusion of racially discriminatory provisions governing the entry, residence and treatment of third-country nationals and stateless persons is incompatible with the effective protection of human rights.

8 See for example: Guild 2000a: 421–2; Lester 2000: 564-5; Bell 2001: 31–2; Goldston 2001: 128; Skidmore 2001: 127–8; Tyson 2001: 209; Toggenburg 2001/2002: 236–8; Bell 2002a: 76–7 and 182–3; Brown 2002: 209–15; Ellis, 2002: 297; Sierra 2002a: 23–9; Brennan 2002/2003: 324–9; Jones 2003: 519–20; McInerney 2003: 14; Brennan 2004; Hepple 2004: 6–7; Ellis 2005: 289–90; Howard 2005: 477–9; Henrard 2007: 23; and Bell 2008a: 67.

The 2003 Annual Report from the European Commission (2003a: 4) discusses the Race and Framework Directives and the Action Programme. It states:

> The two directives outlawing discrimination cover everyone living or working in an EU country, whether they are officially resident there or not. Protection, therefore, is not confined to EU nationals but extends to people from outside the EU who might be visiting for a period, whatever their nationality. (The directives do not, however, affect rules on immigration and do not cover differences in treatment on grounds purely of nationality.)

All this suggests that the Race Directive applies to non-EU nationals and thus protects them against racial and ethnic origin discrimination except in relation to immigration laws or other legal acts covering entry, residence and legal status. Or, as Ellis (2005: 289–90) concludes:

> Nevertheless, one positive message which can be drawn from this provision is that, in situations other than those specified, the Race Directive (and its partner Framework Directive) is intended to apply to all persons within the EU irrespective of their nationality.

Ellis continues, however, that:

> The breadth of the wording used is significant and regrettable; in particular, the final phrase of the provision permits 'any' adverse treatment of third-country nationals and stateless persons which is based on their status.

Therefore, there are significant gaps in the protection of third-country nationals against racial and nationality discrimination. Will the Charter of Fundamental Rights of the Union bring any changes in this respect once it becomes legally binding? Article 20, under the title 'Equality' states that 'everyone is equal before the law'. Article 21 contains a clear prohibition of discrimination:

(a) Any discrimination based on any ground such as sex, race, colour, ethnic or social origin, genetic features, language, religion or belief, political or any other opinion, membership of a national minority, property, birth, disability, age or sexual orientation shall be prohibited.
(b) Within the scope of application of the Constitution and without prejudice to any of its specific provisions any discrimination on grounds of nationality shall be prohibited.

It will be clear from the words 'any grounds such as' that paragraph 1 contains a non-exhaustive or open-ended list of grounds. Although this list is very extensive, it does not contain any reference to nationality or national origin, unlike Article 14 ECHR, upon which it draws. Discrimination on grounds of nationality is instead covered by the second paragraph, which according to the Explanatory Memorandum (CONV 828/1/03, REV 1) 'corresponds to Article 4(2) of the Constitution and must be applied in compliance with that Article'. Article 4(2) of the Constitution echoed the present Article 12 EC and, although the Constitution has now been replaced by the Treaty of Lisbon and Article 12 EC will become Article 18 EC, the text does not materially change in this respect. Therefore, it appears likely that the interpretation of Article 21(2) will follow the interpretation given to Article 12 EC. And, as that article has always been interpreted by the ECJ as covering only EU nationals, the Charter does not extend the protection against nationality discrimination to third-country nationals. Several authors have criticized this (Bell 2003a: 98–9; Waddington 2003a: 23–4; McInerney 2003: 20–3; Howard 2007b: 244–5 and 252–3). According to Bell (2003a: 99), this 'places the Charter in a poor light when compared with Article 14 ECHR'.

Nevertheless, there are some other EU measures which provide protection for third-country nationals and these provisions alleviate somewhat the problems created by the exceptions in Article 3(2) of the Race Directive. First, nationals from countries which have Association Agreements with the EU are protected against nationality discrimination as these Agreements state that the treatment accorded to workers (of Turkish, Tunisian, Moroccan and Algerian nationality) employed on the territory of a Member State shall be free from any discrimination based on nationality, as regards working conditions, remuneration and dismissal, relative to the Member States' own nationals.[9] Some of these Agreements go further and also provide for security of residence or a right to establishment in a Member State.

Second, in November 2003, a Directive on the status of third-country nationals who are long-term residents was adopted. This determines that third-country nationals who have been resident in a EU Member State for five years or more can acquire long-term resident status (Council Directive 2003/109/EC). This status gives them the right to equal treatment with nationals in a large number of areas.[10]

Third, Recital 8 of the Race Directive mentions that the Employment Guidelines 2000 'stress the need to foster conditions for a socially inclusive labour market by formulating a coherent set of policies aimed at combating discrimination against groups such as ethnic minorities'. The 1999 Guidelines consider, under the heading 'promoting a labour market open to all', that

9 See the Association Agreements: Turkey: Council Decision 1963: Article 9; Tunisia: Euro-Mediterranean Agreement 1998: Article 64; Morocco: Euro-Mediterranean Agreement 2000: Article 64; and, Algeria: COM (2002) 157: Article 67.

10 Denmark, Ireland and the UK have opted out of this Directive.

'many groups and individuals experience particular difficulties in acquiring relevant skills and in gaining access to, and remaining in the labour market'. The guideline requires the Member States to:

> Give special attention to the needs of the disabled, ethnic minorities and other groups and individuals who may be disadvantaged, and develop appropriate forms of preventive and active policies to promote their integration into the labour market.[11]

Promoting integration and labour market participation and combating discrimination against people at a disadvantage in that market has been part of the guidelines since then.[12] These employment guidelines thus include ethnic minority groups and they do not specify anywhere that these only include nationals of EU Member States. Therefore, it must be taken that third-country nationals are also included in the Employment Strategy. As Bell (2005: 64) writes: 'To the extent that the Employment Strategy is bringing third-country nationals back into the picture, then it offers a valuable complement to the limits of the Race Directive'. The European Employment Strategy uses the Open Method of Coordination (OMC) procedure. Under the Employment OMC, the Council adopts annual guidelines for employment and the Member States make up National Action Plans to report on their progress towards these guidelines. The Council and the Commission then make up a joint Employment Report which monitors progress and sets priorities for the coming year. Therefore, the Guidelines depend on peer review and exchange of good practices in order to monitor progress towards agreed goals. So, although the Guidelines are not judicially enforceable, they could play an important role in the integration of ethnic minority people, including third-country nationals, at a disadvantage in the labour market.

Article 6 of the Race Directive makes clear that the Directive contains minimum requirements that need to be implemented by the Member States and that 'Member States may introduce or maintain provisions which are more favourable'. Therefore, the Member States could provide protection against racial discrimination to all persons on their territory irrespective of status or nationality without exceptions.

11 Council Resolution 1999: point I–9. For information on the Employment Strategy in relation to the fight against racism see: Bell 2005; and Bell 2008a: 94–103.

12 Employment Guidelines: Council Decisions 2000b: Guideline 9; Council Decision 2001: Guideline 7; Council Decision 2002: Guideline 7. Both the 2001 and 2002 Guidelines mention 'ethnic minorities and migrant workers'; while the 2003 Guidelines (Council Decision 2003: Guideline 7), mention 'immigrants, and ethnic minorities'.

4.2.2.3 Other grounds of Article 13 EC

4.2.2.3.1 RELIGION OR BELIEF

In this section, we discuss the question whether any of the other grounds mentioned in Article 13 EC should be included in the Race Directive. The Race Directive covers racial or ethnic origin discrimination, while the Framework Directive covers discrimination on the grounds of religion or belief, disability, age and sexual orientation. The protection provided against racial or ethnic origin discrimination is more extensive than the protection provided against discrimination on the grounds in the Framework Directive for three reasons. The first difference in protection lies in the material scope: the Framework Directive prohibits discrimination in the following areas: access to employment; access to training; employment conditions; and membership of professional organizations. The Race Directive prohibits discrimination on the grounds of racial or ethnic origin not only in all these areas, but also in the areas of social protection, including social security and health care, social advantages and education. The material scope of the Race Directive is, thus, much wider than that of the Framework Directive.

A second feature which makes the protection against racial or ethnic origin discrimination stronger than the protection against discrimination on the grounds covered by the Framework Directive is that the Race Directive allows for justification of direct discrimination only in very limited and prescribed circumstances: for genuine and determining occupational requirements (Article 4) and for positive action measures (Article 5). Direct racial or ethnic origin discrimination cannot be justified under any other circumstances. The Framework Directive also allows for these exceptions (Articles 4(1) and 7, respectively), but it provides for a number of additional ones. Article 2(5) gives an additional general exception; Article 4(2) contains an exception for occupational activities of organizations with a religious ethos; Article 5 prescribes that reasonable accommodation must be made for disabled persons; Article 6 provides for a general justification and a number of exceptions in relation to age; and Article 15 makes exceptions for the police service and for teachers in Northern Ireland.

The third reason why the protection provided by the Race Directive is wider than that provided by the Framework Directive is that Article 13(1) of the Race Directive imposes a duty on the EU Member States to 'designate a body or bodies for the promotion of equal treatment of all persons without discrimination on the grounds of racial or ethnic origin', but there is no such provision in the Framework Directive.

The protection against sex discrimination is also wider than that under the Framework Directive but not as extensive as that under the Race Directive. As far as the scope is concerned, the prohibition of sex discrimination now covers the same employment and occupation areas as the Race and Framework Directives (in the Recast Directive) and, since 2004, it covers the provision of goods and services. With regard to the exceptions allowed, the Recast

Directive allows for the same exceptions as the Race Directive but also contains some provisions for the protection of women as regards pregnancy and maternity. However, the Equal Treatment (Goods) Directive contains much broader exceptions. Article 4(5) allows for justification of direct discrimination, while Article 3(3) exempts the media, advertising and education and Article 5 allows for an exception in the insurance field. With regard to enforcement, Member States are also under a duty to designate a specialist body or bodies for the promotion of equal treatment between men and women.

Therefore, the scope of the prohibition of sex discrimination is not as wide as the scope under the Race Directive and, in the provision of goods and services especially, much wider exceptions are allowed, while the duty to designate a specialist body exists for both sex and racial or ethnic origin. The protection provided by the Framework against discrimination on the grounds of religion and belief, disability, age and sexual orientation is weaker than that against discrimination on the grounds of sex or of racial or ethnic origin.

However, the first and third differences will disappear once the Commission's 2008 Proposal (COM (2008) 426) has been adopted. This proposal will extend the area covered by the Framework Directive to include all the areas covered by the Race Directive (Article 3(1)); and it will impose a similar duty on Member States to designate a body or bodies for the promotion of equal treatment of all persons irrespective of their religion or belief, disability, age or sexual orientation (Article 12). But, the difference in relation to justifications allowed will remain. Moreover, this Directive needs to be adopted first and then the Member States will, most likely, have three years to implement this, so, for the foreseeable future, the difference in protection provided will remain in place. Also, the 2008 Directive does not cover gender discrimination, so the protection against gender discrimination will still cover less areas than the protection against discrimination on the other grounds.

We already mentioned, in Chapter 1, that the stronger protection afforded by the Race Directive was the result of the political will to go further in the fight against racial and ethnic origin discrimination and we suggested some factors that influenced this political will. The strong and sustained pressure by a large number of NGOs and by the European Parliament for action against racial discrimination mentioned before could also have influenced the stronger protection given to that form of discrimination. But, maybe the 2008 proposal is a sign that the EU is now ready to extend the protection on all prohibited grounds outside the employment field.

But are there differences in character between the grounds that could also have influenced the difference in protection provided? Is race/racial or ethnic origin as a discrimination ground in any way different from the other grounds? Bell and Waddington (2003: 359–63) write that some grounds of discrimination can result in an individual being temporarily not available or not able to do a job or use a good or service. They make a distinction between grounds that are always irrelevant for the employment/access situation, like racial or ethnic origin, sexual orientation and gender; and grounds that are sometimes relevant. The latter category is subdivided between grounds that limit the availability to do a job or use a good or service, like religion with regard to times of worship, religious holidays and periods of pilgrimage; and grounds that can limit both the availability and the ability to do so, like age and disability.

Schiek (2002: 309–10) makes a different distinction; she discerns, first, characteristics that 'only exist as ascriptions – despite being construed as unchangeable'. The most obvious example here is race: 'there is no scientific justification for describing different human groupings as races'. Race is an ascription because racist categorization is beyond the control of the person affected. Other ascriptions are gender '(to be distinguished from sex)', and disability, but the latter only in part. Schiek's second category contains those characteristics 'which are in some way or other referable to a biological basis' and reflect real biological differences, such as sex, age and, under different aspects, disability. These characteristics 'may restrict the market value or employability of persons'. Or, in the words of Bell and Waddington above, they may affect the ability and/or availability of a person to do a job or use a good or service. The third category contains characteristics which reflect a chosen lifestyle or chosen difference in identity, like ethnicity or religion, sexual orientation or political conviction. This category presupposes that persons convey information about themselves, which allows categorization. It is questionable whether religion and sexual orientation (and even ethnicity) is something that a person freely chooses and can control and, also, whether discrimination on these grounds only takes place when the person discriminated against conveys this information about him/herself. Discrimination will often take place because a person is perceived to be of a particular religion, ethnicity or sexual orientation, and then it would come closer to an ascription. Gerards (2004a: 164–5) mentions the 'immutability of the personal characteristic used as a basis for the distinction' and suggests that 'immutability' should be given a broad interpretation 'as to mean all characteristics that cannot be changed without infringing the essence of an individual's identity'. In this broad interpretation, religion and sexual orientation (and possibly also ethnicity) can be seen as immutable characteristics which would come closer to characteristics that are beyond the control of the person affected. But they would still be different in character from race because race is an ascription of something that does not exist, while different religions, ethnicities and sexual orientations do exist.

Although the writers mentioned make slightly different distinctions, the above does suggest that there are differences in character between the grounds and these may justify treating race/racial or ethnic origin differently. We can conclude that race is an ascribed characteristic which is always irrelevant because it does not affect a person's ability or availability to do a job or use a good or service. Discrimination on racial grounds is thus particularly invidious. Of the Article 13 EC grounds, sex and religion can affect a person's availability, while disability and age can affect both a person's ability and the availability to a greater or lesser extent. Sexual orientation, like race, does not affect either, but there is a difference in character between the two, even if we take both to be ascriptions. This would lead to the conclusion that all the grounds covered by the Framework Directive are in some way different in character from racial or ethnic origin and this could thus be an argument for treating the latter ground differently. Or, to put it another way, it could be an argument for keeping the two Directives as they are and for not extending the Race Directive to cover any of the other grounds.

Are there any other arguments for including any of the grounds covered by the Framework Directive in the Race Directive? We would argue that religion or belief should be covered in the same Directive as racial or ethnic origin. The Race Directive has been strongly criticized for omitting this ground from its protected grounds because religion is often closely related to racial and ethnic origin, so it can be difficult to distinguish between the two.[13] Racial discrimination may be interwoven with discrimination on grounds of a person's adherence to a (minority) religion or ethnicity. Therefore, it is often difficult to draw a clear and precise line between racial or ethnic origin and religion or belief.

The following provides an illustration of the problem. In 1993, the European Parliament called on the Council to adopt a Directive introducing national legislation designed to combat racism, xenophobia and anti-Semitism (Resolution 1993). This Resolution does not contain definitions of these terms, but it mentions anti-Semitism and *other forms of religious intolerance* (our italics) (Ibid: para A). This would suggest that the Parliament saw anti-Semitism as a form of religious intolerance. Does this mean that it considered Jews a religious group rather than a racial or ethnic group? The Resolution also mentions 'racism, anti-Semitism, or religious intolerance', which would suggest that anti-Semitism is different from religious intolerance and from racism (Ibid: para 1). Therefore, the European Parliament appears to be unclear whether religious intolerance and anti-Semitism are forms of racism.

In their General Policy Paper on religious discrimination, ENAR expresses the problem very well:

> Discrimination on the grounds of religion or belief and racism are inextricably linked. They can often be fused in the identification of the racialised 'other'; or the line between these forms of prejudice can be blurred.
>
> (ENAR 2005: 1)

13 See for example: Guild 2000a: 416; Fredman 2001b: 158–9; Niessen 2001b: 9; Bell 2002b: 12; Brown 2002: 204–5; Sierra 2002a 23–9; McInerney 2003: 12; Leigl *et al.* 2004: 9; Vickers 2006: 33–5; Howard 2007a: 463–4; and Bell 2008a: 67.

Another reason why the omission of religion or belief in the Race Directive has been criticized is connected to the fact we have mentioned above, that the protection against discrimination on religious grounds under the Framework Directive is not as extensive as the protection against discrimination on racial or ethnic origin grounds under the Race Directive. This difference in protection, and especially the limitation of the material scope of the Framework Directive to the employment sphere, might create a loophole: perpetrators could claim that they discriminate against victims because of their religion rather than because of their racial or ethnic origin and so evade legal action. As the ENAR paper states:

> Religion or belief are often used to justify racial discrimination, and can be used to obscure racist motivations. This reality is compounded by the fact that the perpetrators of racist acts do not necessarily distinguish between nationality, culture or religious background.
>
> (ENAR 2005: 1)

The European Parliament appears to have been aware of this problem as it suggested the following addition to Article 2 of the Race Directive:

> Discrimination on the basis of racial or ethnic origin which is presented as a difference in treatment on the grounds of religion, conviction or nationality is deemed to be discrimination within the meaning of Article 1.
>
> (Opinion European Parliament 2000)

As we have seen, if the 2008 Commission proposal (COM (2008) 426) is adopted, this problem would mostly disappear.

Both Bell (2002b: 25 and 2008a: 23) and Brown (2002: 204–5) suggest that discrimination on the grounds of religion or belief might be covered by indirect racial discrimination under the Directive, because religious discrimination will disproportionately affect people belonging to an ethnic minority. Whether this is indeed the case will ultimately be decided by the ECJ. Of course, the Member States are free to extend the protection against religious discrimination to some or all the areas covered by the Race Directive.

The 'Starting Line', the proposal for a draft directive from the Starting Line Group, covered race, colour, descent, nationality, national and ethnic origin. So it did not include religion as a protected ground (Dummett 1994: 535). However, the 'New Starting Line', the draft proposal the Group issued after the Treaty of Amsterdam inserted Article 13 into the EC Treaty, included religion or belief (Chopin and Niessen 1998: 19). The Group declared that it had opted to cover racial or ethnic origin and religion or belief in one Directive because they had been mentioned together in a number of Declarations made at Community level and because:

> they may arise from overlapping causes: against Jews, for example (are they being identified by the discriminator as a racial or a religious group?)

> and even against Muslims in cases where hostility to north Africans and Turks may spring from one cause or the other, or perhaps both together. (Ibid: 20)

Both definitions of racism given above as examples – in ECRI Recommendation 7 and in the Proposal for a Framework Decision (COM (2001) 664) – also specifically include religion. The inclusion in the ECRI Recommendation shows that the Council of Europe does not differentiate between religious and racial discrimination, whereas the EU sends out mixed signals: the two 2000 Directives suggest that the EU makes a difference, but the Framework Decision 2008 suggests that it does not do so when it comes to criminal measures. The difference in definition appears to have been one of the stumbling blocks in the negotiations of the Proposal for the Framework Decision in the Council and one of the reasons why its adoption took seven years. As Bell (2003b: 34) writes:

> The breadth of this definition was significant, not least because it contrasts with the Racial Equality Directive, which only applies to discrimination on grounds of 'racial or ethnic origin'. Most notably, the Commission sought to include prejudices linked to 'religion or belief' within the concept of racism and xenophobia, whereas discrimination on grounds of religion or belief has been treated as distinct from racial discrimination in the Directives adopted under Article 13EC. … It is not surprising then that this aspect of the proposal has proven highly contentious in the Council.

However, the difference between the grounds covered by the two EU measures aiming to combat racism is likely to create confusion and lead to problems in interpretation.

For the reasons set out above, it is argued that religion or belief should be included in the grounds covered by the Race Directive. The only argument against treating discrimination on the ground of religion and belief the same as that on the ground of race would be that racial or ethnic origin and religion or belief as grounds are slightly different in character. If we take Bell and Waddington's distinction (2003: 359–63) based on a person's ability or availability to do a job or use a good or service, then the two grounds are different: a person's race will not affect this, but his/her religion can affect his/her availability. The inclusion of a duty to make reasonable accommodation in case of religion would solve this problem. For example, providing a place and time for religious worship and adapting patterns of working time could prevent discrimination on religious grounds (Waddington 2000: 178; Bell and Waddington 2003: 360–1). If a duty to make reasonable accommodation is included, there appears to be no reason why the Race Directive could not also cover discrimination on the ground of religion or belief.

Another point needs to be raised at this stage. From the above discussion, and especially from the Reports Brennan (2002/2003: 320–1) writes about: 'that discriminators do not generally know the ethnic or national background of the victim'; from the quote from ENAR 's General Policy Paper No 1 (2005: 1) 'that the perpetrators of racist acts do not necessarily distinguish between nationality, culture or religious background'; and, from the quote from the Starting Line Group cited above that 'these different types of discrimination [on racial or ethnic origin and religion or belief] might arise from overlapping causes: against Jews, for example (are they being identified by the discriminator as a racial or a religious group)' (Chopin and Niessen 1998: 20), it will be clear that discriminators more often than not do not distinguish clearly between race, colour, descent, religion or nationality when they discriminate and that their behaviour may spring from any one or more or all of these causes. This would be another argument for including colour, descent, nationality and religion or belief in the grounds covered by the Race Directive.

However, it might be difficult to reach unanimity on this. Religion or belief appears to be a more contentious issue in many Member States. Why is this so? It is suggested that, although there is a wide variety of traditions regarding the interaction between church and state, the Member States are all traditionally Christian States and, even in countries that have a strict separation, the Christian churches have played and are frequently still playing a major part in the daily life of the society. They often also have quite significant influence in the political process.[14] These churches and religious organizations see legislation against religious discrimination as limiting their freedom to employ only people with the same religion or religious ethos. This is also the likely reason behind the inclusion of Article 4(2) of the Framework Directive.

Article 4(2) adds an extra genuine occupational requirement exception for occupational activities of churches and other organizations with an ethos based on religion or belief. This allows religious organizations to take religion and belief into account in recruitment decisions where national law or practice allows this already, but this 'should not justify discrimination on any other ground'. Article 4(2) also determines that, in regard to existing employees, religious organizations can 'require individuals working for them to act in good faith and with loyalty to the organisation's ethos'.[15] During the negotiations, France and Sweden questioned the need for this second paragraph because it repeats the provision in Article 4(1) (Council of the European

14 For more information on the 15 old EU Member States (Members before 1 May 2004) see European Commission 2004b.

15 Article 4(2) of the final text is considerably different from the proposal and was also changed during the negotiations. See the Framework Directive, the Proposal for this Directive (COM (1999) 565) and Council of the European Union 2000d: 16.

Union 2000d: 16). Waddington (2000: 179) and Ellis (2005: 283) both see Article 4(2) as unnecessary as well. However, the other Member States, probably influenced by pressure from churches and other religious organizations, did see the need for this extra paragraph.

Religion is also a contentious issue because, as Zwamborn writes, many Member States have seen an:

> influx of Islamic migrants who practise and promote their religion in a more prominent and public fashion, going against the general trend among the Christian denominations which is to see one's religion increasingly as a private, publicly less prominent issue.
>
> (European Commission 2004b, Report on the Netherlands: 1)

Zwamborn writes this specifically about the Netherlands, but the same process also appears to be taking or to have taken place in many other EU Member States. On the one hand, most European states are becoming more and more secularized in terms of traditional Christian religious practices and church attendance, but, on the other hand, the Christian values are still entrenched in society and the new migrants are seen as a threat to these values (Vickers: 2006). But they are not only seen as a threat to these Christian values, but also, and even more strongly, as a threat to the liberal value of tolerance.

Because Muslims are often the biggest and most vociferous group amongst the new migrants and because of the events of 9/11 and bombings in several places, many Member States perceive especially Muslims as a threat to their liberal, tolerant, secular societies. Muslims are seen as putting religion and religious laws above these liberal values and above 'the law of the land'. They are seen as a threat because they demand too much in terms of legal concessions in relation to their values, which are considered to clash with the values of the Member State. The debates in many Member States about the wearing by Muslims, especially Muslim women, of traditional dress are illustrative of this. Some European countries have actually introduced or are discussing bans on the display of religious symbols or on signs of dress which openly manifest a religious affiliation.[16]

Therefore, religion is a sensitive issue and it might be difficult to reach the required unanimity for extending the grounds covered by the Race Directive to include religion or belief. It might also be seen as unnecessary now the Commission has proposed extending the protection provided by the Framework Directive to all areas covered by the Race Directive. However, as mentioned, the Framework Directive allows for more justifications and so does the 2008 Proposal. On the one hand, this might make it easier to reach

16 For more information on the way a number of European countries have dealt with the wearing of Islamic headscarves and other clothing and the reasons given for introducing bans, see McGoldrick 2006; Institute of Race Relations 2008: 18–25; and Howard 2009.

unanimity in the Council regarding the Proposal, but, on the other hand, this still leaves a difference in the protection against religious discrimination as compared to the protection against race discrimination.

4.2.2.3.2 SEX, DISABILITY, AGE AND SEXUAL ORIENTATION

Should any of the other grounds of Article 13 EC be included in the Race Directive? Having different instruments means that that there is a need to draw distinct lines between the different grounds, which, as we have mentioned, is not always easy. This is the reason why we have argued for an extension of the grounds covered by the Race Directive to include religion or belief. The other grounds of Article 13 EC are easier to distinguish from racial or ethnic origin and from religion or belief, so they do not need to be included under the grounds covered by the Race Directive for this reason.

However, the different levels of protection provided which, as mentioned, will still be there even after adoption of the 2008 Proposal (COM (2008) 426), do lead to a problem in cases of multiple discrimination: where a person is discriminated against on two or more grounds, for example a woman is discriminated against because she is disabled, black and female. Any one of these might be the reason why she is discriminated against, or it might be because she is all three. If she is discriminated against in education, she could take action because of racial discrimination, but not on the other grounds. If a white disabled woman were treated in the same way, there would be no unfavourable treatment on the grounds of racial or ethnic origin. If a black disabled man or a black able-bodied woman or man were treated differently, there would be no action, because the Recast and the Equal Treatment (Goods) Directives and the Framework Directive do not cover education.[17]

Before we look at how the EU is dealing with multiple discrimination, we will discuss the definition of multiple discrimination.[18] Makkonen (2002: 10–1) distinguishes three forms of multiple discrimination. First of all there is the situation in which a person suffers from discrimination on several grounds, but discrimination takes place on one ground at a time. So a coloured woman might be discriminated against in one situation, for example access to a restaurant, because she is coloured, and in another situation, for example passed over for promotion, because she is a woman. Therefore, discrimination

17 Discrimination on the grounds covered by the Framework Directive (religion or belief, disability, age and sexual orientation) in education will be prohibited once the 2008 Proposal (COM (2008) 426) has been adopted, but it is not covered in the Equal Treatment (Goods) Directive or the Recast Directive.

18 For more information on multiple discrimination see: Fredman and Szyszczak 1992: 221–2; Makkonen 2002; Hannett 2003; Fredman, 2005; McColgan 2005: 32–7; Moon 2006; McColgan 2007; Schiek *et al.* (2007: 171–7); and European Commission 2007.

takes place on the basis of several grounds operating separately. Sometimes the term multiple discrimination is used specifically for this form.

The second form is where a person is discriminated against on more than one ground in the same instance and discrimination on the one ground adds to the discrimination on the other ground to create an added burden. In other words, one ground gets compounded by one or more other discrimination grounds. This is referred to as compound or additive or cumulative discrimination. Schiek *et al.* (2007: 171) give a good example of this: someone is refused access to a pub because he belongs to the Roma community and is accompanied by a young child. The grounds of ethnic or national origin and family status have both affected the negative decision.

The third form takes place where two or more grounds of discrimination interact and discrimination takes place because of this interaction. This is referred to as intersectional discrimination. For example, a disabled woman might experience specific types of discrimination not experienced by disabled men or by women in general. The grounds interact and the discrimination that takes place cannot be captured wholly by looking at discrimination on one ground separately. The grounds are inseparable and discrimination takes place because of the combination of factors. There is also the problem that a combination of factors might have what Makkonen calls the 'trigger effect'. As he writes: 'A person might not in general discriminate against women or immigrants, but the combination of these two factors may trigger discriminatory behaviour' (Makkonen 2002: 14).

How does the EU deal with multiple discrimination? Both the Race and Framework Directives explicitly recognize the possibility of multiple discrimination; they acknowledge the possibility that sex discrimination can go together with discrimination on any of the other grounds covered in the Directives. Recital 14 of the Preamble to the Race Directive states:

> In implementing the principle of equal treatment irrespective of racial or ethnic origin, the Community should, in accordance with Article 3(2) of the EC Treaty, aim to eliminate inequalities, and to promote equality between men and women, *especially since women are often the victims of multiple discrimination* (our italics).

The Framework Directive contains the same in Recital 3, but the term 'multiple discrimination' does not appear anywhere else in either of these Directives and no definition is given nor any indication as to how to deal with cases of multiple discrimination. And, as Fredman (2002: 75) writes, 'no concrete links are made as between the directives, and cumulative discrimination on other grounds … is not dealt with'.

The Community Action Programme 2000 also mentions multiple discrimination. First, Recital 4 is similar to Recital 14 of the Race Directive. Second, Recital 5 states that 'the different forms of discrimination cannot be ranked; all are equally intolerable'; and that the programme is intended, among other things, 'to develop new practice and policy for combating discrimination, including multiple discrimination'. And, third, Article 2 on the objectives of the Action Programme mentions that 'the Programme shall support and supplement the efforts at Community level and in the Member States to promote measures to prevent and combat discrimination whether based on one or on multiple factors …'. The Programme does not give any definition or any further explanation as to how to deal with multiple discrimination, but, in 2006, the Commission announced that three new studies would be conducted to 'improve the understanding of the concept of roots and causes of discrimination'. One would be a study on multiple discrimination, with among its objectives, 'to raise awareness of the particular difficulties victims of multiple discrimination face' (Annual Plan 2005: 2–3). This study came out in 2007 and starts with stating: 'if the reality of discrimination and inequality is to be tackled, workable solutions to combat the existence of Multiple Discrimination have to found' (European Commission 2007: 5). The Report makes a number of Recommendations, and Recommendation 2, on legislation, mentions that 'the scope of the existing anti-discrimination legislation does not provide effective protection against Multiple Discrimination in areas outside employment and occupation' and recommends extending the scope of the areas covered by the Framework Directive to include all areas covered by the Race Directive and 'the new legislation must provide provisions to address Multiple Discrimination' (Ibid: 7).

The 2008 Commission proposal (COM (2008) 426) does extend the areas covered, but does not provide for multiple discrimination although its Recital 13 echoes Recital 14 of the Race Directive. In the Explanatory Memorandum to the proposal, the Commission reports that, in its consultation, attention was drawn 'to the need to tackle multiple discrimination, for example by defining it as discrimination and by providing effective remedies'. However, the Commission then states: 'These issues go beyond the scope of this directive but nothing prevents Member States taking action in these areas' (Ibid: 4). In other words, the EU will not provide for this, it is left to the Member States to do so, which could lead to very different provision in different Member States.

An interesting point is made in the Explanatory Memorandum to ECRI's General Policy Recommendation 7. Paragraph 13 reads:

> Discriminatory actions are rarely based solely on one or more of the enumerated grounds, but are rather based on a combination of these grounds with other factors. For discrimination to occur, it is therefore sufficient that one of the enumerated grounds constitutes one of the factors leading to differential treatment. The use of restrictive expressions such as 'difference of treatment solely or exclusively based on grounds such as …' should therefore be avoided.

ECRI thus recommends that discrimination should be prohibited if it is based on one of the enumerated grounds, no matter whether this is the only factor leading to the discrimination or if it is one of a number of enumerated and other grounds. If national legislation followed ECRI's Recommendation then unlawful discrimination would be found in the case mentioned above of the black disabled woman and it would not be necessary to provide proof that she was discriminated against because of race and sex and disability. Proof of discrimination of any one of these grounds would be sufficient. This appears to suggest that discrimination should be defined as an act based on one or more grounds or a combination of grounds. A national law against discrimination could list the grounds covered and simply add 'or any combination of these grounds' to achieve this.

4.3 Conclusion

In this Chapter, we have analyzed the Race Directive in the context of the concepts of race, racism and racial discrimination discussed in Chapter 3. The negotiations on the Directives show that the terms race and racism are still very much linked to the negative use that was made of them in the past and are, therefore, still problematic for many Member States.

Our analysis has shown that the Race Directive and many national and international measures against race discrimination do not give a definition of race or racism, but only define racial discrimination. It was suggested that this omission might be preferable, because it is difficult to give a definition that would be useful in legal proceedings. However, some definitions exist and there was a EU definition of 'racism and xenophobia': in the 2001 Proposal for a Framework Decision (COM (2001) 664), although that definition was dropped in the Decision that was finally adopted. Naturally, the EU Member States are free to include a definition in their national law if they wish to do so.

A definition of race/racial or ethnic origin is also missing from the Race Directive, but we have suggested that it would be preferable if the terms include colour, descent, nationality and religion or belief, because it is very difficult to draw clear distinctions between any of these grounds and discriminators often do not make such distinctions anyway. Colour and descent are closely related to racial and ethnic origin and it is to be hoped that the ECJ will decide that the Directive implicitly covers these grounds.

The exception for nationality and for provisions governing the entry, residence and treatment of third-country nationals and stateless persons made in Article 3(2) of the Directive has been strongly criticized for being overly broad and for not providing sufficient protection for third-country nationals. This is seen as one of the major problems with the Race Directive and, hopefully, the Member States will introduce legislation which gives more protection than the minimum standard provided by the Directive. We will make some suggestions for changes in Chapter 7.

We have argued for including religion or belief under the grounds covered by the Race Directive because it is difficult to distinguish between these grounds and perpetrators of discriminatory acts do not always do so and because the difference in protection might create a loophole to avoid prosecution. We do, however, foresee problems in reaching agreement of all the Member States on this as religion is a very contentious issue in most Member States. Adding religion or belief to the grounds covered by the Race Directive will most likely also be considered not necessary, as the 2008 Commission Proposal (COM (2008) 426) extends the protection against religion and belief discrimination beyond the employment field anyway.

Adding colour, descent, nationality and religion or belief to the grounds of discrimination covered by the Race Directive would deal with some of the major points of criticism levelled against it and bring it more in line with the definition of the grounds covered by the Framework Decision. The other grounds of Article 13 EC: sex, disability, age and sexual orientation, do not necessarily need to be included in the Race Directive. However, there are differences in the levels of protection afforded by the different Equality Directives which mean that clear lines need to be drawn between the different discrimination grounds. This can lead to problems in cases of multiple discrimination. Of course, the EU Member States can go beyond the minimum requirements laid down by the EU legislation and provide the same protection against discrimination on all the grounds mentioned in Article 13 EC. If the 2008 Proposal (COM (2008) 426) is adopted, they will have to extend their national legislative protection against discrimination on the grounds of religion and belief, disability, age and sexual orientation to cover all areas covered by the Race Directive. The Member States could also extend the protection against sex discrimination to the same areas and they could add other grounds beyond those provided for in EU law if they so wish. The European Commission, in the Green Paper in 2004 (COM (2004) 379), expressed its approval that some Member States had gone beyond the minimum standards set out in Community legislation: some had extended the protection beyond employment to discrimination on the grounds of religion or belief, disability, age and sexual orientation; some had opted for a single legislative framework addressing all grounds; and many had established single equality bodies dealing with all the grounds of discrimination covered by the Directives. What the EU could do to further this trend will be discussed in Chapter 7.

5 Concepts of equality as aims of equality law

5.1 Introduction

For a proper evaluation of anti discrimination legislation, it is necessary to ascertain what concept or concepts of equality are used in, or are the aim of, the legislation. The aim(s) pursued will likely influence not only the measures laid down, but also the enforcement procedures and remedies made available. In other words, different aims call for different provisions, remedies and enforcement strategies. Therefore, in this Chapter, the concept of equality is explored and this is followed in the next chapter by an examination of equality as it appears in the Race Directive. Equality is a key concept in any study on discrimination because it can be seen as the 'flip-side' of discrimination: the right not to be discriminated against or the right to protection against discrimination is seen as a human right based on the principle of equality of all humans. The prohibition of discrimination is based on the fact that people are equal. People should not be differentiated or distinguished from other people in a negative way, because all persons are equal. The right to non-discrimination and the right to equality are therefore often used interchangeably. O'Donovan and Szyszczak (1988: 1–2) call the idea of equality 'the mainspring of anti-discrimination legislation', but write that this idea lacks precision. They discern two uses of the term in political discussions. One is the use in a descriptive way, representing a statement of fact: all persons are equal. The second use is in a prescriptive way, representing a statement of aim: all persons should be equal. According to these authors, the latter, which appears to underlie the objectives of much anti discrimination legislation, is aspirational and is based on an idea of the fundamental equality of all human beings.

Dworkin (1978: 227) makes an interesting distinction in his discussion of an individual's right to equality. He discerns two sorts of rights an individual may be said to have. First, the right to equal treatment, which is the right to an equal distribution of some opportunity or resource or burden. Second, the right to treatment as an equal, which is the right to be treated with the same respect and concern as anyone else. The right to treatment as an equal is a fundamental right, while the right to equal treatment is derivative, according to Dworkin. In certain circumstances the right to treatment as an equal will entail a right to equal treatment, but not, by any means, in all circumstances. Dworkin's right to be treated as an equal appears to correspond with what Feldman (2002: 136) describes as 'moral equality': people should be 'equally entitled to respect for their moral status by virtue of being human beings'.

It will already be clear that the term equality can have different meanings. Dworkin's right to equal treatment falls within the first type of equality distinguished in this chapter: formal equality or equal treatment. The fundamental right to be treated as an equal, to respect for one's moral status, goes beyond formal equality and suggests that differences between people should be recognized and diversity should be respected. The second and third type of equality distinguished, equality of opportunity and equality of results, recognize difference between people, while the fourth type, the pluralist approach to equality, not only recognizes difference but also respects diversity. In this Chapter we examine each of these types in turn. The relationship between equality and difference and diversity will be touched upon as well.

One more point needs to be raised before we embark on this examination: it can be said that all anti discrimination legislation is, as the term itself implies, aimed at fighting discrimination. Laws against racial discrimination, therefore, aim to combat racism and racial discrimination. Fredman (2001a: 15) distinguishes three functions that are required of equality if it is to combat racism:

(a) A means of redressing racist stigma, stereotyping, humiliation and violence;
(b) The redistributive aim of breaking the cycle of disadvantage associated with groups defined by race or ethnicity;
(c) The positive affirmation and accommodation of difference as a part of the right to equal concern and respect.

These three functions of equality will be used to assess the four concepts of equality distinguished in this chapter and will also be used in Chapter 6 and 7 to measure the protection provided by the Race Directive.

5.2 Formal equality

Formal equality, which is also referred to as equal treatment, is based on the idea that every person has a right to be treated in an equal way to any other person in the same situation. This is based on the premise that like should be treated alike, which goes back to Aristotle. In this view, equality lies in consistency. Anti discrimination legislation using the concept of formal equality prohibits different treatment of people in the same situation. It is sometimes referred to as equality in law or equality before the law and is often expressed in international treaties and in the constitution in many countries in a statement similar to Article 7 of the Universal Declaration of Human Rights (1948): 'All are equal before the law and are entitled without any discrimination to equal protection of the law'.[1] As in this statement, proclaiming the right to equal protection against discrimination often follows the right to equality before the law.

At European level, the Charter of Fundamental Human Rights of the European Union also proclaims that 'everyone is equal before the law' (Article 20) and this is followed by a prohibition of discrimination in Article 21. Recital 3 of the Preamble to the Race Directive declares that 'the right to equality before the law and protection against discrimination for all persons constitutes a universal right', as recognized by a number of international human rights instruments.

However, more detailed protection is usually not provided in international or constitutional instruments, rather it is left to other legislation to do this. These other laws aim at formal equality if they prescribe equal treatment or prohibit differential treatment of people in the same or very similar situations. A good example of a law prescribing equal treatment is Article 1 of the Dutch Constitution,[2] which provides that:

> All persons in the Netherlands shall be treated equally, in equal circumstances. Discrimination on the grounds of religion, belief, political opinion, race, or sex or any ground whatsoever, shall not be permitted.

Another example of legislation prohibiting differential treatment is the definition of direct discrimination in Article 2(a) of the Race Directive:

> direct discrimination shall be taken to occur where one person is treated less favourably than another is, has been or would be treated in a comparable situation on grounds of racial or ethnic origin.

Therefore, this concept is expressed most often in either of two ways: a positive duty to treat people equally, or a negative duty not to discriminate, not to treat people unequally or differently. It is suggested that this type of

1 See for example the following international instruments: Article 26 ICCPR; Article 24 American Convention on Human Rights 1969; Article 3 African Charter on Human and Peoples' Rights 1981. For some constitutional examples see Section 15(1) Canadian Charter of Rights and Freedoms; Article 14 Constitution of India; Section 6(1) Finnish Constitution. It should be noted that these three countries accord equality before the law to any person, while some other countries restrict this to citizens only. Examples of the latter are: Article 40(1) Irish Constitution, Article 3 Italian Constitution and Article 13(1) Portuguese Constitution (all three refer to 'citizens'); Article 4(1) Greek Constitution ('all Greeks'); Article 14 Spanish Constitution ('Spaniards').

2 In a sense this is an exception, because it is a constitutional provision. More often this is provided for in other legislation.

anti discrimination legislation is based on the basic meaning of discrimination, which is, as we have seen in Chapter 3, making a distinction or differentiating in some way. The legislation only prohibits making such a distinction if it is based on grounds that are mentioned in the legislation, like 'racial or ethnic origin' in the Race Directive.

The strength of this concept, and one of its main attractions, lies in the fact that it appeals to people's feeling of fairness, of being just and equitable. O'Donovan and Szyszczak (1988: 1) write that 'the idea of equality under the law is a major justification for the rule of law itself'. If formal barriers exist for certain citizens, then these citizens are not equal under the law. If these barriers are upheld by law, then inequality is sanctioned by law. This undermines the rule of law which fails to deliver its promise of equality and this would call the legitimacy of the law into question. Those subjected to legal barriers will deny the law's claim to fairness. Thus, according to O'Donovan and Szyszczak, unequal treatment based on law is seen as unfair. Treating people equally is seen as fair, while unequal treatment is not because it treats one person better and thus another one worse. This feeling of fairness appears to be a very strong human feeling. How often do you hear someone (and not only children!) say: 'It's not fair'? As we have seen, the principle that things that are alike should be treated alike goes back to Aristotle. The sense of unequal treatment as being unfair or unjust can be seen in a quote from him: 'Equality and justice are synonymous: to be just is to be equal, to be unjust is to be unequal' (Barnard 1998: 363). Fredman (2002: 7) writes that the power of this most basic concept of equality 'derives from the even more elementary notion, that fairness requires consistent treatment'. Therefore, the strong point of this concept of equality and legislation prescribing this is its focus on fairness and consistency of treatment.

However, this approach has also been criticized on a number of grounds.[3] First, the concept of formal equality, that like should be treated alike, raises the question: who is like who? The concept thus relies on a comparator: is a person treated unequally compared to another person in the same situation? But to whom should he/she be compared? The choice of a comparator can influence the outcome.[4] There is also the problem, as Barnard (1998: 363) writes, that 'it is a moral judgment as to who is alike'. In a sense, it is different or less favourable treatment from a norm, a standard of what is seen as proper treatment. But this standard or norm is decided by the dominant culture and is often biased towards social or group attributes of the dominant group. Should a black person always be compared with a white

3 See for example: Lacey 1987: 411–21; Gregory 1987; Barnard 1998 and 1999; Barnard and Hepple 2000; Fredman 2001a, 2001b and 2002; Schiek 2002; and Howard 2007b and 2008.

4 For a more extensive discussion of the problems with the comparator concept from a British perspective, see Fredman 2002: 95–102 and McColgan 2005: 49–55.

person? To avoid this problem, Barnard (1999: 386), in her discussion on Article 13 EC, suggests:

> These ideas need to penetrate any interpretation of non-discrimination in legislation adopted under Article 13: that the comparator must not always be a male, white, European, able-bodied, straight man.

The second point of criticism against the notion that like should be treated alike is that it creates strong conformist and assimilationist pressures; pressures to conform to the dominant norms and values of the society. Boyle and Baldaccini write that the formal equality concept 'assumes conformity with the dominant culture' (2001: 157). This concept assumes and promotes sameness and aims at the elimination of difference. If you aspire to be the same, to assimilate into society and to conform to the standard norm, then you have a right to equal treatment with everyone else. Parekh (1998: 2) expresses this in his description of assimilation as follows:

> The choice before the minorities is simple. If they wish to become part of and be treated like the rest of the community, they should think and live like the latter; if instead they insist on retaining their separate cultures, they should not complain if they are treated differently.

Because of its focus on sameness, 'the notion that likes should be treated alike therefore necessarily negates the value of difference' (Fredman 2001b: 155). Schiek (2002: 304–5) writes that, 'as regards ethnic discrimination, the tendency of formal equality principles to further assimilation instead of recognition has been stressed'. Fredman sums this up very well:

> Thus equality in its most familiar sense, that like should be treated alike, could well have the effect of collapsing the principle of equality into one of sameness, devaluing difference and endorsing assimilation and conformity.
>
> (Fredman 2001b: 155)

This concept of equality, therefore, leaves no room for any recognition of the positive aspects of difference or for a requirement that people should be treated appropriately according to their differences.

Third, in this approach, everyone is treated in identical fashion. It is a symmetrical approach that does not look at existing inequalities or social disadvantages. In fact, this approach can even reinforce the inequalities that exist in reality. As Fredman (ibid) writes:

> … an apparently neutral criterion, applied equally to two individuals, can, in fact, exacerbate inequality, because its neutrality disguises a bias towards the social or group attributes of one of them.

Because formal equality is symmetrical, the same right not to be discriminated against, not to be treated differently, is applicable to everyone, black or white, male or female. Black people have the right to be treated equally to white people, but white people also have the right to be treated equally to black people. This leaves no room for positive action measures as these would give preferential, and thus unequal treatment, to certain people. However, this ignores any existing inequalities and social disadvantages. It does not look at any imbalances that have been created by past discrimination. Lacey (1992: 101) writes:

> It is widely recognised that a legal commitment to formal equality is insufficient to guarantee the fair treatment of groups which have suffered a history of prejudice and discrimination.

A fourth point of criticism is that the equal treatment approach will only work if everyone can start from the same starting point. However, cumulative disadvantage may make it difficult for members of some groups to attain the prerequisite merit criteria to compete on the same level. The law may determine that all applicants for a job must be treated equally, but this ignores the fact that some people, because of their race or sex or other ground, have never had the opportunity to acquire the required skills for the job in the first place. In the words of Hepple:

> One is not supplying equality of opportunity if one applies this criterion to people who are unequal because they have been deprived of the opportunity to acquire merit.
>
> (Hepple 1992: 26)

The law prescribing equal treatment does nothing to give the disadvantaged groups the chance to catch up with the dominant group and so to become able to compete at the same level. Therefore, this concept of equality ignores the fact that some groups cannot compete at the same level as others because of past discrimination.

The fifth point of criticism raised against the notion of formal equality is that it is a relative concept, that it does not guarantee a particular outcome. The principle is satisfied as long as likes are treated equally, no matter whether this is equally well or equally badly. Barnard and Hepple (2000: 563) express this as follows:

> A claim to equal treatment can be satisfied by depriving both the persons compared of a particular benefit (levelling down) as well as by conferring the benefit on them both (levelling up).

A good example of levelling down can be found in the ECJ case of *Smith v Avdel Systems Ltd*. In this case there was a difference in pension ages for men (65) and women (60). The Court held that raising the pension age for women to 65 satisfied the principle of equal treatment (para 21).

A sixth problem with legislation prescribing equal treatment or prohibiting unequal treatment is its focus on an individual model of justice: the individual is central in the enforcement procedures and remedies. The model relies on an individual to complain about differential or unfavourable treatment by another individual. The remedies made available by such laws are usually (financial) compensation for the wrong done. The perpetrator of the discrimination is held responsible for the wrong he/she has done to the victim, and, therefore, has to compensate the victim for the loss suffered. Some legal systems allow courts to make certain orders against the discriminator, for example, to reinstate the victim in case of discriminatory dismissal or to reserve the next available post for the victim in case of discriminatory recruitment policies. However, the more usual remedy is compensation. Fredman (2001a: 17) points out:

> the correlative of treating a person only on the basis of her 'merit' is the principle that an individual should only be liable for damage for which he or she is responsible.

In other words, this approach ignores that, often, racial discrimination and prejudice cannot be attributed to any one person. It must be noted that this problem is not exclusively linked to legislation prescribing equal treatment, although it is more likely to occur with such legislation. This does, however, depend on what the legislation itself determines and what remedies are available in general.

All this suggests that this concept of equality as an aim for anti discrimination law is useful as a minimum requirement, addressing the first function of equality (and equality law) as formulated by Fredman (2001a: 15): it can help to redress racist stigma, stereotyping, humiliation and violence. It makes it clear that differential treatment on the grounds of skin colour or racial or ethnic origin is prohibited, that racial prejudice will not be tolerated. But it is a minimum requirement only or, as McInerney (2002: 76) writes, 'equality demands, at minimum, formal equal treatment: that likes should be treated alike, and that deviations from that proportionality be justified'. Fredman's conclusion sums up the role and the limits of the formal equality concept accurately:

> While formal equality or equality of treatment has a role to play, particularly in eradicating personal prejudice, it is clear from the above that it needs to be allied to a more substantive approach.
>
> (Fredman 2002: 11)

These more substantive approaches will be discussed next.

5.3 Substantive equality

In attempts to overcome the problems associated with the notion of formal equality, other concepts of equality have been suggested. Because formal equality is perceived as not touching the substantive inequalities that exist in most societies, or even as reinforcing these, a more substantive equality, which is sensitive to the effects of past and ongoing discrimination, is put forward. Substantive equality aims to compensate for the social inequalities and disadvantages suffered by certain groups. Substantive equality is thus more sensitive to group aspects of discrimination and recognizes that persons are discriminated against as members of a particular group (like ethnic minorities, religious groups, women, disabled persons, etc.). There are extra burdens and barriers to achieving equality for members of disadvantaged groups. As Schiek (2002: 304) writes:

> A substantive, asymmetric notion of equality is ... based on a group-sensitive model of justice, ... The group-sensitive approach purports that discrimination on any of the forbidden grounds is group related. Persons are grouped into a collective and disadvantaged as a 'member' of such a collective. Thus non-discrimination law needs to be sensitive to this group dimension, while avoiding to support forced group membership.

The focus of substantive equality is on the material reality of people's lives. The concept can be in direct conflict with the idea of formal equality because it may require unequal treatment. Bacik (1997: 119–20) writes that the concept of substantive equality is 'based upon difference'. This means that 'in order to create equality, persons must be treated differently according to their needs'. This comes close to Dworkin's right to be treated as an equal (Dworkin 1978: 227).

Substantive equality is also referred to as equality in fact, as opposed to formal equality, which is equality in law. The concept of substantive equality suggests that equality laws should be sensitive to the practical results of equal or unequal treatment. McInerney (2002: 76) follows the statement, quoted above, that 'equality demands, at minimum, formal equal treatment', with:

> Equality can take a more substantive and 'effect-centred' form, demanding that group perspectives be considered, that historical and contextual dimensions of discrimination be accommodated and that remedial action be permitted to redress past discrimination.

Whereas formal equality can be seen as symmetrical, substantive equality is asymmetrical, in that it allows unequal treatment in order to rectify social disadvantages and so achieve the goal of equality in fact. Therefore, laws based on substantive equality concepts try to compensate for these disadvantages and will allow unequal treatment of disadvantaged groups where that is necessary to achieve equality in fact. This unequal treatment or preferential treatment has been referred to as: special measures (often used in international instruments); affirmative action (more often used in the US); or, positive action (more commonly used in (the literature in) Europe). The three terms can be seen as interchangeable. Article 1(4) ICERD is an example of an international measure:

> Special measures taken for the sole purpose of securing adequate advancement of certain racial and ethnic groups or individuals requiring such protection as may be necessary in order to ensure such groups or individuals equal enjoyment or exercise of human rights and fundamental freedoms shall not be deemed racial discrimination, …

Section 9(2) of the South African Constitution reads as follows:

> Equality includes the full and equal enjoyment of all rights and freedoms. To promote the achievement of equality, legislative and other measures designed to protect or advance persons, or categories of persons, disadvantaged by unfair discrimination may be taken.

And Article 5 of the Race Directive, which is headed 'Positive action' determines:

> With a view to ensuring full equality in practice, the principle of equal treatment shall not prevent any Member State from maintaining or adopting specific measures to prevent or compensate for disadvantages linked to racial or ethnic origin.

In this book, we will use the term positive action in the sense given by Fottrell (1999: 183):

> Special measures or affirmative action, in their simplest possible form, involve legalised differential treatment of individuals based on their membership of an historically disadvantaged minority group.

The terms positive or reverse discrimination are also sometimes used but, because of the use of the word discrimination and its negative connotations, this term is not very popular. Sometimes it is used as a synonym for positive action, at other times it is distinguished from the term positive action, in that positive discrimination indicates preferential treatment that goes further than positive action, like, for example, the imposition of quotas or goals. Bacik (1997: 120) writes:

> Generally, policies which seek to achieve equality of opportunity may be described as 'positive action', while those which seek to achieve equality of result are described as 'positive discrimination'.

This indicates that the substantive equality concept embraces two types: equality of opportunity and equality of results. The difference between these two concepts can be said to be one of degree only. Because of the confusion as to its meaning, the terms positive or reverse discrimination will not be used.

It will be clear that both concepts will allow for preferential treatment of historically disadvantaged groups, for positive action measures. However, the main problem with positive action measures is, and it is submitted that this is also one of the reasons why the terms reverse or positive discrimination are unpopular, that they are going against the principle of equal treatment, that they themselves constitute discrimination because preferential treatment of some is worse treatment of others and this is seen as unfair. As Barnard (1998: 373) writes, 'equality comes with a price tag attached. ... improving the position of one group is often to the detriment of another'. And, according to Feldman (2002: 152), such action 'will be seen by the disadvantaged members of previously advantaged groups as a straightforward form of discrimination'. Poulter (1998: 13–4) gives as one of the arguments in favour of varying degrees of assimilation, that the vital principle of equality before the law will be jeopardized if minorities are given special exemptions and privileges. He also states that such equality can be seen as part of the rule of law. Nevertheless, advocates of positive action see it as justified because of the inequalities suffered through historical discrimination.

Anti discrimination legislation providing for positive action can, therefore, aim at either equality of opportunity or at equality of results and it is not always clear from the texts which type of equality is the aim. The reason is that the laws do not often give any further details of the measures that can be taken (see the examples given above) and thus what is allowed depends on the interpretation in secondary legislation or in case law. We will now look at each concept in turn.

5.3.1 Equality of opportunity

This form of equality concentrates on equalizing the starting point for all, on giving everyone the same opportunities. This approach may well involve unequal treatment and unequal finishing points, because it is not concerned with the end result, but only aims to make the starting point equal for all. Equality of opportunity recognizes that the effects of past discrimination can make it very difficult for members of particular groups to even reach a situation of 'being alike' so that the right to like treatment becomes applicable.

Anti discrimination legislation aiming to establish equality of opportunity is sensitive to the position of disadvantage and inequality which some groups of people are in because of the discrimination they have been or are subjected to, and attempts to make up for this (past) inequality by making the starting point equal for everybody. This approach accepts that treating everyone equally, according to merit, cannot be successful if not everyone has been able to, or had the opportunity to, acquire merit. Feldman (2002: 152) expresses this well:

> Inequality of opportunity is particularly likely to result where one group suffers from the effects of a history of systematic discrimination which has limited the educational and economic opportunities open to them.

Thus, the anti discrimination law tries to make up for these missed opportunities. Some groups cannot compete on the same level and they are not at the same starting point because they have suffered disadvantage. The law aims to equalize the starting point so everyone has 'the opportunity to compete on equal terms for the goods which society has to offer' (Townshend-Smith 1998: 73). Once this is achieved, once the starting point is equalized, the competition from then on will be on merit only. The equality of opportunity concept is thus not concerned with the end results of the race as long as anyone can compete at the same level.

Section 14 of Ireland's Equal Status Act 2000 can be seen as an example of an anti discrimination measure aimed at equal opportunity. It reads as follows:

> Nothing in this Act shall be construed as prohibiting–
> (a) …,
> (b) preferential treatment or the taking of positive measures which are bona fide intended to–
>   (1) promote equality of opportunity for persons who are, in relation to other persons, disadvantaged or who have been or are likely to be unable to avail themselves of the same opportunities as those other persons, or …

Article 5 of the Race Directive, quoted above, permits EU Member States to take positive action. The Article itself does not give any indication as to what sort of action is allowed and how far this action can go. We will come back to this in Chapter 6.

The concept of indirect discrimination is, according to some writers, an example of a legislative measure that aims at equality of opportunity, although others refer to it as promoting substantive equality without specifying whether its aim is equality of opportunity or equality of results. Yet others see it as promoting equality of results only. We will discuss indirect discrimination after we have discussed equality of results.

It will be clear that anti discrimination legislation promoting the concept of equality of opportunity remedies some of the problems that we have distinguished in relation to the concept of equal treatment. It recognizes existing inequalities and social disadvantages and allows for preferential treatment to overcome these. It is also asymmetrical in that it takes account of difference and disadvantage and permits unequal treatment. However, the concept of equality of opportunity as a basis for anti discrimination laws has been criticized for the following reasons. First, as we already mentioned, it appears to go against the principle of equality and non-discrimination as it requires preferential treatment of, for example, a black person or a woman, which would discriminate against white people or men.

Second, once the starting point has been equalized for all the competition from then on will be based on merit. O'Donovan and Szyszczak (1988: 3–4) write that the role of the state here is to equalize the rules of entry and thereafter 'to hold the ring for free competition'. The question with this competition on merit is: what is merit and who determines this? Townshend-Smith (1998: 77) writes that the notion of merit is deep-rooted in our society, and that 'merit has historically been determined in [white] male terms'. Feldman (2002: 138–9) points out that 'the opportunities which systematically disadvantaged groups seek might not be those which are traditionally favoured by the dominant set of values'. This ignores that:

> what at least some members of the underprivileged group (women or ethnic minorities) really desire is not the opportunity to be like the previously dominant group (men, whites, Christians, etc.) but rather the freedom to pursue their own values in their own ways.
>
> (Ibid: 139)

Lacey (1987: 420) calls the notion of equality of opportunity a 'manipulable notion'. She advocates abandoning equality of opportunity as an underlying principle of equality law because:

> The opportunity ideal's presupposition of a world of autonomous individuals starting a race or making free choices has no cutting edge against the argument that men and women are simply running different races.

The above suggests that the disadvantaged group, in the terminology of Lacey, is not running the same race and might well not want to run the same race and that, therefore, equalizing the starting point for all will not lead to a more equal society.

Fredman (2001a: 21) describes the two views of equality of opportunity as distinguished by Williams. On a procedural view, it would require 'the removal of obstacles to the advancement of women and minorities', but this would not 'guarantee greater substantive fairness in the result'. A substantive view of equality of opportunity would require 'measures to be taken to ensure that persons from all sections of society have a genuinely equal chance of satisfying the criteria for access to a particular social good'. This would require a 'reconsideration of existing criteria of merit'. It is submitted that equality of opportunity on a substantive view would go some way towards remedying the criticism against the notion described above. It would also get closer to a notion of equality of results.

This concept of equality also does not guarantee a particular result. It is not concerned with the outcome of the competition: different finishing points are not seen as a problem, as long as everyone can compete equally on merit. This is the reason why this concept rejects the setting of quotas and targets to correct imbalances in the workforce or in the allocation of housing, which aim at equalizing the results. It aims at the removal of barriers, but does ignore that this might not necessarily equip the disadvantaged group to move forward. Equalizing the starting point may not necessarily lead to a more equal society. Townshend-Smith (1998: 73) describes equal opportunity as giving everyone 'the opportunity to compete on equal terms for the goods which society has to offer'. He continues:

> The problem, though, is that reliance on equal opportunity alone provides no guarantee that, in practice, those goods will not remain disproportionately in the hands of white males.

This equality concept does focus more on groups and thus could lead to a more group sensitive model of justice, but whether it allows for group action depends on the legislation and the legal system. If this solely focuses on an individual model of justice, than the same objections that applied to the equal treatment concept also apply here.

A last point that needs to be discussed in relation to the equality of opportunity concept is the sort of remedies this could permit or prescribe. These remedies could include: compensation; orders to change policies; and contract compliance or withholding of licences: where a public body has the authority not to make contracts with or give licences to companies unless they have an equality of opportunity policy in place or to end contracts with and withdraw licences from companies who do not respect equality principles. However, whether these sorts of remedies are available again depends on the legislation itself and the legal system it is part of. Sometimes, neither the anti discrimination law itself nor the legal system will allow for anything but compensation.

5.3.2 Equality of results

This concept is also referred to as equality of outcome or impact. It is based on a system of justice which takes account of past or present discrimination and concentrates on correcting maldistribution and achieving a more representative participation of all groups in public life. Its aim is thus redistributive; the laws aim to establish a fairer distribution of goods and resources in society. Townshend-Smith (1998: 61) describes equality of outcome as 'a notion which pays at least some regard to the distribution of outcomes between the various different groups'. Later on he writes that 'equality of outcome implies an equitable division of the economic cake between different groups in society' (Ibid: 73).

This equality concept 'looks to the results of competition and then raises questions about the rules of entry' (O'Donovan and Szyszczak 1988: 4). A good example of legislation trying to achieve fair participation in employment of both Protestants and Catholics is the Fair Employment and Treatment (Northern Ireland) Order 1998 which determines under the heading 'Affirmative Action' in Section 4(1):

> In this Order "affirmative action" means action designed to secure fair participation in employment by members of the Protestant, or members of the Roman Catholic, community in Northern Ireland by means including:
> (a) the adoption of practices encouraging such participation; and
> (b) the modification or abandonment of practices that have or may have the effect of restricting or discouraging such participation.

This involves redressing imbalances and under-representation between the two communities in Northern Ireland. The aims are 'to secure greater fairness in the distribution of jobs and opportunities'.

Anti discrimination legislation aiming at equality of results would also allow for positive action measures, but, in this case, they would go further and include the setting of targets and quotas. An example of such a law aimed at equality of results is Section 46 of the Police (Northern Ireland) Act 2000 which contains a quota system for the recruitment of police trainees and support staff. Its aim is to reverse the under-representation of Catholics in the police force. Section 46(1) requires the appointment of one Catholic person for every person of another religion who is awarded a post. According to Section 47(1), these provisions were temporary for three years but they have been extended twice and are now in place until 2010. However, the other paragraphs of Section 46 empower the Secretary of State to amend the above requirements if not enough people can be appointed.

Another example is the Canadian Employment Equity Act of 1995. According to Article 2 on the purpose of the Act, 'employment equity means more than treating persons in the same way but also requires special measures and the accommodation of differences'. Article 5 of this Act puts the following obligation on employers:

> Every employer shall implement employment equity by
> (a) ...; and
> (b) instituting such positive policies and practices and making such reasonable accommodations as will ensure that persons in designated groups achieve a degree of representation in each occupational group in the employer's workforce that reflects their representation in
>   i. the Canadian workforce, or
>   ii. those segments of the Canadian workforce that are identifiable by qualification, eligibility or geography and from

> which the employer may reasonably be expected to draw employees.

In other words, employers must use positive policies and practices and make accommodations to ensure that women, aboriginal peoples, persons with disabilities and members of visible minorities – Article 3 gives this as the meaning of 'designated group' – are represented in their workforce in the same numbers as they are represented in the Canadian workforce as a whole or in those segments of the workforce that the employer may reasonably be expected to recruit employees from, looking at qualifications, eligibility and geography. Therefore, if 5 per cent of the Canadian workforce as a whole or of that segment is of a visible minority, then the workforce should also have about 5 per cent of visible minority people, and not just the workforce of the employer as a whole but also each occupational group. This can be seen as a clear target: 5 per cent should be of visible minorities. However, is this duty on employers as results-oriented as it first appears from Article 5? This is indeed questionable; first, part (b)(ii) could mitigate the duty on the employer, depending on how it is interpreted. Second, even if part (b)(ii) does not do so, Article 6 certainly does. It contains the following exceptions:

> The obligation to implement employment equity does not require an employer
> (a) to take a particular measure to implement employment equity where the taking of that measure would cause undue hardship to the employer;
> (b) to hire or promote unqualified persons;
> (c) with respect to the public sector, to hire or promote persons without basing the hiring or promotion on selection according to merit in cases where the Public Service Employment Act requires that hiring or promotion be based on selection according to merit; or
> (d) to create new positions in its workforce.

So, Article 5, as it is aiming to achieve fair participation in the workforce for minority groups, can be seen as an example of a results-oriented measure. However, its effect could be mitigated by the interpretation of its part (b)(ii), and is definitely mitigated by the exceptions of Article 6. Therefore, both the Police (Northern Ireland) Act 2000 and the Canadian Employment Equity Act 1995 allow for exceptions.

The concept of indirect discrimination will now be discussed as it is seen as a measure which aims at promoting substantive equality. Indirect discrimination occurs, according to Article 2(2)(b) of the Race Directive:

> … where an apparently neutral provision, criterion or practice would put persons of a racial or ethnic origin at a particular disadvantage compared with other persons …

Article 2(2) of the Belgian Act of 25 February 2003 Pertaining to the Combat of Discrimination and to the Amendment of the Act of 15 February 1993 Pertaining to the Foundation of a Centre For Equal Opportunities and Opposition to Racism, states:

> Indirect discrimination occurs when a seemingly neutral provision, measure or practice has harmful repercussions on persons on which one of the grounds for discrimination set out in para 1 applies, ...

From these definitions it will be clear that indirect discrimination takes account of differences. In cases of indirect discrimination, people are treated equally, the same provision is applied equally to everyone, but some people will find it more difficult or impossible to comply. Therefore, the concept of indirect discrimination recognizes that equal treatment can have a discriminatory effect on some as a result of historical and structural impediments to equality. For example, requiring applicants for a job to pass literacy tests even if this is not necessary for doing the job can be discriminatory against those who did not have the educational opportunities to become literate. The concept does, therefore, aim to compensate for past or current inequalities and disadvantages. By defining as prohibited discrimination apparently neutral provisions, criteria and practices that have a disparate effect and, therefore, by taking these barriers away as irrelevant, laws against indirect discrimination make the starting point more equal for everybody and make it easier for everyone to compete on the same level. In this sense, such legislation can be seen as aiming at equality of opportunity. However, not all barriers are against the law. The reason for this is that legislation against indirect discrimination allows for justification: there is no discrimination if the provision, criterion or practice is 'objectively justified by a legitimate aim and the means of achieving that aim are appropriate and necessary' (Article 2(2)(b) of the Race Directive). Such justification clauses are a feature of many legislative measures against indirect discrimination.[5] So, even if there is a disadvantage or a barrier, this might not be unlawful if business or administrative interests objectively justify it.

The definitions show that indirect discrimination takes account of the impact, the results of seemingly neutral provisions or measures applied to all persons equally. It focuses on the practical result of a measure: if it has 'harmful repercussions' it may be considered discrimination. In this sense, indirect discrimination takes differences into account and is result-oriented. Does this mean that it aims at equality of results? Fredman (2001b: 161) writes, 'this focus on impact may be used in different ways, the aim not necessarily being equality of results'. Elsewhere, Fredman (2001a: 19) writes that equality of

5 See for example: Section 1(1)(b)(ii) of the British Race Relations Act 1976 and Article 2(1) of the Dutch Equal Treatment Act 1994. The Belgian law quoted contains a similar clause.

results can be used in three different ways. The first focuses on the impact on the individual, with the aim of obtaining a remedy for that individual, rather than achieving equality of results. This would not touch the discriminating structure. The second use focuses on the results to the group. However, this aims to demonstrate the existence of obstacles to entry rather than prescribing an outcome pattern. The third and strongest meaning of equality of results is a demand for an equal outcome. This is a more obviously redistributive aim, although even here, as Fredman points out, the notion of equality is not fully in focus: often 'it is not equality, but proportionality, fairness or balance which is required' (Ibid).

If we take the first way which focuses on the effect of the equal treatment on the individual, then the concept of indirect discrimination involves equality of results, because the focus is on the 'particular disadvantage' or the 'harmful repercussions' for the individual. The second sense focuses on the results to the group. In this sense too, the concept can be said to involve outcome equality. As Barnard and Hepple (2000: 564) write:

> The essential characteristic of indirect discrimination is that an apparently neutral practice or criterion has an unjustifiable adverse disparate impact upon the group to which the individual belongs.

The third sense of equality of results assumes that the end result should be equal, proportional and fair, that the outcome is equal. In this last sense, the concept of indirect discrimination is not redistributive because the end result may remain unequal. For example, a finding of indirect discrimination against an employer requiring literacy tests for a job when this is not necessary to do the job might not result in the person who was discriminated against getting the job. And, even if this were the result, it would not change the fact that some people never had the opportunity to become literate because of past or ongoing discrimination in education. Requiring literacy tests might in other cases be justified for the interest of the business. With Fredman (2002: 115) we can conclude that:

> The aims of the concept of indirect discrimination are ambiguous. … its goals are not necessarily the achievement of equality of results. … If indirect discrimination is only partially about equality of results, is it instead about equality of opportunity in that it aims to equalise the starting point? Again, this is only partially true.

We can add to this, however, that indirect discrimination 'has been characterised as an important step away form a formal equality approach towards a substantive notion' (Schiek 2002: 305). Therefore, when anti discrimination legislation prohibits indirect discrimination, it moves away from a formal equality concept to a more substantive one, whether that is equality of opportunity or equality of results.

Equality of outcome or results can thus be used in different ways. In the first two uses, the aim of redistribution, of an 'equitable division of the economic cake', will not be reached. Even if the concept is used in the third sense, full equality of outcome might not be the result. Therefore, it will be clear that equality of results is not without its problems. The following objections have been made against it. First, like equality of opportunity, it requires preferential treatment of some people and thus involves unequal treatment.

Townshend-Smith (1998: 80) points out a second problem with equality of results. Its aim of redistribution of wealth is intertwined with the relief of poverty. But why then should only certain victims of poverty (black people, women) and not others be entitled to such relief?

The third problem is that, despite the fact that this concept of equality aims at redistribution, this might not necessarily be the result because the outcome depends on the way the concept is used. This can be seen in the paper by Menski (1992: 300–43) on the policy of protective discrimination of traditionally disadvantaged groups that was laid down in the Constitution of India in 1950. Articles 14–16 of the Constitution of India explicitly allow preferential treatment for certain groups and Article 16(4) allows the reservation of appointments or posts in favour of any backward class of citizens. The constitutional provisions aimed to accelerate the process of building an egalitarian social order. However, the Constitution does not give any indication as to how these policies of protective discrimination are to be implemented and 'the implementation of the policies is apparently far from perfect' (Ibid: 310–1 and 313). And, as Menski writes, 'the social reformer's dream of an egalitarian society as the result of "equalizing policies" … has clearly not been achieved in modern India' (Ibid: 307).[6]

Fredman (2001a: 20) writes about equality of results that the 'underlying redistributive aims may only be partially achieved'. She gives two reasons for this: first, 'monitoring of results does not necessitate any fundamental re-examination of the structures that perpetuate discrimination'; and, second,

> there is a danger that a focus on equality of results pays too little attention to the equally important notion of equality of diversity; or the duty to accommodate diversity by adapting existing structures.

A fourth problem is that there are disadvantages linked to the setting of quotas. Gregory (1987: 64–5) mentions:

> Although a system of quotas produces rapid and dramatic results, its application in the job market would tend to accentuate rather than dissipate racial hostility. If it entailed the selection of people with inferior

6 For more information on how the policies were implemented and why they did not have the desired effects, see the paper.

> qualifications merely because they were black or female (or both), those selected might feel patronized and those not selected might see themselves as a new class of victim.

Menski calls this the 'efficiency argument': the public perception in India is 'that the effect of reservation policies has been to bring about lower standards and to encourage inefficiency' (Menski 1992: 324–5).

MacEwen (1995: 24) criticizes quotas thus:

> In particular the results may involve the less well-qualified, and potentially less deserving, getting a job, a house or a promotion to make up the numbers, and in doing so discriminating against better qualified white applicants who feel no great need to shoulder the burden of rectifying historical disadvantage. Such reverse discrimination is often unlawful, but perhaps more importantly it is seen to be unfair; it denies everyone a fair chance and is in breach of the concept of natural justice.

Thus, again, the importance of treatment being seen to be fair and just is stressed.

The last problem is whether it is really possible to achieve equality of results through legislation. O'Donovan and Szyszczak (1988: 6) write that 'the creation of outcome equality would require a major social revolution. … Liberals object that equality of outcomes could be maintained only at a substantial cost to liberty'. This is because 'the maintenance of strict equality would require continuous coercive interference to maintain an egalitarian distribution pattern'. A second question is whether legislation can aim purely at equality of results. We can put this question in a different way: can we have legislation that uses the notion of equality of results as defined in Fredman's third way above, as requiring a redistributive outcome, an 'equal outcome, that is that the spread of women and minorities in a category should reflect their proportions in the workforce or the population as whole'?

It is suggested that we can have such a legislative aim, that we can have laws that aim at a more equal distribution and a fairer participation, but that legislation alone can never reach full equality of results. Section 46(1) of the Police (Northern Ireland) Act 2000, Section 4(1) of the Fair Employment and Treatment (Northern Ireland) Order 1998, and Article 5 of the Canadian Employment Equity Act, cited above, can all be seen as examples of legislation with such an aim. However, as we have seen, the Police (Northern Ireland) Act 2000 provides for exceptions when not enough people are available and Article 5 of the Canadian Act is mitigated by Article 6. The Fair Employment and Treatment (Northern Ireland) Order 1998 defines affirmative action as action designed to secure fair participation by means of adopting practices that encourage it and abandoning practices that discourage or restrict it. Therefore, this Order focuses more on encouraging fair participation, rather than setting strict rules and quotas as to how to achieve this. The reason that anti discrimination legislation alone cannot establish full equality of results is that there are always conflicting interests at work. First, there is the conflict between the different groups that should be given preferential treatment: why some groups (like, for example, black people or women) and not others (like, for example, religious groups)? And even within the groups selected, preferential treatment often goes to the more privileged people within that group (Menski 1992: 331; Pitt 1992: 284; Fredman 2002: 152; Costello 2003: 210). To be truly redistributive, all disadvantaged people should be given such treatment, irrespective of the group they belong to or even if they don't belong to any group at all.

Second, there is the conflict, already mentioned, between preferential treatment and the feeling of fairness and justice. Positive action is seen to be unfair and to go against the principle of equal treatment of every person.

Third, there is also the conflict between the redistribution of goods and resources and the business interests of an employer. This is clear in Article 6 of the Canadian Employment Equity Act, where an employer does not have to take an employment equity measure if it 'would cause undue hardship to the employer' or if it meant hiring or promoting unqualified persons. The problem can be illustrated by an example: in a country, 10 per cent of the population is from a racial or ethnic minority origin. Because this group of people is involved in employment in only a very small percentage, a law determines that every employer must make sure that 10 per cent of his workforce and of each category in his workforce is from such a minority origin. How quickly should an employer comply (the law could give a time scale)? Should an employer make some people redundant and replace them with people of the racial or ethnic minority if financial restraints will not make it possible for the employer to create new jobs? What if there are not enough people of the racial or ethnic minority who are qualified and suitable to do the job?

This suggests that legislation can be based on the concept of equality of results in that it can aim at a more equitable distribution and a fairer participation, but that these legislative measures need to be supported by measures in a number of other areas, such as the social, political and educational field.

As for remedies, the same range would apply here as was discussed for laws aiming at equality of opportunity: compensation; orders to change policies; and contract compliance or the withholding or withdrawing of licences. It could also allow orders to reach certain targets or quotas before the expiry of a certain time.[7] But, again, which remedies are allowed depends on the legislation and the legal system it is part of.

7 For a way of dealing with non-compliance see Part II of the Canadian Employment Equity Law, Articles 22–34. Part III (Articles 35–40) determines monetary penalties for employers who do not comply.

It can be concluded that both substantive concepts of equality as goals of anti discrimination law go some way towards remedying the problems that occur with the equal treatment concept, but that they are not without problems themselves. It will also be clear that it is not always possible to draw a sharp line between equality of opportunity and equality of results because measures can contain aspects of both. Where the concepts differ is that equality of opportunity focuses on equalizing the starting point for everyone without being concerned about the outcome, while equality of results concerns itself with an equal outcome. Positive measures may fit in with either concept: they might only attempt to create fair procedures in job applications without giving a person a right to a job. Or they may go further and actively encourage people from disadvantaged groups to apply without guaranteeing any specific outcome in their favour. Both these type of measures would fit in the concept of equality of opportunity. On the other hand, positive measures could not only encourage applications from certain groups, but could also determine that a set number of jobs should be given to people of that group. In this case, the measure fits in with the concept of equality of results.

5.4 Pluralist approach to equality

Some writers suggest a more pluralist approach to equality. Such an approach would aim to create a society where differences and diversity between groups and individuals are considered an asset and everyone is treated with the same respect. Townshend-Smith (1998: 80–1) writes that an approach based on pluralistic political philosophies is far more appropriate. In such an approach 'the law must take account of the differences between groups which affects their capacity for equal competition in the market place'. Fredman (2001a: 3) suggests that a central challenge is to fashion a concept of substantive equality that can encompass positive diversity. Bacik (1997: 119–20) appears to support this pluralist view, when she writes that substantive equality is based on difference and that people should be treated differently according to their needs.

It is suggested that this pluralist concept of equality can be related to Dworkin's right to treatment as an equal (Dworkin 1978: 227), the right to be treated with the same respect and concern as anyone else. O'Donovan and Szyszczak write about the distinction made by Dworkin:

> If this passage is taken as suggesting that people and their needs are different, then it seems to follow that rights to equality do not mean treating people in the same way. This is an argument for pluralism. … It is an argument against the assimilationist ideal [O'Donovan and Szyszczak (1988: 6)]. … If treatment as an equal implies respect for others, avoidance of stereotypes and viewing the world from another's point of view, then pluralism goes further than equal treatment.
>
> (Ibid: 7)

Dine and Watt (1996: 5) also discuss Dworkin's distinction between 'equal treatment' and 'treatment as an equal'. They ask what it means to treat people as equals and write:

> ... all that is needed is a recognition that individuals have different incommensurable abilities, goals and aspirations, and that 'treating people as equals' means giving equal weight to each person's own 'plan of life', i.e. treating people as equals means recognizing their autonomy.

So, according to this, treating people as equal means respecting their goals and aspirations, their 'plan of life', whatever people choose this to be. This appears to be close to Feldman's concept of moral equality. He writes that treating people as moral equals is 'seen as demanding respect for (even celebration of) difference, rather than its elimination'. And the 'willingness to treat someone as an equal only if he or she adopts one's own system of beliefs and values is a denial of moral equality rather than an expression of it' (Feldman 2002: 139). Feldman thus also appears to favour a pluralist notion of equality and to reject assimilationist ideas.

Mason (1995: 2 and 127) writes about the distinction between difference, which is often seen as a problem and has assimilationist assumptions, and diversity, which is a positive perspective. He concludes that the choice between fearing difference and embracing diversity is a major challenge for the future. To choose to embrace diversity would fit in a pluralist approach to equality.

Legislation based on a pluralist concept of equality would aim to establish a society where difference and diversity are celebrated as positive assets and where every individual is treated with equal respect. In such a society, there would be acceptance of distinctive cultures and identities and people would be treated in accordance with their own requirements and aspirations. Society would be based on respect for and tolerance of differences and diversity and strive to integrate minority communities rather than assimilate them. The idea is not new: in a speech in 1966, Roy Jenkins (then Home Secretary) described integration thus:

> I do not regard it as meaning the loss, by immigrants, of their own national characteristics and culture. ... I define integration therefore, not as a flattening process of assimilation but as equal opportunity, coupled with cultural diversity in an atmosphere of mutual tolerance.
>
> (Jenkins 1967: 267)

The above suggests that, in a pluralist view, equality laws should be based on respect for difference and diversity and should prescribe that everyone is treated with equal respect and concern. But is it possible to put this down in legislation? As O'Donovan and Szyszczak (1988: 7) write, 'in terms of legislative policy pluralism may be impossible to implement'.

Equality legislation grounded in a pluralist concept of equality would aim to create 'an atmosphere of mutual tolerance' between people of different groups. One way of doing this is by prohibiting intolerance and its manifestations, like discrimination. In this sense all laws against discrimination aim to promote tolerance. But legislation based on this concept of equality would go further. It could contain a government statement that cultural diversity is to be respected or it could put a positive duty on authorities and employers to eliminate discrimination and to respect diversity. It could also lay down a policy of mainstreaming equality and diversity: a duty to take combating discrimination and promoting equality and respect for diversity into account in every policy and executive decision, thus making equality and diversity factors that always need to be considered. Mainstreaming could fit in with the other concepts of equality, but this depends on what is mainstreamed. We will discuss this in more detail in Chapter 6.

An example of legislation aiming at a pluralist concept of equality is the Canadian Multiculturalism Act 1985. The Preamble states that:

> the Government of Canada recognizes the diversity of Canadians as regards race, national or ethnic origin, colour and religion as a fundamental characteristic of Canadian society and is committed to a policy of multiculturalism designed to preserve and enhance the multicultural heritage of Canadians while working to achieve the equality of all Canadians in the economic, social, cultural and political life of Canada.

Article 3(1)(a) and (e) and 3(2)(a), under the heading 'Multicultural Policy of Canada' are the most relevant for our discussion. These declare that it will be the policy of the Government of Canada:

- To 'recognize and promote the understanding that multiculturalism reflects the cultural and racial diversity of Canadian society and acknowledges the freedom of all members of Canadian society to preserve, enhance and share their cultural heritage' (Article 3(1)(a));
- To 'ensure that all individuals receive equal treatment and equal protection under the law, while respecting and valuing their diversity' (Article 3(1)(e));
- that all federal institutions shall 'ensure that Canadians of all origins have an equal opportunity to obtain employment and advancement in those institutions' (Article 3(2)(a)).

Here, the aim of a multicultural society in which everyone, whatever their cultural heritage, has a right to equal treatment and equal protection under the law as well as a right to respect for their diversity, is laid down in law as a government policy. The Act does not define what a multicultural society is. Parekh (1998: 1) describes a multicultural society as 'a society which includes several distinct cultural, ethnic and religious communities'. According to Watson (2000: 1), a multicultural society denotes a society in which there exist several cultures; and culture refers to a common language, a shared history, a shared set of religious beliefs and moral values, a shared geographical origin, all of which taken together define a sense of belonging to a specific group. Watson writes that other terms have been used to describe such a society: plural, cosmopolitan, multi-ethnic, poly-ethnic or multi-racial.

The Dutch system of 'verzuiling' (pillarization)[8] is often mentioned as an example of a democratic, pluralist society where tolerance for others was laid down in law. The system was based on the existence of four pillars, a Roman-Catholic, a Protestant, a Socialist and a Liberal or neutral one, where members of each pillar accorded rights and deference to members of other pillars. The pillars had their own organizations at all levels of life: politics, unions, education, health, youth, media and sports. The system was a result of the Pacificatie (peaceful settlement) of 1917, which established a politics of accommodation. In that year, the Dutch Constitution was changed in three respects: first, all public and all denominational schools were given the same financial status (in other words, they were all financed by the Government in the same way) (Article 23); second, universal (male) suffrage was introduced (followed in 1919 by universal female suffrage) (Article 54); and, third, the electoral system was changed to a system of proportional representation (Article 53).

The seven main rules that taken together describe how this system worked were (Bagley 1973: 17–19; Lijphart 1975: 122–38; Blom 2000: 154):

(a) The business of politics: practical politics aimed at achieving results;
(b) The agreement to disagree: acceptance of the spiritual disunity of society; the fundamental convictions of other pillars must be tolerated if not respected;
(c) Summit diplomacy: top-level discussion, especially to solve crises;
(d) Proportionality as the principle for solving crises (distributional equity);
(e) Depoliticization of issues that are loaded ideologically or in terms of political principles, thus turning them into practical technical issues;
(f) Secrecy when seeking solutions, to enable compromises to be reached;
(g) The Government's right to govern: the Government is elected to get a job done, in the business-like traditions of Dutch politics. It has the power and the duty actually to apply solutions. To do this it needs a lot of room for manoeuvre.

8 See "Verzuiling" www.parlement.com/9291000/modules/g72bd2vo (accessed 8 April 2009). The above is only a very short summary. For more extensive information, including on the depillarization or deconfessionalization that took place in the 1960s, see Bagley 1973; Bryant 1981; Lijphart1995: 275–87; Bryant 1997; Pennings 1997; de Rooy, 1997; Wintle 2000; Blom 2000; and Toonen 2000.

The above is a very short and simplified description of the Dutch system of pillarization, mentioned as an example of a plural society where sections of the population lived together and tolerated and respected the differences between them. The term 'living apart together' has been used frequently in this context.

However, there are some problems with pluralism and the pluralist concept of equality as an aim of anti discrimination law. We can discuss these by using Poulter's arguments for assimilation, which can be seen as arguments against minorities retaining their separate customs and traditional practices, as they would do in a pluralist society (Poulter 1998: 13–14).

One of his arguments, that the principle of equality before the law will be jeopardized if minorities get special treatment by the legal system, has already been mentioned when we discussed positive action measures. This argument goes back to the feelings of unfairness and injustice about unequal treatment in whatever form.

Another of Poulter's arguments is that members of minority groups may not so easily be able to attain economic advancement and break free of the cycle of disadvantage and discrimination if they insist upon retaining their separate customs. This is mainly because employers will not employ them out of fear that they will make cultural or religious demands or will not fit in with other employees. Is this an argument against a pluralist society? It is submitted that this is not, as such a society is all about tolerating and respecting diversity, about accommodating and making room for differences. The problem would not exist in a truly pluralist society. Anti discrimination or equality legislation would aim to establish tolerance and respect, so would aim to remedy the problem Poulter points at here.

This leaves us with Poulter's other two arguments: one is the concern that failure to assimilate to certain important shared values will mean a departure from minimum standards of acceptable behaviour. This is connected with the other argument, that 'the active promotion of separate identities may foster divisiveness and be incompatible with the degree of social cohesion required for the maintenance of a sense of national unity'. These arguments both suggest that there are limits to cultural diversity. The Swann Committee Report (1985: 5–6) expressed this as follows:

> We would ... regard a democratic pluralist society as seeking to achieve a balance between, on the one hand, the maintenance and active support of the essential elements of the cultures and lifestyles of all the ethnic groups within it, and, on the other, the acceptance by all groups of a set of shared values distinctive of the society as a whole. This then is our view of a genuinely pluralist society, as both socially cohesive and culturally diverse.

Rex (1986: 133) writes about the 'secular civic culture as a common and necessary component of all cultures in advanced industrial societies. ... The possibility of different cultures coexisting depends upon them all accepting this shared set of common ideals'. And Verma (1990: 56) concludes, in relation to Britain, that 'the type of pluralist society for which we must strive is one that stresses core values but allows for diversity within an agreed framework'.

But what are these shared values, core values or shared set of common ideals? Parekh (1998: 11) considers that minority values and practices 'should be tolerated subject to such collectively agreed minimum principles as respect for human life and dignity'. Other writers have mentioned human rights norms, like freedom of expression and religion and the legal and moral equality of all persons, and democracy and the rule of law as minimum standards to be maintained. Poulter (1990: 16–7) advocates the use of human rights and suggests that two questions of principle should be asked. First, does a particular ethnic practice demand legal recognition because to refuse it would be tantamount to a denial of human rights? This question sees it as a human right to have one's culture and traditions respected if one so wishes and sees a denial of such recognition and respect as a breach of fundamental human rights. Human rights are thus used as an argument for respecting diversity. Second, does an ethnic tradition require automatic non-recognition because the practice itself constitutes a violation of human rights? Poulter gives as examples here slavery, female circumcision and barbarous punishments.

All this suggests, therefore, that human rights values can provide a limit on diversity in a society. However, it must be kept in mind that these values, the core values of society, must not automatically be the values of the dominant group in that society. As Poulter (1998: 24–5) writes: 'the relationship between "shared values" ... and minority cultures ... should be seen as a reciprocal one. ... These values are not immutable'. In other words, these two influence each other constantly and both are always developing.

As Rex (1986: 134) points out, 'the creation of a multicultural society must involve an element of voluntarism'. This means that those who want to assimilate should be allowed to do so, while those who prefer to keep their own culture should also be allowed to do just that. The important point is 'to create the kind of society in which all people may choose their cultural affiliations'. Every person and every group should be respected in the choices they make about their culture. People should not be labelled by outside agencies as belonging to a group and therefore as having a certain culture.

The Preamble to the Canadian Multiculturalism Act mentions that 'the Canadian Human Rights Act provides that every individual should have an equal opportunity with other individuals to make the life that the individual is able and *wishes to have* [our italics], ...'. The words 'wishes to have' indicate that the decision of what life a person wants to make should not be made by the government or by the majority.

Therefore, a person's cultural affiliation should not be defined or decided by an outside body because that would mean imposing certain values on that person and the group or community he/she belongs to. In all this it should be noted that it is often not a clear-cut choice between following either the minority culture or the majority culture. Ethnic minorities follow strategies of adaptation and often follow a hybrid of their own culture and the dominant culture.[9]

The last point to be raised is whether legislation can promote pluralism and achieve the aim of establishing a plural society. It is suggested that legislation can aim to create acceptance of and respect for whatever culture or mixture of cultures people would want to follow, it can aim to promote tolerance and participation and it can aim to establish the circumstances in which a plural society can blossom. However, legislation alone cannot establish such a society. As with legislation based on the other concepts of equality, legislation based on the pluralist approach needs to be supported by measures in other areas.

It can be concluded that the pluralist concept of equality as an aim of anti discrimination law, although it remedies some of the objections made against the other concepts, also raises some problems of its own.

5.5 Conclusion

It will be clear that there are several different concepts of equality. Anti discrimination laws, sometimes referred to as equality laws because they prohibit discrimination or prescribe equality, are often promoting a notion of formal equality, or equality of treatment: like people should be treated alike. However, they can also aim for a more substantive equality which is sensitive to existing inequalities produced by past and on-going discrimination. This substantive equality can take the shape of equality of opportunity or equality of results. The first aims to give everyone the same opportunities, and therefore aims to equalize the starting point. This can involve unequal treatment and unequal outcomes. Equality of results is aiming to equalize the end results and therefore has a more distributive aim. The lines between the two forms of substantive equality are not always easy to draw. If one takes a more substantive view of equality of opportunity one comes close to equality of results, especially as that can be used in a less or more redistributive way. Pluralism is another possible approach to equality, which sees diversity as a positive attribute of society and which accords equal respect and concern to every person and to his/her values and way of life.

In the introduction to this Chapter, we mentioned the three functions required of equality if it is to combat racism as distinguished by Fredman (2001a: 15). If we return to these three functions we can see that the first

9 Menski and Ballard have written extensively on this process of adaptation and the creation of a hybrid culture. For more information on this the reader is referred to: Ballard 1994 and 1996; and Menski 1993; 2001; and 2002a and b.

function – a means of redressing racist stigma, stereotyping, humiliation and violence – could be said to correspond to formal equality: equal treatment without differentiating on the grounds of racial or ethnic origin. The second function – the redistributive aim of breaking the cycle of disadvantage associated with groups defined by race or ethnicity – corresponds to substantive equality in both its forms: equality of opportunity and equality of outcome or results. And the third function – the positive affirmation and accommodation of difference as a part of the right to equal concern and respect – corresponds to the pluralist approach to equality.

This suggests that equality in all its types is needed to fight racism and racial discrimination. Does this mean that anti discrimination legislation should protect equality in all these forms?

Lustgarten (1992: 455–7) discuses the question where anti race discrimination law in Britain should be going and approaches this question by asking: what are the goals of racial equality policy? It is submitted that these goals are not limited to Britain, but can be applied to (racial) equality policies in general. Lustgarten describes three aims: the first aim should be the just treatment of individuals, in other words no unfavourable treatment on grounds such as race or ethnicity. This should involve more than formal equality and go towards a conception of substantive equality. The equality of all humans is the bedrock here. The reason for fair treatment is, according to Lustgarten, that 'the value of fairness in the sense of formal equality is one that is deeply rooted in British culture' and has been the driving force behind efforts to counter discrimination. Again this does not appear to be limited to British culture and can be applied more widely.

Lustgarten's second aim is group distributional equality: the income distribution of each racial or ethnic group of significant size should be proportionally equivalent to whites and the rates of unemployment of people in these groups should be roughly equal. The third aim is 'the acceptance in principle of the equality of cultural norms and beliefs, which means adjustment and accommodation to customs and practices of significant minority groups'. Lustgarten makes this subject to two provisos: first, that human rights norms are paramount; and, second, that there operates some notion of proportionality, 'which will balance the seriousness of the minority's interest against the degree of disruption the accommodation will cause'. Lustgarten adds that he 'would equally insist on the principle that each individual retains the right of self-definition about group membership or identity'.

Lustgarten's aims of equality policies correspond with the concepts of equality and the aims of anti discrimination law which we have described and they can be seen as a good summary thereof. The first aim covers formal equality and goes some way towards equality of opportunity. The second aim covers equality of results, while the third aim corresponds with the pluralist concept of equality. The provisos show that Lustgarten also accepts limits on cultural diversity.

It is submitted that equality policies and anti discrimination laws should aim at establishing all four concepts of equality distinguished in this Chapter. However, we deliberately use 'equality policies and anti discrimination law' together, because we would argue that legislation alone can never be enough to achieve a more equal society without racial and other forms of discrimination. A number of writers express the same view. For example, MacEwen (1995: 23) writes that 'it is generally accepted that law alone will be inadequate to effect change; legislation must be integrated with complimentary policy measures'. And Niessen (2001b: 15)[10] writes:

> Legislation is important, but it is only one of the instruments available to combat racial discrimination. Legislation should be embedded in a comprehensive approach that includes other policy measures against discrimination, the promotion of equal treatment and the valuing of diversity.

The European Commission shares this view as well, which is clear from the following consideration in the proposal for the Community Action Programme (COM (1999) 567: 1):

> to combat discrimination, the Community needs to use all the instruments at its disposal, in a co-ordinated and integrated strategy. Legislation is a key component of such a strategy, but it is only one component.

The existence of this Action Programme, which accompanied the Race and Framework Directives, is itself recognition that legislation is only one component of action to combat discrimination, as the 2004 Green Paper (COM (2004) 379: 7) points out. This paper goes on to state that 'support for a range of positive measures is also necessary in order to challenge discriminatory behaviour and promote a change of attitude over time'.

The view that legislative measures should be taken together with other measures thus appears to be quite widespread and lies behind the ICERD as well. Article 2(1)(d) ICERD puts a duty on States to 'prohibit and bring to an end, by all appropriate means, including legislation, as required by circumstances, racial discrimination by any persons, group or organisation'. Article 2(2) mentions measures in the 'economic, cultural and other fields'. Article 7 is interesting as well. It states:

> States Parties undertake to adopt immediate and effective measures, particularly in the field of teaching, education, culture and information,

10 See also: Lustgarten 1986; Lacey 1992; Townshend-Smith 1998; and Nickel *et al.* 2003: 41.

> with a view to combating prejudices which lead to racial discrimination and to promoting understanding, tolerance and friendship among nations and racial or ethnical groups …

The following quote from MacEwen (1997: 10) sums up the opinion that law should be accompanied by other measures in a clear way:

> … it is clearly optimistic to expect that an anti-discrimination law, in itself, will have anything other than a marginally ameliorative impact on improving the real life chances of black and ethnic minority communities. … at best, anti-discrimination laws may provide protection against the worst abuses and facilitate a remedy where wrong has been identified. Unless they are accompanied by government policies and strategies which imbed the legislative provisions in a more holistic approach to discrimination, substantial change is unlikely to be effective.

In other words, legislation against discrimination can be useful to give victims a remedy and to put pressure on people not to discriminate, but it is only one part of a broader strategy to combat discrimination and to counter inequality. Legislation in this field, and this applies to legislation based on any of the four concepts of equality distinguished, is thus not to be seen as the only way of tackling the problem of discrimination, but as one of a number of different, mutually interacting strategies. With this in mind, we will next examine which concept or concepts of equality can be detected in the Race Directive.

6 The Race Directive and concepts of equality

6.1 Introduction

In Chapter 5, we discussed the different concepts of equality which can be the objective of anti discrimination measures and stated that it was important to ascertain what such measures are aiming at because this influences the type of provisions, remedies and enforcement strategies laid down. We distinguished four concepts of equality as aims of equality law. First, laws aiming for formal equality aim to prevent people in the same or similar situations being treated differently on prohibited grounds. Second, legislative measures based on equality of opportunity aim to achieve equal opportunities for everyone; they aim to equalize the starting point so that historically disadvantaged groups can compete on an equal footing with people who did not suffer such disadvantage, by prescribing or permitting preferential treatment of these groups. Measures against discrimination based on equality of results aim for an equal outcome; aim for a fairer distribution of goods, resources and opportunities in society and for the equal participation of all. This also involves preferential treatment of the disadvantaged groups. The equality of opportunity and equality of results concepts are together referred to as substantive equality. Finally, legislation with a pluralist approach to equality as objective aims to create a society that welcomes and celebrates diversity and in which each person is respected equally. In this Chapter we will examine the concept(s) of equality which can be detected in the Race Directive.

In the conclusion in Chapter 5, it was suggested that equality in all its concepts is needed to fight racism and racial discrimination and that anti discrimination law should aim at all four types of equality in order to fulfil the three functions required of equality as distinguished by Fredman (2001a: 15). These functions were, first, a means of redressing racist stigma, stereotyping and humiliation; second, the redistributive aim of breaking the cycle of disadvantage associated with groups defined by race or ethnicity; and, third, the positive affirmation and accommodation of difference. These three functions will be used in the analysis of the equality concepts in the Race Directive.

The question of what types of equality should be the aim of the equality legislation at the EU level did not appear to feature in any explicit form in the discussions and negotiations before the Directive was adopted, although there seems to have been a consensus that legislative prohibitions on discrimination should include both direct and indirect discrimination and that there should be room for positive action.[1] The concepts of indirect discrimination and positive action were familiar from the existing sex discrimination legislation and had been part of the proposals for a Community Directive made by the Starting Line Group (Dummett 1994; Chopin and Niessen 1998: 23–32).

As mentioned in Chapter 1, this group, together with the European Parliament, played an important role in lobbying for action against racism and racial discrimination in the EU. The Kahn Commission also recommended that indirect discrimination should be prohibited in EU anti discrimination legislation and that this legislation should make provisions for positive action (European Consultative Commission 1995: 39 and 59).

At the time the Race Directive was proposed and during the negotiations, the main focus appears to have been on achieving the adoption of legislation at EU level in order to lay down minimum standards for all Member States. As the Commission itself stated in the Explanatory Memorandum to the Proposal for the Race Directive, that Directive would ensure 'that people in all Member States enjoy a basic level of protection against discrimination' (COM (1999) 566: 3). Once these minimum standards were laid down in EU legislation and the deadline for implementation of the Race and Framework Directives had passed, the language within the EU started to shift towards an awareness of the limitations of formal equality and the need to go beyond this. This shift in language and the question whether this is translated into concrete measures will be discussed in this Chapter. First, the Race Directive is examined in relation to each of the equality concepts in turn.

6.2 Formal equality

Anti discrimination legislation aiming at formal equality prohibits differential treatment of people who find themselves in similar situations. Can we detect the concept of formal equality in the Race Directive? According to Article 2(2)(a):

> direct discrimination shall be taken to occur where one person is treated less favourably than another is, has been or would be treated in a comparable situation on grounds of racial or ethnic origin.

This reflects very clearly a formal notion of equality, prohibiting less favourable treatment than a person in a comparable situation.

1 The Explanatory Memorandum to the Proposal for the Race Directive does recognize that some groups suffered disadvantage because of discrimination (COM (1999) 566: 6). We discuss this further when we analyze the positive action provisions of the Race Directive.

This definition of direct discrimination did not appear to cause particular difficulties in the negotiations of the Race Directive (Tyson 2001: 202).[2] It is close to that used in S 1(1)(a) of the British Race Relations Act 1976 and what has been understood as direct discrimination by the ECJ in its case law on sex discrimination. This case law was the only guideline at EU level as there were no legislative measures containing a definition of direct discrimination until the Race Directive. The case law asks for a comparison to be made between a man and a woman in the same or a comparable situation. In the case of *Defrenne v Sabena No. 2*, the ECJ held that direct discrimination may be 'identified solely by reference to the criteria laid down by Article 119 (now 141) EC' (para 21). This Article prescribes equal pay for men and women doing equal work or work of equal value, which means that a comparison has to be made. The ECJ continues that these forms of discrimination 'may be detected on the basis of a purely legal analysis of the situation. This applies even more in cases where men and women receive unequal pay for equal work carried out in the same establishment or service …' (paras 21 and 22). In *Macarthys v Smith*, the ECJ used a comparative test; it considered that in a situation of direct discrimination, 'the decisive test lies in establishing whether there is a difference in treatment between a man and a woman performing "equal work"' (para 11). The ECJ mentions that 'comparisons are confined to parallels which may be drawn on the basis of concrete appraisals of the work actually performed by employees of different sex within the same establishment or service' (para 15).

Therefore, the definition makes it necessary to identify a 'comparable situation', but there is no indication as to the meaning of this. The test has been used in sex discrimination cases, but not always without problems. In the previous chapter, one of the problems identified in relation to the concept of formal equality was the need to find someone in a comparable situation. But who is in a comparable situation? The choice of comparator is important because it can influence the result.[3] The use of the words 'would be' in the definition in the Race Directive suggests that a hypothetical comparator can be accepted,[4] although the ECJ has rejected such a comparator in sex discrimination cases. The ECJ has made an exception in cases of discrimination on grounds of pregnancy, where it has held that no comparator is required.[5]

2 Tyson writes, erroneously in our view, that the definition of direct discrimination was taken almost verbatim from the Burden of Proof Directive, but this Directive does not contain a definition of direct discrimination. It only defines indirect discrimination.

3 For a good example of this see the British case of *London Borough Council of Lewisham v Malcolm*.

4 This opinion is also expressed by Waddington and Bell 2001: 592; Bell 2002a: 75; Schiek 2002: 295–6; Liegl *et al.* 2004: 9; Parmar 2004: 143; Ellis 2005: 165; Schiek *et al.* 2007: 218.

5 In *Dekker v Stichting Vormingscentrum voor Jong Volwassenen (VJV Centrum) Plus*, the ECJ held that discrimination on grounds of pregnancy contravenes the equal treatment principle and

However, it seems likely that the situation in sex discrimination cases has changed because of the 2002 Equal Treatment (Amendment) Directive. As Ellis (2005: 165) writes, as a result of the amendment of the Equal Treatment Directive, 'this now defines discrimination so as to embrace hypothetical comparison'. She continues that 'the Race Directive and the Framework Directive expressly permit hypothetical comparisons over the whole field of their respective application'. Moreover, the Recast and the Equal Treatment (Goods) Directives contain the same definition, including the words 'would be' (Article 2(1)(a) of both Directives). In many cases of direct discrimination, it will be easier to find a hypothetical comparator and the possibility of using such a comparator in cases of discrimination on all Article 13 EC grounds, including sex, will alleviate one of the problems with the formal equality concept.

The prohibition of direct discrimination or of unequal or less favourable treatment on the grounds of racial or ethnic origin can be seen as performing the first of the functions of equality, as distinguished by Fredman (2001a: 15) and is, therefore, important because it is the minimum first step to attack racial prejudice and prohibit behaviour based on such prejudice.

The concept of formal equality was, as mentioned in Chapter 5, criticized for being a relative principle which does not guarantee any particular outcome, as treating two people equally can mean treating them both equally well or equally badly. Article 6 of the Race Directive might remedy this problem to some extent. This article contains a so-called 'non-regression clause': the implementation of the Directive shall under no circumstances constitute grounds for reducing the already existing level of protection. This can be seen as a 'prohibition on levelling-down', so equal treatment can no longer be achieved by limiting or taking away existing benefits (McColgan 2005: 58; Bell and Waddington 2003: 14–15). However, the Directive is addressed to the Member States, and therefore only binds these States. Article 6 does not prevent levelling-down by individual employers or service providers.

The equal treatment concept can also be seen in the Charter of Fundamental Rights of the Union, which states in Article 20 that 'everyone is equal before the law'. The Explanatory Memorandum (CONV 828/1/03) mentions that this 'corresponds to a general principle of law which is included in all European constitutions and has also been recognised by the Court of Justice as a basic principle of Community law'. It corresponds to similar articles in many of the international human rights instruments discussed in Chapter 2 and is a clear expression of an anti discrimination measure aiming at formal equality or equality in law.

that there is no need for a comparator in such a case (para 12). See also *Webb v EMO Air Cargo (UK) Ltd*: paras 24–5.

6.3 Substantive equality

The Race Directive's title indicates that its aim is 'to implement the principle of equal treatment', while Article 1 states as its purpose: 'to lay down a framework for combating discrimination on the grounds of racial or ethnic origin, with a view of putting into effect in the Member States the principle of equal treatment'. The Framework and the Equal Treatment (Goods) Directives and the 2008 Proposal (COM (2008) 426) contain the same purpose in their Article 1. In this, all four measures follow the 1976 Equal Treatment Directive,[6] and the 2002 amendments did not change this purpose. So, the expressly stated aim of these EU legislative measures against discrimination is to put into effect or to implement the principle of equal treatment. The 2006 Recast Directive's purpose goes beyond this: 'to ensure the implementation of the principle of equal opportunities and equal treatment …' and its title mentions the same principle. The Recast Directive replaces the 1976 and 2002 Equal Treatment Directives. The ECJ has also held that the objective of the 1976 Equal Treatment Directive is to arrive at real equality of opportunity for men and women (*Marshall v Southampton No. 2:* para 24; *Coote v Granada:* para 27). Does this mean that the purpose of EU gender discrimination legislation in the employment field is wider than that outside the employment field or against the other Article 13 EC grounds of discrimination?

There are a number of arguments which would suggest that this is not the case. First of all, the phrase 'put into effect' can be read as meaning that the Directives aim at more than formal equality. As Schiek (2002: 305) writes:

> All of the directives have the purpose *to 'put into effect' the principle of equal treatment* [her italics]. Thus they are not merely concerned with equality in law but also with equality in fact.

Second, all the Directives and the Proposal explain that the principle of equal treatment means that 'there shall be no direct or indirect discrimination based on racial or ethnic origin'. Third, Bell (2008a: 27) writes: 'in EU jargon, "equal opportunities" traditionally equates with gender equality, whereas "non-discrimination" is understood as discrimination based on other grounds', which suggests that it simply is a matter of different expressions used in different areas. Therefore, the use of the words 'put into effect', the inclusion of a concept of indirect discrimination in the meaning of the principle of equal treatment, the opinion of the ECJ on the 1976 Equal Treatment Directive, whose wording about the purpose was followed in the Race,

6 This Directive was followed by a number of Directives implementing the principle of equal treatment for men and women in different areas, see Council Directives 79/7/EEC, 86/378/EEC, and 86/613/EEC. All these Directives state as their purpose: to implement the principle of equal treatment.

Framework and Equal Treatment (Goods) Directives and the 2008 Proposal and the quote from Bell, all suggest that the purpose of the EU Equality Directives goes beyond the formal concept towards a more substantive concept of equality. In the previous Chapter, two substantive concepts of equality were distinguished: equality of opportunity and equality of results. Can either of these concepts be found in the Race Directive?

6.3.1 Indirect discrimination

As we have seen, legislation prohibiting indirect discrimination can be seen as a step away from formal equality towards a more substantive concept, which has elements of both equality of opportunity and equality of results. Article 2(2)(b) of the Race Directive determines that:

> indirect discrimination shall be taken to occur where an apparently neutral provision, criterion or practice would put persons of a racial or ethnic origin at a particular disadvantage compared with other persons, unless that provision, criterion or practice is objectively justified by a legitimate aim and the means of achieving that aim are appropriate and necessary.

The Race Directive follows the definition of indirect discrimination given by the ECJ in relation to the free movement of persons in the *O'Flynn* case (paras 20–1). In this case, the Court considered that:

> ... unless objectively justified and proportionate to its aim, a provision of national law must be regarded as indirectly discriminatory if it is intrinsically liable to affect migrant workers more than national workers and if there is a consequent risk that it will place the former at a particular disadvantage. It is not necessary in this respect to find that the provision in question does in practice affect a substantially higher proportion of migrant workers. It is sufficient that it is liable to have such an effect.

Tyson (2001: 202–4) writes that the definition in the Directive did not follow the definition given in the Burden of Proof Directive (Council Directive 1997) and that this caused some concern to a number of Member States.[7] The Burden of Proof Directive defines indirect discrimination in Article 2(2):

> indirect discrimination shall exist where an apparently neutral provision, criterion or practice disadvantages a substantially higher proportion of

7 For the suggestions made by different Member States in relation to the definition of indirect discrimination see Council of the European Union 2000a,b and c.

> the members of one sex unless that provision, criterion or practice is appropriate and necessary and can be justified by objective factors unrelated to sex.

Tyson (2001: 202) explains that this definition means that, for a finding of indirect sex discrimination, it is necessary to show that a greater proportion of one sex than the other is affected and this involves statistical evidence. In the case of sex discrimination, obtaining statistical evidence is usually not a problem because all Member States collect statistics on gender. However, as was mentioned in Chapter 4, statistics about racial or ethnic origin are not collected in all Member States. As a result of the misuse of racial and ethnic information in the 1930s and 1940s, there is widespread opposition to the collection of such data and in some Member States it is unlawful 'as it is seen either to be an infringement of personal privacy or as a racist act in itself' (Ibid: 203).

The definition in the Race Directive would thus remove the burden of providing statistical proof. This was the intention of the European Commission, as is clear from the negotiations. In answer to the remark from some of the Member States that the definition was broader than that in the Burden of Proof Directive, the Commission answered that this 'takes new case law into account, which leaves out the reference to numbers' (Council of the European Union 2000a: footnote 9). The same intention was clearly stated by the Commission's Director General for Employment and Social Affairs, Odile Quintin, in her evidence to the House of Lords Select Committee on European Union (House of Lords 2000: para 80). She 'defended the new definitions on the grounds that it removed the need to demonstrate statistically that indirect discrimination had in fact occurred', which would make the definition easier to use because the 'statistical assessment is something which is extremely complicated to develop for other areas of discrimination'. But some Member States wanted to retain the definition of the Burden of Proof Directive because they did not want a definition that made it apparently easier to win a case of racial discrimination than a case of sex discrimination (Council of the European Union 2000b: footnote 16). Recital 15 was added to the Race Directive as a compromise. This Recital declares:

> The appreciation of the facts from which it may be inferred that there has been direct or indirect discrimination is a matter for national judicial or other competent bodies, in accordance with rules of national law or practice. Such rules may provide in particular for indirect discrimination to be established by any means including on the basis of statistical evidence.

This allows, but does not oblige, Member States to require statistical evidence. However, it means, as Tyson (2001: 204) points out, that different tests for indirect discrimination could be applied in different Member States. This problem could be solved by removing the Recital as the reason for the addition of the Recital now no longer exists because the Equal Treatment (Amendment) Directive contains the same definition of indirect discrimination as the Race Directive, as do the Framework and Equal Treatment (Goods) Directives. Support for the argument that the Recital (and a similar Recital 15 in the Framework Directive) are no longer necessary can be found in the fact that the two Equality Directives adopted on the basis of Article 13 EC after the Race and Framework Directives – the Equal Treatment (Amendment) and the Equal Treatment (Goods) Directives – do not contain a reference to statistical evidence in their Preamble. The Recast Directive does not mention statistical evidence in relation to indirect discrimination either, although Recital 37 mentions:

> For the sake of a better understanding of the different treatment of men and women in matters of employment and occupation, comparable statistics disaggregated by sex should continue to be developed, analysed and made available at the appropriate levels.

This could even be read as inferring that statistics are no longer required to prove indirect sex discrimination but that these can be useful and thus 'should continue to be developed', etc. However, the 2008 Proposal (COM (2008) 426) retains the reference to statistical evidence in its Recital 14, which echoes Recital 15 of the Race Directive. The situation thus seems to be that statistical evidence is no longer required in cases of indirect sex discrimination both in and outside the employment field, while such statistics are readily available in all Member States, but national law can determine that such evidence is required to prove indirect discrimination on the grounds of racial or ethnic origin, religion or belief, disability, age and sexual orientation in all areas covered, while such statistics in relation to these grounds are often not readily available.[8]

According to the definition, indirect discrimination is not unlawful if it is 'objectively justified by a legitimate aim and the means of achieving that aim are appropriate and necessary' (Tobler 2008). The Burden of Proof Directive also allowed for justification: indirect discrimination is not established where the 'provision, criterion or practice is appropriate and necessary and can be justified by objective factors unrelated to sex'. Both these exceptions follow the case law of the ECJ. In the *Bilka* case, the ECJ decided that it was for the national court to determine whether there was an objective justification, but it laid down a three-tier test: the measures chosen must, first, fulfil a real need on the part of the undertaking; second, be appropriate with a view of achieving the objectives pursued; and, third, be necessary to that end (paras 36–7).

8 See further on statistical evidence: Barnard 2001: 969–70; Waddington and Bell 2001: 594; Bell 2002a: 75; Brown 2002: 206–7; Schiek 2002: 296; Liegl *et al.* 2004: 10; Schiek *et al.* 2007: 400–24; and Tobler 2008: 40–1.

The Race Directive does not allow for justification of direct racial or ethnic origin discrimination with two exceptions, for genuine and determining occupational requirements (Article 4) and for positive action (Article 5), but it does allow for justification of indirect discrimination. As we saw in Chapter 2, most international instruments prohibit discrimination as such, and do not make a distinction between direct and indirect discrimination. Indirect discrimination is taken as falling under the instrument's prohibition of discrimination, usually via the case law or via advice or recommendations of the body designated to oversee the instrument. The international measures allow for justification of discrimination in general, so this includes both direct and indirect discrimination. The Race Directive did not follow the international measures in this but instead it followed the then existing EU legislation on sex discrimination and thus gives separate definitions of both direct and indirect discrimination.

So why does it only allow for justification of indirect discrimination? Perhaps it is because the EU legislators saw direct discrimination as 'worse', as more offensive and repugnant than indirect discrimination. The EU legislator might have reasoned that direct discrimination is a more overt and noticeable form of making a difference in treatment. It can be seen as openly flouting the rule that one should not discriminate. Indirect discrimination, on the other hand, can be seen as not quite such an infringement because it is a more 'accidental' result of a rule or practice. The prohibition of direct discrimination, of unequal or less favourable treatment, is the basic, most fundamental concept and the first requirement to fight racism and racial discrimination and, therefore, justifications should be strictly limited and prescribed by law. But, because indirect discrimination can be seen as a lesser infringement of the rules, it should not be prohibited in all situations, or, in other words, justification should be permitted, but only if it has a legitimate aim and the means of achieving that aim are appropriate and necessary. In cases of indirect discrimination, other interests play a role as well and a balancing of interests must take place between prohibiting the indirectly discriminatory practices and business interests and policy and administrative considerations. These interests might be present in direct discrimination cases as well, but they should never be given priority in such cases because that form of discrimination is so much more openly against the rules and offensive. This might be the reason why direct racial or ethnic origin discrimination under the Race Directive cannot be justified.

Although the European Court of Human Rights allows for justification for both direct and indirect discrimination, in its determinations whether a difference of treatment contravenes the anti discrimination clause of article 14 ECHR, it appears to deal with certain grounds of discrimination in a different way. As de Schutter (2005: 14–15) explains:

> although, in most cases, a difference of treatment will pass the test of non-discrimination if it pursues a legitimate aim by means of presenting

> a reasonable relationship of proportionality with that aim, where differential treatment is based on a 'suspect' ground, it will be required that it is justified by 'very weighty reasons' and that the difference in treatment appears both suited for realizing the legitimate aim pursued, and *necessary* [his italics].

The European Court of Human Rights thus requires 'very weighty reasons' before it will consider that a difference in treatment on suspect grounds is justified. Gerards (2004b: 38–57) writes that this Court will scrutinize the suspect classifications more carefully, while it will leave a wider margin of appreciation in the case of other classifications. In her own words, 'if the right is fundamental in character, the Court will mostly apply a very strict test' (Ibid: 44). But are not all Convention rights fundamental or core rights? Gerards deduces from the case law that 'the Court seems to characterize aspects of Convention rights as core rights especially if they prove to be essential to the well functioning of a pluralistic and democratic society', and that, as a general rule, 'political rights and rights that are closely linked to human dignity belong to the core rights protected by the Convention' (Ibid: 45–6).[9] Both de Schutter (2005: 15) and Gerards (2004b: 26) write that the Human Rights Court appears to consider race a suspect ground.

Even though the European Court of Human Rights allows for justification of both direct and indirect discrimination, it is suggested that the ECJ should use the distinction between suspect and non-suspect grounds when considering whether indirect discrimination is justified and scrutinize such justification more strictly when a suspect ground is involved (Howard 2006). As mentioned, the Race Directive only allows for justification of indirect discrimination, as does the Equal Treatment (Amendment) Directive, but the Framework and the Equal Treatment (Goods) Directives contain more exceptions and both also allow for some justification of direct discrimination. From this, we could infer that the EU has made racial or ethnic origin into a suspect ground, while sex has also been made suspect, but only in relation to the employment fields. For this reason, we would argue for a very strict scrutiny of all justifications put forward for indirect discrimination on racial or ethnic origin grounds.

Another reason why we advocate that the ECJ applies a very exacting test to justifications for indirect discrimination based on racial or ethnic origin is that such justifications can be used in different ways. They can be used to support a multicultural approach as well as an approach supporting or reinforcing assimilation. For example, rules that hair must be covered in places where food is handled can be justified on the basis of health and safety requirements. But is an employer justified in requiring all employees to wear a specific type of headgear, or should he/she allow any headgear as long as it

9 For more information on the case law, the reader is referred to the paper by Gerards.

covers all hair? If he/she requires all employees to wear specific headgear, this could be indirectly discriminatory against Sikhs who wear turbans. Such a requirement would support an assimilationist approach. Allowing Sikh employees to wear turbans (and, if necessary also provide for surgical type masks to cover facial hair), would comply with health and safety rules, but, at the same time, would support a diverse and multicultural workforce. The requirement that all employees wear specific headgear should not pass the justification test under the Race Directive because, although the aim of the rule is legitimate (health and safety), the means of achieving that aim cannot be said to be appropriate and necessary, since the same aim could be achieved by different means which would not indirectly discriminate against Sikhs. Therefore, the court should conclude that the rule is not objectively justified and make a finding of indirect discrimination against the employer.

Schiek (2002: 297) writes that the objective justification test in the Race Directive stresses 'a little more that a strict standard of proportionality is required', and that, 'as regards gender equality, the jurisdiction of the European Court of Justice has been contradictory in this respect'. In relation to gender discrimination, the ECJ has in most cases, according to Schiek, applied a strict proportionality test in relation to the practices of individual employers, while it has used a much less exacting test for Member States legislation (Ibid). Finlay (2003: 143–4) argues the same, but Parmar (2004: 146–7) seems to argue the opposite: 'that the Court is applying a higher standard of scrutiny when the objective justification exception is raised by Member States'.[10] This shows clearly that there are contradictions in the case law and that the situation under the 1976 Equal Treatment Directive is far from transparent. This might change as 'these regrettable developments are now likely to be halted by the more concise wording, which will also be inserted into the Gender Equality Directive' (Schiek 2002: 297). The more concise wording should, therefore, lead the ECJ to scrutinize all justifications of indirect discriminatory measures, whether advanced by employers or by Member States, very closely.

The definition of indirect discrimination in the Race Directive does recognize that an apparently neutral provision can have a disparate impact on some people and, in this respect, it fits in a substantive concept of equality. But does it fit in with equality of opportunity or equality of results? It focuses on results in that it takes account of the disparate effect of a seemingly neutral provision, criterion or practice, applied to all equally. Therefore, the Directive's aim appears to be equality of results. However, the end result of a finding of indirect discrimination under the definition of the Race Directive may well remain unequal because the Directive's aim is not redistributive.

10 All three authors (Schiek, Finlay and Parmar) cite cases in support of their argument. For these, see the papers.

In other words, equality of results is not the end the Directive's provisions are aiming for. An unequal impact is not always discriminatory: if no exclusionary provision, practice or criterion can be shown or if the inequality can be objectively justified by reference to business needs or administrative interests, there will be no finding of indirect discrimination. So the Directive's prohibition of indirect discrimination cannot be said to aim fully at equality of results, it only does so to the extent that it takes the result of a measure into account.

Does the Directive's prohibition of indirect discrimination then fit in the concept of equality of opportunity because it makes the starting point equal for all? By prohibiting indirect discrimination, it makes the barriers certain people face unlawful. These barriers are, therefore, taken out of, for example, the recruitment process and, in this aspect, the prohibition makes the starting point more equal for everybody. The prohibition of indirect discrimination thus fits in with equality of opportunity. However, the barriers are not unlawful if they are objectively justified by business or administrative interests and thus indirect discrimination is not always unlawful. A finding that an employer has, in the recruitment process, indirectly discriminated against an individual or against the group he/she belongs to, does not necessarily lead to the individual obtaining the job after all; and, even if he/she would get the job, it does nothing about the disadvantaged position of the group. If the legal system of the Member State only allows individuals to complain about (indirect) discrimination, then the remedy, if the claim is successful, will only apply to that individual. Moreover, the remedy may well be compensation, rather than a duty to refrain from the discriminatory behaviour in future. So, there is no obligation on the employer to abstain from applying the discriminatory practice in future recruitment processes, although the risk of another adverse court finding might stop him/her doing so. There is also no duty on the employer to create equality of opportunity by making sure that the members of the group can compete on an equal footing in that process. Therefore, here again, indirect discrimination is only partially about equality of opportunity. On the other hand, as we concluded in Chapter 5, the concept does move away from formal towards substantive equality, with some elements of both equality of opportunity and equality of results.

6.3.2 Positive action

The Race Directive allows, but does not require, Member States to take positive action measures. Article 5 of the Race Directive determines:

> With a view to ensuring full equality in practice, the principle of equal treatment shall not prevent any Member State from maintaining or adopting specific measures to prevent or compensate for disadvantages linked to racial or ethnic origin.

Recital 17 expands on this:

> The prohibition of discrimination should be without prejudice to the maintenance or adoption of measures intended to prevent or compensate for disadvantages suffered by a group of persons of a particular racial or ethnic origin, and such measures may permit organisations of persons of a particular racial or ethnic origin where their main object is the promotion of the special needs of those persons.

The Explanatory Memorandum to the Race Directive's Proposal (COM (1999) 566: 6) states with regard to 'Article 5: Positive Action':

> Equal treatment by itself may not be enough if it does not overcome the weight of accumulated disadvantage suffered by discriminated groups. Article 4 allows Member States to authorise legislative or administrative measures which are necessary to prevent or correct situations of inequality. (In our view Article 4 in this quote should read Article 5, as the title above this passage suggests.)

Article 5, Recital 17 and the Memorandum thus all express a fairly clear idea of substantive equality: they recognize the accumulated disadvantage suffered by some groups and allow Member States to take measures to make up for this. That positive action measures aim at substantive equality is confirmed by the case law of the ECJ on Article 2(4) of the 1976 Equal Treatment Directive. This Article allowed Member States to take 'measures to promote equal opportunity for men and women, in particular by removing existing inequalities which affect women's opportunities', in other words, to take positive action measures for women. The ECJ has recognized that Article 2(4) allows measures which 'are intended to eliminate or reduce actual instances of inequality which may exist in the reality of social life' (*Commission v France*: para 15).[11] It has also held that 'the result pursued by the Directive is substantive, not formal equality' (*Caisse Nationale*: para 26).[12]

By providing for positive action, Article 5 of the Race Directive thus moves towards a more substantive concept of equality but there is no indication in the article, the proposal or the recital, as to what type of positive action measures are allowed. The original proposal for the Race Directive (COM (1999) 566) also allowed for positive action but it was formulated in

11 This is repeated in *Kalanke*: para 18; and, *Marschall v Land Nordrhein-Westfalen*: para 26.

12 The following cases all combine what the ECJ held in *Commission v France* and in *Caisse Nationale: Badeck's Application*: para 32; *Abrahamsson and Anderson v Fogelqvist*: para 48; and *Serge Briheche:* para 25.

a different way. Under the Heading 'Article 5 Positive Action' it determined:

> This Directive shall be without prejudice to the right of Member States to maintain or adopt measures intended to prevent or compensate for disadvantages suffered by a group of persons of a particular racial or ethnic origin.

In the final text of the Race Directive 'with a view to ensuring full equality in practice' is added. These opening words are the same as those of Article 141(4) EC, although Article 5 of the Race Directive does not follow this article fully. Article 141(4) EC was added to the EC Treaty by the Treaty of Amsterdam in 1997 and was the first primary legislation to refer to positive action. Article 141(4) EC reads:

> With a view to ensuring full equality in practice between men and women in working life, the principle of equal treatment shall not prevent any Member State from maintaining or adopting measures providing for specific advantages in order to make it easier for the under-represented sex to pursue a vocational activity or to prevent or compensate for disadvantages in professional careers.

The fact that the final text of the Directive corresponds more closely to Article 141(4) EC could be an indication that the Commission and the Member States intend to give the same interpretation to the two positive action provisions. Does this help us in deciding what sort of positive action is allowed and how far this action can go?

The answer will depend on the interpretation of Article 5 by the ECJ. If the ECJ interprets this article in the same way as it has interpreted Article 2(4) of the 1976 Equal Treatment Directive[13] and Article 141(4) EC, then it will exclude programmes which involve automatic preferential treatment at the point of selection for employment, although it does seem to accept a wide range of measures prior to that point. The ECJ has also held that positive measures should be limited to the period necessary to overcome the disadvantage.[14]

13 Article 2(4) of the Equal Treatment Directive (Council Directive 76/207/EEC) was replaced by Article 2(8) of the Equal Treatment (Amendment) Directive. Both are now replaced by Article 3 of the Recast Directive 2006, under the heading 'Positive action'; this Article determines that 'Member States may maintain or adopt measures within the meaning of Article 141(4) of the Treaty with a view to ensuring full equality in practice between men and women in working life'.

14 See, for example: *Kalanke; Marschall v Land Nordrhein-Westfalen*; *Badeck's Application*; and *Abrahamsson and Anderson v Fogelqvist*. For a detailed discussion of positive action and the different concepts of equality, including the cases mentioned, see Fredman 2002: 125–60; and Schiek *et al.* 2007: 801–25.

And it sees positive action as derogation from the principle of equal treatment and as such it should be interpreted strictly.[15] In other words, in the sex discrimination field, the ECJ appears to hold that positive action aiming at equality of opportunity is allowed but that positive action which goes further and pursues equality of results is not. As Poiares Maduro (2005: 25) writes: 'the case law of the ECJ regarding affirmative action measures has therefore been framed largely by the notion of equality of opportunities'.

If this interpretation is indeed followed, then Article 5 of the Race Directive can be seen as aiming for equality of opportunity. However, Schiek (2002: 299) points out that the Race and Framework Directives – Article 7(1) of the latter contains the same provision as Article 5 of the Race Directive – both allow for positive measures 'with a view to ensuring full equality in practice' and do not use the terminology of the Equal Treatment Directive. This, as Schiek argues, appears to indicate that these directives do go further and are aiming for equality of results:

> Neither of the directives thus uses the term 'equal opportunity' from the old Gender Equality Directive, which led both Advocates General Tesauro and Jacobs in their conclusions on *Marschall* and *Kalanke* respectively to assume that positive action measures aiming at results are inadmissible. On the contrary, aiming to 'ensure full equality in practice', the directives appear to envisage result-oriented as well as procedural measures.

So Schiek argues for a different interpretation of the Race and Framework Directives because their text differs from the older Equal Treatment Directive's text. Article 3 of the Recast Directive and Article 6 of the Equal Treatment (Goods) Directive both refer to Article 141(4) EC and contains the same words – 'with a view to ensuring full equality in practice' – in relation to gender discrimination and, following Schiek's reasoning, this should allow for a wider interpretation of the positive action provisions in relation to all the grounds covered by EU anti discrimination law.

The ECJ, in the *Abrahamsson* case (para 55), considered Article 141(4) EC separately and held:

> Even though Article 141(4) EC allows the Member States to maintain or adopt measures providing for special advantages intended to prevent or compensate for disadvantages in professional careers in order to ensure full equality between men and women in professional life, it cannot be inferred from this that it allows a selection method which appears on any view to be disproportionate to the aim pursued.

15 *Johnston v Chief Constable of the Royal Ulster Constabulary*: para 36.

This might mean that the ECJ sees Article 141(4) EC as going beyond Article 2(4) of the Equal Treatment Directive, but, unfortunately, it does not really give any indication as to whether Article 141(4) EC allows for broader positive action. Ellis (2005: 312) writes that the language of the Race and Framework Directive appears to be more permissive than that of Article 2(4) of the Equal Treatment Directive, but weaker than that of Article 141(4) EC, which suggests that Article 141(4) EC is more permissive than Article 2(4).

Therefore, it remains to be seen whether the ECJ will use the same interpretation for positive action as it has done in gender equality cases under the new Equality Directives or whether it will allow for more far-reaching measures that aim more clearly at equality of results. Will it make a distinction between the different Article 13 EC Directives in this area? Apart from the argument that the words 'with a view to ensuring full equality in practice' are more permissive, another argument for allowing a broader interpretation in relation to all Article 13 EC grounds is that the case law of the ECJ is partly based on its interpretation of Article 2(4) of the 1976 Equal Treatment Directive, but the Equal Treatment (Amendment) Directive (and now the Recast Directive) has replaced this Article. Poiares Maduro (2005: 26) uses the same arguments where he writes that the scope of Article 141(4) EC and the Article 13 EC Directives might broaden the scope of admissibility of affirmative action measures.

There might also be some room for a broader interpretation in the case of racial or ethnic origin discrimination because the scope of the Race Directive goes beyond the employment field. The ECJ might decide to allow broader positive action measures in the other areas covered. Support for this can be found in the *Lommers* case (para 37) in which the ECJ upheld an employer's scheme that provided subsidized nursery places only for female employees (save in exceptional circumstances).[16] Some (tentative) support for a broader interpretation in relation to racial and ethnic origin discrimination might be found in the Explanatory Memorandum (COM (1999) 566: 6), as quoted above, that Article 5 of the Race Directive allows 'Member States to authorise legislative or administrative measures which are necessary to prevent or correct situations of inequality'.

However, it can also be argued, as Brown (2002: 216) and Ellis (2005: 312), mentioned above, do, that the text of the Race and Framework Directives is weaker than Article 141(4) EC. Waddington and Bell (2001: 602) write that the text of the Race Directive is more restrictive than Article 141(4) EC because 'it omits the positive element of that Article, notably the possibility of conferring specific advantages to make it easier for the under-represented

16 This argument can also be used in relation to the Equal Treatment (Goods) Directive and, once the 2008 Proposal (COM (2008) 426) is adopted, in relation to the other Article 13 grounds.

sex to pursue a vocational activity'. These authors anticipate 'that the Court will seek to extend these general principles on positive action to the other grounds of discrimination enumerated in Article 13 EC', although they do admit that 'there remains a variety of positive action schemes that have yet to be tested'.

In another paper, Bell and Waddington (2003: 355) write that 'an assumption that such result-oriented measures [programmes involving preferential treatment at the point of selection] will be difficult to justify under the Article 13 Directives may be inferred from two derogations from the positive action clause'. These derogations are, first, an additional exception in Article 7(2) of the Framework Directive for disabled people, which 'has been interpreted as permitting states to retain quota based schemes'; and, second, a specific exception in Article 15(1) of the Framework Directive 'for recruitment into the Police Service of Northern Ireland, in order to protect legally the "50:50" quota system introduced to increase Catholic participation' (See S 46 of the Police (Northern Ireland) Act 2000, discussed in Chapter 5). Therefore, Bell and Waddington argue that the fact that the Framework Directive makes exceptions for two cases where quotas are allowed would indicate that quotas are not allowed in any other cases.

Therefore, there are arguments to be found both for and against an extension of the permitted positive action measures under the EU Equality Directives. It is suggested that the arguments for an extension are stronger for the Race Directive because, first, its field of application goes beyond the employment field and, second, because the derogations mentioned by Bell and Waddington are both made in the Framework Directive and there are no such derogations in the Race Directive. The Race Directive generally contains less exceptions and derogations than the other Equality Directives. Are there any other arguments that could be used for allowing wider positive action for racial groups than for groups characterized by the other grounds in Article 13 EC? Is race in any way different from the other grounds?

In Chapter 4, we discussed the difference in character between discrimination grounds. As we mentioned there, Bell and Waddington (2003: 359–63) looked at the influence a ground could have on the ability or availability to do a job or use a good or service, while Schiek (2002: 309–10) distinguished between characteristics which only exist as ascriptions, characteristics which reflect real biological differences and characteristics that reflect a chosen lifestyle or difference in identity. We concluded that race is an ascribed characteristic which is always irrelevant because it does not affect a person's ability or availability to do a job or use a good or service. Of the Article 13 EC grounds, sex and religion can affect a person's availability, while disability and age can affect both a person's ability and the availability to a greater or lesser extent. Sexual orientation, like race, does not affect either. Schiek put religion, ethnicity and sexual orientation in the third category, but, by following Gerards' (2004a: 164–5) suggestion that a characteristic should be considered as immutable if it 'cannot be changed without infringing the essence of an individual's identity', we argued that religion and sexual orientation – and possibly ethnicity – are immutable characteristics in this sense and so would come closer to the first category because they are beyond the control of the person affected. We could, therefore, argue that discrimination on the grounds of race/racial or ethnic origin, religion and sexual orientation is particularly repugnant and malicious, because these characteristics can be seen as being beyond the control of a person.

But does this justify allowing for different levels of acceptable positive action? In our view, the difference in character and the fact that discrimination is more repugnant on these grounds could well be used as an argument for allowing more far-reaching positive action in relation to racial, ethnic and religious groups, but not in relation to homosexual groups. As we have argued in Chapter 4, the Race Directive should be extended to cover religion or belief as well and, therefore, religion or belief should be treated in the same way as racial or ethnic origin. Positive action measures are taken to make up for structural disadvantages suffered by particular groups in society. In this sense, homosexual people cannot be said to have suffered such disadvantages as a group, but racial, ethnic and religious groups have.

Other possible differences between the grounds that might justify the provision for broader positive action measures are the size of the group affected, the disadvantage suffered by this affected group and the extent of the discrimination. All these factors are difficult to assess accurately, but it might be the perception that these differences exist that influence the decision on how to deal with the different grounds. The perception may lead to the conclusion that some grounds need to be dealt with more urgently and/or more extensively than others.

The perception that the number of people affected by racial discrimination in the EU was and is very large and that racial discrimination was and is particularly widespread and invidious, appears to have played a role in the quick adoption of the Race Directive with its stronger protection. This perception – influenced no doubt by the strong lobbying by NGOs and the European Parliament for legislative action against racial discrimination – most likely strengthened the political willingness to take action to combat racism and racial discrimination in a wide area. Support for this can be found in the fact that the European Council mentioned the importance of the fight against racism and xenophobia at the Maastricht Summit in 1991, the Edinburgh Summit in 1992 and the Copenhagen Summit in 1993,[17] while the Corfu Summit in 1994[18] resulted in the setting up of the Kahn Commission.

17 EC Bulletins 12–1991, 12–1992 and 6–1993.

18 Corfu Summit Conclusions, http://www.europarl.europa.eu/summits/cor1_en.htm#justice (accessed 1 April 2009)

The designation of 1997 as the European Year Against Racism and the establishment of the European Monitoring Centre on Racism and Xenophobia also lend support to this view, as does the opinion of the European Commission that 'a comprehensive coverage is necessary to make a serious contribution to curbing racism and xenophobia in Europe' (COM (1999) 566: 3). Thus, the perception in the EU that racial discrimination affects a large number of people and that such discrimination is particularly widespread and invidious, could well be used as another argument for allowing broader positive action measures in relation to racial/ethnic groups under Article 5 of the Race Directive.

Therefore, a number of arguments can be advanced for a broader interpretation of Article 5 of the Race Directive, allowing for more result-oriented measures than what is allowed under the old Equal Treatment Directive and the other Equality Directives. Unfortunately, the European Commission, in its report on the application of the Race Directive under Article 17 (COM (2006) 643: 7–8), states in respect of Article 5 that 'it is worthwhile stressing the difference between positive action measures, which are allowed, and so-called "positive discrimination" measures, which are not compatible with the Directive'. It continues:

> On the one hand, positive action measures aim to ensure full equality in practice by preventing or compensating for disadvantages linked to having a certain racial or ethnic origin. These measures may include, for example, providing specific training to people belonging to groups that do not usually have access to such training, or taking particular steps to ensure that certain racial or ethnic groups are fully informed about job advertisements, including, for example, publishing adverts in publications targeting these groups. On the other hand, 'positive discrimination' measures give automatic and absolute preference (for example in access to employment) to members of a particular group over others for no other reason than belonging to that group.

This suggests that the Commission does not want to accept broader positive action measures under Article 5 of the Race Directive, nor does it appear to want to go beyond the case law of the ECJ in sex discrimination cases. This is, in our view, an undesirable development and, in Chapter 7, some alternative paths will be discussed.

One last point needs to be made in relation to positive action measures. Article 5 allows, but does not require, Member States to take such action. This contrasts with the ICERD which requires, in Article 2(2), States Parties to take such measures. Under EU law there is no obligation on the Member States to do so and if they don't they are not contravening any EU legislation. This means that there could, and, because of a variety of attitudes towards positive action in the Member States, more than likely would, be significant differences between the individual Member States, with some taking extensive positive action measures while others do not. Some calls for mandatory positive action in the EU Directives have been made. Cahn (2005: 3), for example, writes:

> In light of the fact that both Article 1(4) and Article 2(2) [ICERD] comprise components of European Union Member States' obligations to end racial discrimination, the currently diminished EU standard will need to change, and the sooner the better, to end a situation in which states are faced with discord between requirements flowing from the EU acquis on the one hand, and their international obligations on the other.

It could thus be argued that as all EU Member States are required to take positive action measures under the ICERD, the lower standard in the Directives does not matter, because the duty exists anyway. In Chapter 2 we have seen, however, that enforcement of a duty imposed by an international instrument is not easy.

Another organization that has advocated mandatory positive action under the Race Directive is the European Network against Racism (Bell 2008b: 12). According to ENAR, 'without mandatory positive action the anti-discrimination model espoused by the Directive will never be fully effective, particularly for the most vulnerable groups in society'. ENAR recommends that: 'the Directive be enhanced through the promotion of mandatory positive action, which is responsive to the individual national contexts'. The latter part appears to indicate that ENAR is in favour of allowing the Member States more discretion in what measures they take.

The fact that the EU Equality Directives allow Member States to take positive action measures, but do not require them to do so, most likely reflects the diversity of views on the subject and the lack of unanimity between the Member States for mandatory positive action.

Positive action is mentioned in the Charter of Fundamental Rights of the EU in Article 23, which determines that 'the principle of equality shall not prevent the maintenance or adoption of measures providing for specific advantages in favour of the under-represented sex'. This article appears to be a general statement which does not add anything to the provisions for positive action in Article 141(4) EC or Article 3 of the Recast Directive. The Charter does not mention positive action in relation to any of the other grounds of Article 13 EC.

Therefore, the positive action provisions of the Race Directive move it towards a substantive concept of equality but it remains to be seen whether the Member States will be allowed to go beyond measures aiming at equality of opportunity and take positive action which aims at equality of results.

6.4 Pluralist concept of equality

Recital 8 of the Race Directive mentions 'a socially inclusive labour market' and 'combating discrimination against groups such as ethnic minorities'. Recital 12 explains that the scope of the Race Directive should go beyond the employment field and cover other areas 'to ensure the development of democratic and tolerant societies which allow for the participation of all persons irrespective of racial or ethnic origin'. A socially inclusive labour market means a labour market in which all groups in society, including groups such as ethnic minorities, participate. The recognition of discrimination against groups and the stress on their participation in society fit in a pluralist concept of equality.

Articles 11 and 12 of the Race Directive determine that the Member States should promote dialogue with the social partners (Article 11(1)) and with NGOs which have 'a legitimate interest in contributing to the fight against discrimination on grounds of racial or ethnic origin' (Article 12) with a view to fostering and promoting equal treatment; or with a view 'to address different forms of discrimination and to combat them', as Recital 23 explains. Article 17 provides for Reports from the Commission on the application of the Directive, which 'shall include, if necessary, proposals to revise and update this Directive'. According to Article 17(2), the Commission's report shall take into account, among other views, the viewpoints of the social partners and relevant NGOs. Dialogue with and considering the viewpoints of the social partners and NGOs involved in the fight against race discrimination gives these partners and organizations – and through them employers, employees and (groups of) victims – a chance to participate in the implementation of the Race Directive and in policy making in relation to the fight against race discrimination. Articles 11, 12 and 17 and Recital 23 can thus be seen as promoting participation, and thus a pluralist concept of equality.

We have mentioned above that ECRI (General Policy Recommendation 7: para 5) recommends that Member States should provide for temporary special measures (or positive action). These measures should be allowed either 'to prevent or compensate for disadvantages suffered by persons designated by the grounds enumerated in paragraph 1b)' – the Recommendation uses the same wording as the Race Directive here – or 'to facilitate their full participation in all fields of life'. Legislation providing for positive action measures aimed at participation would aim at a pluralist concept of equality.

The Treaty of Lisbon changes the TEU and the new Article 2 gives the Union's values:

> The Union is founded on the values of respect for human dignity, freedom, democracy, equality, the rule of law and respect for human rights, including the rights of persons belonging to minorities. These values are common to the Member States in a society in which pluralism, non-discrimination, tolerance, justice, solidarity and equality between women and men prevail.

Equality and respect for the rights of persons belonging to minorities are thus explicitly mentioned as values on which the Union is founded. The new Article 3 determines that the Union, among other things, 'shall combat social exclusion and discrimination, and shall promote social justice and protection, equality between women and men, solidarity between generations' and 'solidarity among Member States'. It shall 'respect its rich cultural and linguistic diversity' and 'contribute to peace, ... solidarity and mutual respect among peoples'. Both these Articles have elements of the pluralist notion of equality: respect for human dignity and the rights of minorities; a pluralist and tolerant society; respect for diversity; and the stress on solidarity and mutual respect between peoples. The placing of these Articles, at the beginning of the TEU, makes a clear statement that the Union values equality and diversity.

Three articles in the Charter of Fundamental Rights also contain statements of intent to respect diversity: Articles 22 ('the Union shall respect cultural, religious and linguistic diversity'), 25 ('the Union recognises and respects the rights of the elderly ...'), and 26 ('the Union recognises and respects the rights of persons with disabilities ...'). Therefore, there are elements of the pluralist concept of equality in the Treaty of Lisbon and the Charter but both the statements in Articles 2 and 3 and those in the Charter are general statements without creating clear legal rights, so they could remain mere rhetoric.

6.5 Other provisions

Some parts of the Race Directive and the Treaty of Lisbon could be seen as aiming for different concepts of equality, depending on the way they are interpreted or implemented by the Member States or on the legal system of the Member State in question. We will discuss these parts in this section.

6.5.1 Enforcement provisions of the Race Directive

As the experience in the EU with sex discrimination had shown that enforcement is often problematic, the new Equality Directives give considerable attention to enforcement and contain a number of provisions to alleviate the problems experienced by victims in bringing cases. Article 7(1) of the Race Directive puts a duty on Member States to make 'judicial and/or administrative procedures, including where they deem it appropriate conciliation procedures', available to all persons who feel discriminated against, even after the relationship in which the discrimination is alleged to have occurred has ended. The second paragraph provides victims with support in bringing actions. It determines that associations, organizations or other legal entities with a legitimate interest may bring enforcement actions, 'either on behalf or in support of the complainant, with his or her approval'. Therefore, the

Directive does not provide for organizations to bring cases in their own name, but, as it contains minimum requirements only, the Member States can give them the right to do so.

Article 8 of the Race Directive shifts the burden of proof onto the respondent once facts from which it may be presumed that there has been direct or indirect discrimination have been established before a court or any other competent authority. This Article echoes Article 4 of the 1997 Burden of Proof Directive, which laid down in law the shift in the burden of proof developed by the ECJ. The reason for this shift is that in many discrimination cases, especially in employment related cases, it is the respondent (the discriminator) and not the victim who holds the relevant information. This provision is, again, a minimum requirement and Member States can introduce rules of evidence which are more favourable to the plaintiff.

Article 9 of the Race Directive provides for protection against victimization:

> Member States shall introduce into their national legal systems such measures as are necessary to protect individuals from any adverse treatment or adverse consequence as a reaction to a complaint or to proceedings aimed at enforcing compliance with the principle of equal treatment.

This Article protects not only victims of discrimination, but also others who support victims by reporting an act of discrimination or by acting as a witness (Tyson 2001: 214). The reason for including protection against victimization is that the fear of retaliation often works as a real deterrent to making a complaint of discrimination.

One of the problems for victims of discrimination has proved to be that they do not know about their rights to take action. To alleviate this problem, Article 10 of the Race Directive determines that the Member States should take care to disseminate information to all persons concerned on provisions adopted pursuant to the Directive or on provisions already in place.

All the above provisions appear to be mainly aiming to make it easier for individual victims of discrimination to bring a case against a discriminator. In this sense, the provisions do not appear to go beyond formal equality as there is nothing in the Directive that provides for actions by groups. However, nothing in the Directive prevents or prohibits Member States to allow actions by groups of individuals as well, and the provisions above are equally applicable to such groups. Allowing for group actions would move towards a more substantive concept of equality.

Article 13 of the Directive can be considered to go beyond formal equality, as it prescribes that:

> Member States shall designate a body or bodies for the promotion of equal treatment of all persons without discrimination on the grounds of racial or ethnic origin. These bodies may form part of agencies charged

at the national level with the defence of human rights or the safeguarding of individuals' rights.

The use of the word 'shall' means that it is compulsory for the Member States to designate such a body or bodies (Council of the European Union 2000a: footnote 27).

Article 13(2) gives the competences of the body/bodies as: providing independent assistance to victims of discrimination in pursuing complaints about discrimination; conducting independent surveys concerning discrimination; and publishing independent reports and making recommendations on any issue relating to such discrimination. Article 12(2) of the Proposal for the Race Directive (COM (1999) 566) did include: 'receiving and pursuing complaints from individuals' and 'commencing investigations or surveys concerning discrimination', but this was dropped in the final text. According to Tyson (2001: 216), the EU Member States were concerned that 'the proposal overstepped the line between setting objectives and telling Member States how to achieve them (so contravening the principle of subsidiarity)'. This suggests that the Member States preferred to leave the precise structure and tasks of the body/bodies to be decided at national level.

The final text of the Race Directive is different from the Proposal in another aspect: in the latter, the Article was entitled: 'independent bodies' and the first paragraph put a duty on Member States to provide for an *independent* body or bodies, which may form part of *independent* agencies. The second paragraph gives the tasks of these *independent* bodies (our italics). In the final text, the word independent is omitted from Article 13(1) and the opening part of Article 13(2), but then added to each task in the second paragraph. During the negotiations, the Member States expressed their concern about the independence of these bodies, but the Commission responded that the key point was to enshrine the existence of these bodies in legislation so that governments could not abolish them without consent of Parliament. Their independence could be ensured in different ways and was not incompatible with the obligation to report to Ministers and/or financing by the State, according to the Commission (Council of the European Union 2000b: footnote 42). The change in the text does not appear to make the situation with regards the independence of these bodies any clearer.[19]

Both the Equal Treatment (Goods) and Recast Directives prescribe the designation of 'a body or bodies for the promotion, analysis, monitoring and support of equal treatment of all persons without discrimination on the grounds of sex' with the same competences as given in Article 13(2) of the

19 ECRI has composed basic principles concerning specialized bodies to combat racism, xenophobia, antisemitism and intolerance at national level. Principle 5 concerns the independence of such bodies. See appendix to ECRI, General Policy Recommendation 2 (ECRI 2007: 21). See on this also Cormack and Niessen 2005.

Race Directive. The Framework Directive does not contain such a duty and this omission has been criticized in the literature (Skidmore 2001: 129; Waddington and Bell 2001: 608; Schiek 2002: 301; Barry 2003: 418; Higgins 2003: 401–2). There appears to be no sound reason why victims of sex and racial or ethnic origin discrimination need such a body more than victims of discrimination on the grounds covered by the Framework Directive. However, the practice in many Member States appears to be to designate a body or bodies with competence to deal with all the Article 13 EC grounds of discrimination (Liegl *et al.* 2004: 12; COM (2004) 379: 7; European Commission 2006). Article 12 of the 2008 Proposal to extend the area covered by the Framework Directive (COM (2008) 426) will remedy this omission.

The Directives leave it to the Member States to decide whether they want to designate a single body covering one or more grounds or more than one body each covering a single ground. The advantages of having a single equality body which deals with all the grounds of discrimination covered by the national legislation are, first, that a single body would provide a 'one-stop-shop' for victims of discrimination and for persons who seek information about discrimination, thus making it easier to obtain information or help. Second, a single body could deal much better with cases of multiple discrimination. With single ground bodies, a victim of multiple discrimination will either have to decide which ground he/she wants to pursue or he/she will have to go to different bodies. Third, a single body could keep an overview of all the grounds covered, while a number of single ground bodies would fragment the overall picture. Fourth, a single body would also be better able to handle possible clashes between different grounds. And, finally, a single body would have the advantage of scale and could probably work more efficiently financially because it would avoid possible overlap between objectives and tasks, including administrative tasks. However, having a number of smaller bodies for each specific ground has the advantage that each body only has to concentrate on a narrow area and thus it can quickly build up special expertise in this area. With a single body there is also a risk that some grounds of discrimination will be given more attention and that other grounds will be neglected, especially if resources are insufficient.

The establishment of national bodies for the promotion of equal treatment is important because they provide independent assistance to victims of discrimination in pursuing complaints and so make it easier for the victims to pursue a claim. This assistance of victims can take the form of supporting cases in court, but many equality bodies only support a small number of court cases and these are often chosen on the basis of the importance of the legal point at issue (COM (2006) 643: 5). This is called 'strategic litigation' and, through such litigation, the bodies can test or establish important legal issues, for example on the interpretation of key terms. The assistance to victims can also take the form of providing opinions or recommendations on complaints. Often these have strong persuasive value and will be followed but, if they are not followed, the victim can take legal action before the courts which will take the opinions and recommendations of the body into account. Some bodies established in the Member States also provide mediation services and some can even provide legally binding recommendations on complaints submitted to them (European Commission 2006: 21). In this way, through opinions, recommendations or mediation, complaints are often solved before they reach the court or tribunal stage. Through the strategic litigation and through their opinions and recommendations, these bodies can influence and support the development of national and EU anti discrimination legislation.

But the national bodies are also important because, through the other tasks mentioned in Article 13 (2) of the Race Directive – conducting surveys, publishing reports and making recommendations – the bodies can influence policy making at both national and European level and play a part in the development of new legislative and non-legislative measures. The bodies in the Member States have been given a variety of tasks. The Dutch Equal Treatment Commission, for example, undertakes investigations on its own initiative and organizes training sessions, lectures and conferences on the Equal Treatment Legislation. The British Commission for Racial Equality, which has now become part of the Equality and Human Rights Commission, issued codes of practice which provide guidance on how to avoid unlawful discrimination and achieve equality. These codes aim at preventing discrimination as well as informing people about the legal steps they can take once discrimination has taken place.

The work of these bodies can thus be said to go beyond establishing formal equality because it is proactive and preventative and it aims at eliminating discrimination and at promoting and establishing factual equality. Whether these bodies work towards equality of opportunity, equality of results and/or pluralism depends on the competences given to them by the Member States.

6.5.2 Mainstreaming duty

The Treaty of Lisbon, if ratified, will establish a strong legal basis for the mainstreaming approach in relation to all the grounds of discrimination mentioned in Article 13 EC. Article 8 of the *Consolidated Version of the Treaty on the Functioning of the European Union* (TFEU) echoes the present Article 3(2) EC and reads:

> In all its activities, the Union shall aim to eliminate inequalities, and to promote equality between women and men.

Article 10 TFEU extends the mainstreaming duty to all the grounds of Article 13 EC as it states:

> In defining and implementing its policies and activities, the Union shall aim to combat discrimination based on sex, racial or ethnic origin, religion or belief, disability, age or sexual orientation.

These mainstreaming duties were also part of the Draft Constitution for Europe (Articles III–116 and III–118) and, in his discussion of those articles, Bell (2004: 255) points out the strength of these mainstreaming duties. He writes:

> the equality mainstreaming duties go beyond an obligation to 'take into account', but instead integrate equality as an *aim* [his italics] of all policies. ... placing equality as an aim conveys the need for all policies to be actively engaged in achieving equality.

He does mention that translating this duty into practice is not easy. But putting such a duty down in law is a positive step because, rather than providing an individual victim with a means of redress, a mainstreaming duty is a more forward-looking, pro-active and positive mechanism, which moves beyond the need to identify an individual victim and perpetrator and thus beyond a formal equality concept. Bell (2008a: 2) writes that, in practical terms, mainstreaming in order to combat racism and promote equality:

> implies that policy makers in all fields should ensure: (1) that any measures taken do not discriminate on grounds of racial or ethnic origin; and (2) law and policy instruments are actively used to promote equality for all persons, irrespective of racial or ethnic origin.

So a legislative mainstreaming duty can be seen as moving beyond formal equality, beyond the prohibition of unequal treatment, because it moves away from the focus on the individual and because it aims to prevent discrimination rather than acting after this has taken place.

But does it aim to establish substantive equality (either equality of opportunity or equality of results) or pluralism? This is often not very clear for two reasons. The first reason is that it depends on what is being mainstreamed. Is it non-discrimination and equality or is it diversity? A duty to mainstream non-discrimination and equality, to assess the impact of all decisions and policies on non-discrimination and equality means that an authority must ask itself if its policy or decision promotes non-discrimination and equality. This could mean promoting equal treatment or equal opportunities or equal results. If it does no more than promote equal treatment, it would not really go much beyond formal equality, although it would go beyond just prohibiting discrimination and would be more preventative. It would go further if it promoted equal opportunities or equal outcomes or if it imposed a duty to mainstream equality of opportunity or equality of results.

On the other hand, if the duty is to mainstream diversity and/or social and political participation and/or social inclusion, it would fit in a pluralist equality concept. For example, in the 1998 Action Plan against Racism, the

Commission mentions that it will 'actively develop a mainstreaming approach to combating racism and discrimination and *promoting integration across all relevant sectors*' (our italics) (COM (1998) 183: 3).

The second reason why it is not always clear what the aim of a legislative mainstreaming duty is, is that the concept itself, although it is a popular concept, is vague and open to a wide variety of interpretations and that it is not easy, to use Bell's words mentioned above, to translate the duty to mainstream into practice. What exactly does a duty to mainstream equality mean? We mentioned that it means that an authority must ask itself if its policy or decision promotes equality. But what happens if it doesn't? Does the mainstreaming duty include a duty to change the policy or decision in such a way that it does? Shaw (2004: 5) points out that the 1998 Action Plan mentioned above lists many areas where the fight against racism should be incorporated into policy considerations – employment strategy; structural funds; education, training and youth; Justice and Home Affairs cooperation; information, communication, culture, audiovisual and sport; public procurement; research activities; external relations; and Commission staff policy. On paper, this, according to Shaw, 'amounts to a substantial commitment to a policy of mainstreaming'. She continues: 'Yet, despite the rhetoric and these paper policies, there has been little solid action to bring the fight against racism to the forefront of the EU policy concerns'. This suggests that the commitment to a mainstreaming policy or even a mainstreaming duty imposed by law is not always as effective as it might at first appear. This very much depends on how this duty is interpreted and how or even whether it is put into practice.

However, if the duty in Article 10 TFEU is interpreted, as Bell (2004: 255) appears to do, as meaning that all policies need 'to be actively engaged with achieving equality' then it could be useful to have such a duty as it would mean a greater focus on equality issues. It is, therefore, argued here that the addition of a mainstreaming duty for all the grounds of Article 13 EC is a positive development.[20]

6.5.3 EU developments after adoption of the Race Directive

As we have suggested in Chapter 1, since the end of 2004, there appears to be a shift at the EU level in the language in relation to anti discrimination policies and the term 'equal opportunities' is used more frequently. This shift in language concerns anti discrimination policies in general rather than specifically mentioning measures against racial or ethnic origin discrimination, but the shift is important because it can influence the interpretation of the Race Directive and the future development of new legislative or other

20 For more information on mainstreaming racial equality see Bell 2008a.

measures against racial or ethnic origin discrimination. The Commission also refers a number of times to disadvantaged ethnic minorities.

The shift can be seen, for example, in the fact that the new European Commission, installed in 2004, has a Commissioner for Employment, Social Affairs and Equal Opportunities (Mr. Spidla). This is the first time that equal opportunities are specifically mentioned in the title of a Commissioner. A group of Commissioners responsible for fundamental rights, anti discrimination and equal opportunities was also created (Barroso 2004: 3).

Commissioner Spidla himself mentioned equal opportunities and the need to tackle patterns of inequality on a number of occasions. In his opening address to the Dutch EU Presidency Conference on Anti-discrimination, he said:

> I would like, above all, to push for the incorporation of equal opportunities in all policies – commonly referred to as 'mainstreaming'. The group of Commissioners with responsibility for fundamental rights, anti-discrimination and equal opportunities, announced by President Barroso, will be the driving force behind this new policy approach.
>
> (Spidla 2004: 4)

In June 2005, at a Conference on 'Mainstreaming Diversity', Spidla ended his speech with: 'Europe cannot be content with formal equality. It must work towards achieving genuine equality for everyone' (Spidla 2005).

This use of the 'language of equal opportunities' in the Community anti discrimination context appears to be even stronger in the Commission's Communication on the Framework Strategy for Non-discrimination and Equal Opportunities for All (COM (2005) 224) and the Proposal to designate 2007 as the European Year of Equal Opportunities for All (COM (2005) 225).

The introduction to the Communication describes the EU legislation against discrimination as 'some of the most comprehensive and far-reaching anti-discrimination legislation to be found anywhere in the world'. The Commission emphasizes that full and effective implementation and enforcement of this legal framework must be ensured.

However, this is followed by the consideration that:

> It is clear that the implementation and enforcement of anti-discrimination legislation on an individual level is not enough to tackle the multifaceted and deep-rooted patterns of inequality experienced by some groups. There is a need to go beyond anti-discrimination policies designed to prevent unequal treatment of individuals. The EU should reinforce its efforts to promote equal opportunities for all, in order to tackle the structural barriers faced by migrants, ethnic minorities, the disabled, older and younger workers and other vulnerable groups.
>
> (COM (2005) 224: 2)

Later in the Communication, the Commission states:

> … it is difficult for legislation alone to tackle the complex and deep-rooted patterns of inequality experienced by some groups. Positive measures may be necessary to compensate for long-standing inequalities suffered by groups of people who, historically, have not had access to equal opportunities.
>
> The EU experience in the field of gender equality strongly suggests that protection of individual rights must be backed up by accompanying measures in order to bring about lasting change and to promote genuine equal opportunities for all.
>
> (Ibid: 6)

The Commission suggests as one of the accompanying measures the promotion of mainstreaming of non-discrimination and equal opportunities for all in relevant EU policies. The Commission will also seek to promote exchanges of good practice, cooperation and networking between all stakeholders in the field of discrimination.

The Communication then announces:

> In order to drive forward the agenda outlined in the Communication for *a more positive approach to equality* [our italics], the Commission is proposing to designate 2007 as the European Year of Equal Opportunities for All …
>
> The Year will aim to: inform people of their rights to protection against discrimination under European and national law; celebrate diversity as an asset for the EU; and to promote equal opportunities for all in economic, social, political and cultural life.
>
> (Ibid: 8–9)

The Commission recognizes that 'enlargement has increased the EU diversity in terms of culture, language and ethnicity' and that 'one of the key challenges facing the enlarged EU is the need to develop a coherent and effective approach to the social and labour market integration of ethnic minorities'. To deal with this, the EU 'needs to develop appropriate responses to the different needs of new migrants, established minorities of immigrant origin and other minority groups' (Ibid: 9–10). The Commission thus stresses the need for the integration of established and new ethnic minority groups.

The conclusion reiterates that 'in addition to the legal protection of individual rights, this Communication sets out a strategy for the positive and active promotion of non-discrimination and equal opportunities for all' (Ibid: 12).

Which concepts of equality can be detected in all this? The Communication recognizes the need to go beyond the prevention of unequal treatment, in other words, beyond a mere formal concept of equality. It acknowledges that positive action may be necessary to compensate for the structural barriers and long-standing and deep-rooted inequalities that some groups experience which have denied these groups access to equal opportunities. This shows clearly a substantive notion of equality. The Commission itself calls the Communication an agenda for 'a more positive approach to equality', and stresses the importance of the promotion of equal opportunities for all in economic, social, political and cultural life, which also suggests a substantive approach including positive action. The aims of the Year include the celebration of diversity as an asset for the Union. This and the focus on the social and labour market integration of ethnic minorities and the development of appropriate responses to their different needs, all fit in a pluralist approach to equality.

The Commission will aim to ensure that a range of EU funding instruments contribute to the promotion of non-discrimination and equal opportunities for all. The Commission also proposes an annual high-level Equality Summit to bring together key stakeholders. If this leads to greater participation of disadvantaged groups, it would fit in the pluralist notion of equality. To support policy development to tackle discrimination and social exclusion faced by disadvantaged ethnic minorities, the Commission plans to establish a high-level advisory group on social and labour market integration of these disadvantaged ethnic minorities (Ibid: 10). Here again, there is a focus on ethnic minorities, which shows that the Commission recognizes that there are disadvantaged ethnic minorities. This fits in the substantive concept of equality, and if the recommendations of this group actually lead to policy development to create greater inclusion, then it would also fit in the pluralist notion of equality. Therefore, the Communication contains clear elements of both the substantive and the pluralist concepts of equality. Can we also detect such elements in the Proposal for the Year of Equal Opportunities for All?

The Explanatory Memorandum to the Proposal for the Year (COM (2005) 225: 2) states:

> The global objective of the Year will be to raise awareness of the benefits of a just, cohesive society where there is equality of opportunity for all. This will require tackling barriers to participation in society and promoting a climate in which Europe's diversity is seen as a source of socio-economic vitality.

It considers that the Year 'will provide an opportunity to promote a more cohesive society that celebrates differences within the framework of EU core values' (Ibid: 4). Article 2 gives the specific objectives of the Year: rights, representation, recognition and respect and tolerance. 'Rights' refers to the raising of awareness on the right to equality and non-discrimination and of the existing anti discrimination legislation.

'Representation' means the promotion of full and equal participation of all groups in society. 'The disadvantages experienced by some communities … are so wide-scale and embedded in the structure of society, that positive action may be necessary to remedy the nature of their exclusion' (Ibid: 4–5). 'Recognition' indicates the celebration and accommodation of diversity. As Article 2(c) states:

> The European Year will highlight the positive contribution that people, irrespective of their sex, racial or ethnic origin, religion or beliefs, capacities, age and sexual orientation can make to society as a whole, in particular by accentuating the benefits of diversity.

'Respect and tolerance' relates to the promotion of a more cohesive society. Key to this will be the promotion of good relations between different communities and building trust and understanding, and work to eliminate stereotypes and prejudices (Ibid: 2–5 and Article 2).

Under the heading 'delivering change' it states that the Year:

> will target common barriers and inequalities affecting several communities … It will seek to encourage the promotion of good relations among different communities, building trust and understanding that will contribute to a more cohesive society.
>
> (Ibid: 5)

There are also some interesting points in the legislative financial statement. Where this looks at the specific objectives, it mentions that 'a key challenge will be to demonstrate that the notion of "equality" does not mean "sameness" but rather taking account of differences and diversity to ensure equal treatment'. It also states that 'equal opportunities policy is not simply limited to the elimination of discrimination. It also requires equalising the opportunities to full and equal participation for all' (Both ibid: 25).

Therefore, the proposal also clearly contains elements of the concepts of substantive equality: a society where there is equal opportunity for all and where structural disadvantages, barriers and inequalities affecting several communities may necessitate positive action. Three elements fit in the pluralist approach to equality: the tackling of barriers to participation to aim at the full and equal participation of all groups in society; the celebration and accommodation of diversity; and the promotion of good relations, trust and understanding between different communities.

Thus, elements of both the substantive and pluralist concepts of equality are appearing in the 'equality' language of the EU. A recognition is emerging that the deep-rooted patterns of inequality experienced by some groups need to be tackled. But is this use of the 'language of equal opportunities' translated into practical policies?

The Communication proposes the development of tools to promote mainstreaming of non-discrimination and equal opportunities for all in relevant EU policies, not only in relation to gender discrimination, but also in relation to discrimination on the other grounds of Article 13 EC. It mentions that the

Commission does an 'impact assessment': any proposal for legislation and any draft instrument to be adopted will, when being prepared under the normal decision-making procedures, be scrutinized for compatibility with the EU Charter of Fundamental Rights.[21] As mentioned, the Charter contains a right to equality before the law and a prohibition of discrimination on a large number of grounds, including all those mentioned in Article 13 EC. Therefore, any draft instruments will be scrutinized for compatibility with the right to equality and non-discrimination and there appears to be a commitment to assess the impact of all proposals for legislation on non-discrimination and equal opportunities which fits in with the concept of equal opportunity. This impact assessment suggests that the mainstreaming policy is more than mere 'rhetoric and paper policies' (Shaw 2004: 5).

Both the Communication and the Proposal mention repeatedly the need for positive action measures to tackle the inequalities and structural barriers suffered by some groups. However, these statements could remain mere rhetoric as there are no specific policies or measures requiring or promoting positive action. Because there will be no proposals for changes in the legislation in the near future, the current provisions allowing for, but not requiring, positive action, will, therefore, not be changed or strengthened. Article 3 of the Recast Directive and Article 5 of the 2008 Proposal (COM (2008) 426) allow for, but do not require, positive action. The Explanatory Memorandum to the 2008 Proposal mentions in relation to Article 5: 'The Member States have different traditions and practices regarding positive action, and this article lets Member States provide for positive action but does not make it an obligation' (Ibid: 9).

The 2005 Communication and the Proposal have been followed up by some action. The first action was specifically directed at ethnic minority groups. It was the establishment, in January 2006, of a High-level Advisory Group with the task to analyze how to achieve better social integration of ethnic minorities and their full participation in the labour market within the EU (Commission Decision 2006 and Press Release IP/06/149). This Group submitted its report in December 2007 and one of the recommendations to 'the European Commission, the other European Institutions, the Member States' authorities at all appropriate levels, social partners and organisations of civil society' is to 'pursue equality and gender mainstreaming' (High Level Advisory Group 2007: 99). The report also states:

> Equal rights are a first step towards an inclusive society. Equal rights alone, however, do not automatically entail equality. An inclusive society, thus, aims at bridging the gap between formal and real equality, provides equal opportunities for all its members and actively promotes diversity'. (Ibid: 8)

21 SEC (2001) 380: 2. A methodology for systematic and rigorous monitoring, based on this SEC document, has been set out in COM (2005) 172. See also Press Release IP/05/494.

Second, in its Resolution on the Follow-up of the European Year of Equal Opportunities for All (2007), the Council notes that 'in order to make real progress towards achieving equality in practice ... equal opportunities need to be mainstreamed' (Council Resolution 2007: 6). The Council also invites the Member States: to continue their efforts in the field of equal opportunities and discrimination and to ensure implementation of existing anti-discrimination legislation; to promote awareness of the legislation and of the benefits of equal opportunities for all; to engage civil society and the social partners in these processes; and 'to make full use of the possibilities for positive action in order to overcome existing equalities and achieving full equality in practice' (Ibid: 9–10).

Third, the evaluation report of the 2007 European Year of Equal Opportunities for All (European Commission 2008) appears to be positive as to the results of the Year and emphasizes as particularly positive the decentralized approach, with National Implementing Bodies in each Member State designing national strategies, and the positive contribution of having to address all six grounds of discrimination at once. The latter created an increased understanding of the need to join forces (Ibid: 4). However, the report points out that the effects of the Year on valuing the benefits of diversity and the need for positive representation were more limited and that reaching the business sector seemed particularly difficult (Ibid: 5). Overall, though, the results obtained by the Year were sustainable and likely to continue beyond 2007 (Ibid: 6).

Lastly, in 2008, the Commission brought out a Communication on 'non-discrimination and equal opportunities: a renewed commitment' (COM (2008) 420), together with the Proposal to extend the scope of the Framework Directive beyond the employment field (COM (2008) 426). In the communication it is stated that 'better legislative protection against discrimination must be accompanied by an active strategy to promote non-discrimination and equal opportunities' (COM (2008) 420: 1). Under the heading: 'Strengthening policy tools for active promotion of equal opportunities' the Commission states:

> Mainstreaming principles should apply across all grounds covered by Article 13 EC if the inequality and discrimination suffered by all groups is to be reduced. ... The Commission will build on these achievements [of mainstreaming actions in relation to gender and disability] by promoting the systematic incorporation of non-discrimination and equal opportunity concerns on all Article 13 grounds into all policies, in particular within existing coordination mechanisms for employment, social inclusion, education and training.
>
> (Ibid: 6–7)

In relation to positive action, the Commission 'will use the permanent dialogue with Member States to promote the full utilisation of the possibilities of positive action, in particular in access to education, employment, housing and health care' (Ibid: 8).

The above suggests that the EU is moving towards a more substantive concept of equality. There is a realization that prohibiting discrimination and prescribing equal treatment is not enough to tackle the patterns of inequality suffered by some groups in society and recognition that there are structural barriers to full participation faced by vulnerable groups such as migrants, ethnic minorities, the disabled, older and younger people and others. Why has this shift taken place? As mentioned, in the discussions and negotiations before the adoption of the Article 13 EC Directives, questions about concepts of equality do not appear to have played any great role. It is submitted that the Commission wanted to establish a common minimum standard of protection against discrimination across the EU, and anti discrimination measures aiming at formal equality are seen as providing this minimum standard of protection as a first step in the fight against discrimination. To a large extent, the Directives followed the existing legislation in the field of gender discrimination, where formal equality was the main aim, supplemented by provisions against indirect discrimination and for positive action. These minimum standards were set in 2000 (in the Race and Framework Directives). Now the Member States have become more familiar with anti discrimination rules, the idea of going beyond formal equality has started to crop up in the language of the Commission. This idea is not new: as we have seen, it was mentioned by the ECJ in a number of cases. Similar discussions on what aims equality laws should pursue took and are taking place in many Member States. The shift in emphasis is based on the EU experience in the field of gender discrimination that formal equality is not enough to tackle existing inequalities.

However, it appears that, despite the emphasis on the need for positive action measures to tackle the inequalities and structural barriers suffered by some groups, this shift in language is not going to be reflected in the near future in any new legislative measures. Other, non-legislative measures and policies could and will, hopefully, go further towards substantive and pluralist notions of equality and in this way complement the formal equality idea in the EU legislation. The Open Method of Coordination, which we mentioned in Chapter 5 in relation to the Employment Guidelines, might be a useful process in this area by setting common objectives and benchmarks and providing for the exchange of good practices.

The European Commission is, in its own words, looking for 'a more positive approach to equality'. However, where do the Member States stand in this? Will the Year create enough political determination to take further action against discrimination? The Commission appears to be using the language of equal opportunities and to be emphasizing the idea of equal opportunities for all more and more often. It is suggested that it is doing so with the idea that if this language of equal opportunities is used and repeated often enough, the terms might become so familiar to the Member States that they will accept more and stronger measures to tackle inequality and barriers in society. In this way the use of the language might act as a catalyst for more EU action, both legislative and non-legislative, against discrimination.

6.6 Conclusion

In this Chapter, we have analyzed which concepts of equality can be detected in the Race Directive. The definition of direct discrimination is a clear example of formal equality. However, the definition in the Directive goes some way towards remedying some of the problems identified in relation to the formal equality concept. First, it allows for a hypothetical comparator and this will make it easier for victims to prove discrimination. Second, the non-regression clause of Article 6 prohibits Member States from complying with the principle of equal treatment by levelling-down the protection provided. Levelling-down by private actors, however, does not fall under this clause.

Although its stated purpose seems to suggest that the Directive aims at equal treatment, there are indications that it goes in fact beyond the formal concept towards a more substantive concept of equality. The inclusion of a concept of indirect discrimination recognizes that an apparently neutral provision can have a disparate effect on some people because they have faced historical and structural impediments to equality. The definition of indirect discrimination in the Directive is thus partly about equality of opportunity and partly about equality of results, but, even though it is a step away from formal equality, it does not quite fit in with either concept. The Directive allows for justification of indirect discrimination, but we have argued that such justification should only be allowed in very limited circumstances and, therefore, every justification must be subjected to a very strict scrutiny.

It is clear from Article 5, Recital 17 and the Explanatory Memorandum to the Proposal for the Race Directive (COM (1999) 566) on positive action, that these provisions promote substantive equality as they recognize the accumulated disadvantage suffered by some groups and allow Member States to take measures to make up for this. This is confirmed by the case law on positive action under Article 2(4) of the Equal Treatment Directive. However, the Directive itself does not give any indication of how far such measures can go, and neither are there any indications in the other Article 13 EC Equality Directives. The case law in the sex discrimination field suggests that positive measures aiming at equality of opportunity are allowed, but that positive action which goes further and aims at equality of results is not. We advanced a number of arguments for allowing a broader interpretation, especially in the case of positive measures permitted under the Race Directive, although there are also arguments against this.

However, the Commission's Report on the application of the Race Directive under Article 17 (COM (2006) 643) suggests that the Commission does not want to go beyond the case law in sex discrimination cases and accept broader positive action measures under Article 5 of the Race Directive.

A pluralist concept of equality can be detected in Recitals 8 and 12 of the Race Directive, which stress the importance of participation of all groups, and in Articles 11, 12, 17 and Recital 23, which can be seen as promoting participation. It can also be found in the changes made by the Treaty of

Lisbon and in a number of articles in the European Charter of Fundamental Rights stressing equality and respect for diversity, pluralism, tolerance and solidarity. But, these are all very general statements which could very well remain mere rhetoric.

However, the mainstreaming duty in relation to all Article 13 EC grounds laid down in Articles 8 and 10 TFEU could be useful, because it makes authorities focus on equality and non-discrimination issues. If the duty is interpreted as an obligation to promote equality, diversity and tolerance in all policies and decisions then it would aim at substantive and pluralist concepts of equality.

We showed that a shift is taking place in the EU in the language about equality and that the EU is moving towards a more substantive concept of equality. Prohibiting discrimination and prescribing equal treatment are no longer seen as sufficient to tackle patterns of inequality and disadvantage suffered by some groups. There is recognition that vulnerable groups face barriers to full participation in society. At the time of adoption of the Race Directive, the Commission's main concern appeared to be to create common minimum standards of protection in all Member States. Once these standards were laid down, the notion of different concepts of equality entered the discussion. The EU experience in the field of gender discrimination that formal equality is not enough to tackle existing inequalities influenced this development.

Despite the fact that this shift in language is not likely, in the near future, to lead to an extension of the EU legislation against discrimination towards more substantive and pluralist concepts of equality – for example by requiring rather than allowing positive action – it could be significant for two reasons. First, it might influence non-legislative measures and policies. We suggested that, for example, the Open Method of Coordination could be useful in the anti discrimination field, by setting common objectives and benchmarks and providing for the exchange of good practices. Second, by frequently using the language of equal opportunities and emphasizing that patterns of disadvantage and barriers to participation of ethnic minorities and other disadvantaged groups need to be tackled, this language might become common currency in the Member States and their willingness to work towards a more substantive equality for all might grow. The shift in the language might, in this way, lead to stronger and more effective measures – both legislative and non-legislative – against discrimination.

7 Conclusions and proposals for change

7.1 Introduction

In Chapter 1, the history of the fight against racism and racial discrimination in the EU was discussed and this was followed, in Chapter 2, by an analysis of the protection against (racial) discrimination provided by international and European human rights instruments. These two chapters not only set the scene for the subsequent closer examination of the Race Directive in relation to definitions of race, racism and racial discrimination in Chapters 3 and 4 and to different concepts of equality in Chapters 5 and 6, but they also provided a set of standards against which to measure the Directive in this Chapter.

The first part of this Chapter contains conclusions based on the previous chapters including the gaps in protection left by the Race Directive as it is at present. The second part gives an assessment of the question whether the Race Directive has improved the protection against discrimination on the grounds of racial or ethnic origin. The concluding part contains a number of suggested proposals for changes which should be made to the Race Directive to make it a more effective tool to fight racism and race discrimination in the EU.

It is important to bear in mind that the Race Directive cannot be seen as a completely separate entity which was adopted and exists in a vacuum. This is precisely the reason why the Race Directive has weaknesses and leaves gaps in the protection it provides. It is not a theoretical exercise to make the perfect legislation against racial or ethnic origin discrimination but it is a practical instrument. The Directive was the product of negotiations and required unanimity for its adoption. In the negotiations, developments in thinking about the notions of race and racism and concepts of equality, existing national and EU measures against discrimination, like the EU sex discrimination provisions, and developments in international human rights played an important role. It must be stressed that not only is there a degree of overlap between these areas, but also that these areas have been both influenced by and are influential on each other, in other words, all these areas must be seen as mutually interacting.

7.2 Conclusion

7.2.1 The EU and the fight against racial discrimination

Chapter 1 traced the development of the fight against racism and racial discrimination within the EU. Until the early 1990s, there was no real commitment to take Community action except in the European Parliament and within NGOs. The other EU institutions appear to have made some very general statements but these were not followed by any legislative or other measures or action against racial discrimination. However, from the early 1990s, support for Community action began to grow. In 1994, the Council of the EU set up a Consultative Commission on Racism and Xenophobia, which, in its final report in 1995, recommended amendment of the EC Treaty to explicitly establish the Community's competence to act against discrimination. This amendment took place with the Treaty of Amsterdam in 1997, which came into force on 1 May 1999. The Treaty added Article 13 to the EC Treaty and so established competence for the Community to 'take appropriate action to combat discrimination based on sex, racial or ethnic origin, religion or belief, disability, age and sexual orientation'. The Commission used this competence very quickly and proposed, in November 1999, the adoption of two directives – the Race and Framework Directives – and an Action Programme. The Race Directive was adopted in June 2000, followed in November of the same year by the Framework Directive and the Action Programme. The latter was designed to complement and support the two Directives because a combination of legislation and practical action was thought to be the most effective in fighting discrimination.

During the drafting of the Proposals and the negotiations that followed, there did not appear to be much discussion about what concepts of equality the measures were aiming for. The Commission was guided by existing EU sex discrimination measures and by the legislation against racial discrimination that existed in some of the Member States and focused on achieving the adoption of the proposals. As both indirect discrimination and positive action were familiar from the EU sex discrimination legislation, there appears to have been a consensus that these should be included in any legislation against discrimination on other grounds. Therefore, the legislative measures adopted on the basis of Article 13 EC all prohibit both direct and indirect discrimination and provide for positive action.

In December 2000, the Charter of Fundamental Rights for the European Union was proclaimed at the Council meeting in Nice. This Charter is important for our subject because it lays down the guarantee that everyone is equal before the law and has a right to equal protection of the law. It also contains a clear prohibition of discrimination on an extensive and open-ended list of grounds which includes race, colour and ethnic or social origin. Once the Treaty of Lisbon comes into force, the Charter will become legally binding.

From late 2004 onwards, a shift in the language on equality and non-discrimination can be detected in the EU. People started to use the term equal opportunities rather than the term equal treatment which was common currency until that time. The European Commission also showed an interest in going beyond formal equality or equal treatment towards a more substantive equality concept.

2008 saw the issue of a Commission proposal to extend the protection against discrimination on the grounds covered by the Framework Directive – religion or belief, disability, age and sexual orientation – and the adoption of the Framework Decision on Combating Certain Forms and Expressions of Racism and Xenophobia by means of Criminal Law.

As far as implementation of the Race Directive goes, after a slow start, it appears that all but one of the Member States have transposed the Directive and the Commission is in contact with a number of Member States to ensure correct and complete transposition.

7.2.2 *International human rights instruments to combat discrimination*

In Chapter 2, we examined the anti discrimination clauses in international human rights instruments. The ravages of World War II, with its abuse of theories of race and racism, were to be avoided in future and to this end the UN and the Council of Europe were established. Fundamental human rights were seen as vitally important in achieving greater unity between all nations and, therefore, the UDHR, the ICCPR, the ICESCR and the ECHR were adopted. These measures can be seen as setting international standards of human rights. Because these fundamental human rights should be enjoyed by everyone without discrimination, anti discrimination clauses can be found in all these instruments.

According to Article 6 TEU, one of the founding principles of the Union is respect for human rights and fundamental freedoms. The Lisbon Treaty will add a new Article 2 to the TEU which expresses this even stronger: 'The Union is founded on the values of respect for human dignity, freedom, democracy, equality, the rule of law and respect for human rights…'. Article 6 TEU also determines that the Union shall respect the fundamental rights guaranteed by the ECHR and the rights that result from the constitutional traditions common to the Member States. As all Member States are parties to most of the international instruments discussed in Chapter 2, the rights guaranteed in these measures can be said to be part of their common constitutional traditions.

The EU institutions have always placed the right to equality and non-discrimination firmly within the wider European and international human rights measures. This explicit adherence to international human rights standards gives the EU anti discrimination legislation more legitimacy and improves the image of the EU in both the Member States – towards its own citizens – and on the international scene. And, as the prohibition of racial discrimination is part of *ius cogens*, the EU shows, in legislating against such discrimination, that it respects international law.

The ICERD has been signed and ratified by all Member States and has had an impact on their laws because it prescribes in Article 2(d) that States Parties shall prohibit and bring to an end racial discrimination by any persons, group or organization, by all appropriate means, including legislation. The ICERD prohibits both direct and indirect discrimination, like the Race Directive, and it puts an obligation on State Parties to take positive action measures. On positive action the Convention, therefore, goes further than most legislative instruments against discrimination, including the Race Directive, which allow but do not require positive action.

The ECHR is particularly important within the EU because both Article 6 TEU and the European Charter of Fundamental Rights specifically refer to it and because the EU will accede to this Convention when the Treaty of Lisbon comes into force. In Chapter 2, we discussed that the Charter determines that, when Charter rights correspond to the rights guaranteed by the ECHR, the meaning and scope of the rights will be the same as that of the ECHR rights. According to the Explanatory Memorandum to the Charter (CONV 828/1/03 REV 1), the reference to the ECHR covers not only the text of the Convention and the Protocols to it, but also the case law of the European Court of Human Rights and of the ECJ. The Convention and its case law are, therefore, important aids in interpreting the Charter and the EU anti discrimination legislation.

Like the Race Directive, all the international measures discussed in Chapter 2 prohibit both direct and indirect discrimination and allow – in the case of the ICERD require – positive action measures. They thus have elements of both formal and substantive equality concepts. Most also contain general statements about tolerance and respect which fit in the pluralist concept of equality. The big difference between these measures and the Directive lies in their enforcement. International measures are often not strictly legally enforceable and sanctions for non-compliance are largely ineffective, but they have a more political and persuasive force. Many states sign and ratify them to improve their public image both at home and on the international stage, and they stick to them because they do not want to look bad. In contrast, the Race Directive is binding on the EU Member States, which have a legal duty to implement it. They can be taken to the ECJ when they do not (fully) comply with this duty or when Member States' interpretations of substantive obligations under the Directive are challenged.

The international human rights instruments are thus important for the Race Directive and for EU anti discrimination law because they are part of its historical foundation; because adherence to the international standards of human rights that they set provides the EU with legitimacy; and because they can act as an aid to interpretation.

7.2.3 Definitions of race, racism and racial discrimination and the Race Directive

In Chapter 3, definitions of race, racism and racial discrimination were analyzed and, in Chapter 4, this analysis was used to assess the Race Directive in relation to these terms. The terms are central to a discussion of the Directive, but their meaning, as used within the EU, is not always very clear or consistent. The terms race and racism are historically and socially specific and should, therefore, always be studied within the time and society in which they occur. Before the eighteenth century, the term race was not very commonly used, but if it was used it denoted a group of people with a common line of descent or a common ancestry. In the eighteenth century, race became a subject of the biological sciences, which saw the world's population as being made up of people of different races, each with their own biological characteristics. However, this biological distinction became linked to ideas that some races were superior to other races and that it was, therefore, justified to exclude, suppress or exterminate people of inferior races. The extermination of Jews and Gypsies during World War II and the *Apartheid* regime in South Africa are clear examples.

The term racism is used in two distinctive ways; either to denote the belief that races have distinctive biological or cultural characteristics determined by hereditary factors and that this endows some races with intrinsic superiority; or to indicate not only this belief but also the behaviour based on it. In studying racism and racial discrimination it should be kept in mind not only that some people do make the distinction, but also that, in practice, the terms racism and racial discrimination are often merged with little apparent difference between the two.

In the 1930s, scientists disproved the theories about biological differences and it now appears to be generally accepted that there is no scientific evidence that supports theories that there are different, separate, biological races. Despite this, biological notions of race appear to persist in both political discourse and popular thinking. Because of the abuse/misuse of theories of race, both the terms race and racism are negatively loaded. Ethnicity is, therefore, sometimes used instead of race and xenophobia instead of racism because these terms appear to have a less negative connotation. Ethnicity or ethnic (origin) is also used together with race, especially in the EU, as in Article 13 EC and the Race Directive. The term discrimination is also most commonly used in a negative way as it is linked to a moral judgment that discrimination is unjustified and unlawful.

The negotiations for the Race Directive show clearly that, in many Member States, the terms racism and racial discrimination are still very sensitive issues because the term race is still very much associated with theories of race and the atrocities of World War II they gave rise to. This is confirmed by the explicit rejection, in Recital 6, of theories which attempt to determine the existence of separate human races. And it was not only the (then 15) EU Member States which felt the need for such an explicit statement, as is clear from ECRI General Recommendation 7 which contains a similar statement.

The fact that race and racism were and still are sensitive subjects might help explain, first, why it took the EU such a long time to take action against racism and racial discrimination. And, second, it helps explain why a definition of the key terms race, racism and racial or ethnic origin are notably absent from the Directive. The problems during the negotiations suggest that it might have been too difficult to reach a consensus on the definitions of these terms. However, as the Race Directive contains minimum requirements only, the Member States can go beyond these if they wish to do so and they are thus free to define race and racism in their national laws.

The terms race and racism are usually not defined in legislation, while racial discrimination often is. It was suggested that it might well be better for the legislator not to give a definition of racism, but to define racial discrimination only. The reason for this is that it is difficult to define an ambiguous and social constructed concept like racism in a way that would be useful in court proceedings. It might be better to define those acts which are based on racist beliefs as unlawful race discrimination.

We concluded that Article 3(2) of the Race Directive means that there are gaps in the protection of third-country nationals against racial or ethnic origin discrimination and that these gaps are not remedied by the provisions of the European Charter of Human Rights. In the third part of this chapter, we will suggest some ways of filling this gap.

Within the EU, the protection against racial or ethnic origin discrimination is stronger than the protection provided by the Framework Directive against discrimination on the grounds of religion or belief, disability, age or sexual orientation, because the Race Directive has a wider material scope, only allows for very limited exceptions and includes a duty to establish an equality body/bodies. The first and third of these differences will disappear once the 2008 Proposal (COM (2008) 426) to extend the protection against discrimination on the grounds of religion and belief, disability, age and sexual orientation outside the employment field has been adopted, although the prohibition of gender discrimination will still have a more limited coverage than the other Article 13 EC grounds. The stronger protection provided by the Race Directive in 2000 was partly the result of the then existing strong political will to combat as many aspects of racial discrimination as possible.

The question whether there were differences in character between the discrimination grounds which could justify a difference in protection was discussed and it was concluded that race does not affect a person's ability or availability to do a job or use a good or service and it is an ascription of something that does not exist. This might make race particularly invidious as a ground for discrimination and this might also justify stronger protection against racial discrimination.

However, the difference in levels of protection could lead to problems because it necessitates clear distinctions between the grounds. This is especially problematic with the grounds of racial or ethnic origin and religion or belief, because these grounds are often very closely related and overlapping, especially in the mind of discriminators. The difference in protection can also lead to a problem in cases of multiple discrimination.

7.2.4 Concepts of equality and the Race Directive

In Chapter 5, we distinguished four concepts of equality which could be the goal of equality or non-discrimination law: formal equality, two concepts of substantive equality, equality of opportunity and equality of outcome, and pluralism. In Chapter 6, we examined which of these can be detected in the Race Directive. The formal equality concept can be clearly seen in the definition of direct discrimination as less favourable treatment of a person on the grounds of racial or ethnic origin. However, the Directive addresses some of the problems of the concept of formal equality identified. First, the Race Directive allows for a hypothetical comparator, as all the Article 13 EC Equality Directives do, and this should make it easier for victims to prove discrimination. Second, the non-regression clause in Article 6 of the Race Directive – a similar clause is found in the other Equality Directives – prevents levelling down by the Member States. Unfortunately, private actors are not covered by this prohibition. And, third, the problem that the formal equality concept ignores existing inequalities and social disadvantages created by past discrimination is partially addressed by the inclusion of a prohibition of indirect discrimination and a provision for positive action.

The Directive does not appear to do anything to avoid the problem that legislation aiming at formal equality leads to strong conformist and assimilationist pressures nor does it create any room for respect for difference or for the recognition of its positive aspects. The Directive also does not appear to go beyond a focus on the individual in enforcement procedures and remedies, but the provisions leave the details of this to the Member States.

Can the Race Directive be said to have substantive equality as its aim in any of its provisions? If so, is this equality of opportunity or equality of results or both? Three points suggest that the Directive goes beyond the formal concept towards a more substantive concept of equality. First, the use of the words 'put into effect'; second, the inclusion of a concept of indirect discrimination in the meaning of the principle of equal treatment; and, third, the opinion of the ECJ that the 1976 Equal Treatment Directive aimed to arrive at real equality of opportunity. As the stated purpose of the 1976 Directive was followed in the Race, Framework and Equal Treatment (Goods) Directives and the 2008 Proposal, the opinion expressed by the ECJ should be applicable for these measures as well.

The Directive's prohibition of indirect discrimination takes account of differences and of the unequal impact of seemingly neutral provisions or measures, applied to all persons equally, and, therefore, it goes beyond formal equality towards a more substantive concept, although it is not always clear whether the aim of the provision is to establish equality of opportunity or equality of results. The move towards substantive equality is somewhat tempered by the possibility of justification: indirect discrimination is not unlawful if it is objectively justified by a legitimate aim and the means of achieving that aim are appropriate and necessary. Therefore, business or administrative interests could objectively justify treatment that has an adverse impact on some people. We have argued that the national courts and the ECJ should always scrutinize justifications of indirect racial or ethnic origin discrimination very strictly, both because race can and should be seen as a suspect ground and because justifications can be used to promote either pluralism/multiculturalism or assimilation.

The Race Directive allows the Member States to take positive action measures 'to prevent or compensate for disadvantages linked to racial or ethnic origin'. It thus permits preferential treatment of historically disadvantaged groups and aims at substantive equality. Whether this aims at equality of opportunity or at equality of results will depend on what the ECJ is prepared to accept as permitted positive action. The discussion has shown that there are arguments both for and against a broader interpretation than the ECJ has allowed in sex discrimination cases up to now, which could go further towards equality of results. However, the Commission's Report under Article 17 of the Directive (COM (2006) 643) indicates that the Commission is not prepared to allow for a broader interpretation. We submitted that this is unfortunate and will make suggestions as to how the EU could deal with this in the third part of this Chapter.

There are also some traces of the pluralist concept of equality to be found in the Race Directive in Recitals 8 and 12 of the Preamble and Articles 11, 12 and 17 and Recital 23, which can all be seen as promoting participation.

We discussed some provisions of the Race Directive that move it beyond a concept of equal treatment, like the duty imposed on the Member States by Article 13 of the Directive to designate a body or bodies for the promotion of equal treatment. The work of these bodies is proactive and preventative as they aim at promoting and establishing factual equality. These bodies can influence policy-making at national and EU level and can be involved in the development of new anti discrimination measures. The Member States are under the same duty in relation to gender equality and such a duty has also been proposed in relation to religion or belief, disability, age and sexual orientation (COM (2008) 426).

The mainstreaming duty in relation to all Article 13 EC grounds which will be introduced when the Lisbon Treaty comes into force moves beyond formal equality. However, the question whether a mainstreaming obligation aims at equality of opportunity, equality of results or at a pluralist concept of equality, depends very much on how it is implemented and interpreted. Nevertheless, a mainstreaming duty laid down in legislation – like the mainstreaming duty to be introduced by the Treaty of Lisbon – is a positive step which clearly goes beyond formal equality.

When the Race Directive was adopted there appeared to be little consideration of the different concepts of equality. However, from the end of 2004, a shift in the language at EU level towards more substantive and pluralist ideas of equality can be detected. There is now recognition of the need to go beyond the prevention of unequal treatment and of the fact that positive action may be necessary to compensate for the structural barriers and long-standing and deep-rooted inequalities that some groups experience. The term equal opportunities has been mentioned more frequently and there is also a greater emphasis on mainstreaming non-discrimination and equal opportunities. The 2005 Communication (COM (2005) 224) and the Proposal for a European Year of Equal Opportunities for All (COM (2005) 225) also stress the importance of social inclusion and of the promotion of full and equal participation of all groups in society.

There is thus a definite shift in the language towards equal opportunities and more substantive and pluralist concepts of equality and, although it appears unlikely that this shift in language will lead to legislative changes in the near future, it might well lead to other measures and policies and so, in time, to further legislation. The shift in the language is important because it will make the terms equal opportunities and positive action common currency and this might lead to the Member States becoming more familiar and, following on from this, more willing to accept legislation based on substantive and pluralist concepts of equality. That the Commission is proposing to extend the protection against discrimination on the grounds of religion or belief, disability, age and sexual orientation beyond the areas of employment and occupation is a sign that developments have taken place in the Member States since the adoption of the Race and Framework Directives. In 2000, it was considered that this extended protection was only possible and likely to be accepted against racial or ethnic origin discrimination but the Member States have now moved on from that and the Commission must consider that the time is right to go further.

7.3 Has the Race Directive improved the protection against racial or ethnic origin discrimination within the EU?

The second part of this Chapter examines whether the Race Directive improves the protection against discrimination on the grounds of racial or ethnic origin for people within the EU using the in-depth evaluation of the Directive and the standards provided in the previous Chapters.

In our view, the answer is yes, the Race Directive has improved the protection of victims of racial or ethnic origin discrimination in the EU. It has established common minimum standards and has put the EU Member States under a legally enforceable duty to ensure that their national laws conform to this minimum standard. In doing so, the Directive has added value to the protection against racial or ethnic origin discrimination provided for at both national and international level. At national level, all Member States had to adopt new legislation or amend existing legislation.[1] For some Member States, the transposition of the Directive meant that completely new legislation against discrimination had to be adopted while other countries already had laws in place, but these laws needed to be amended to bring them in line with the Directive.

In its imposition of a legally enforceable obligation to adopt legislation, the Directive goes beyond the international human rights instruments because their enforcement is problematic. The ICERD also imposes duties on Member States, including an obligation to take positive action measures but, again, the enforcement provisions are vague and the sanctions provided are largely ineffective. Article 14 ECHR is problematic because it is accessory in character and can only be used in conjunction with another article of the ECHR. To compound the problem, the European Court of Human Rights did not find a breach of Article 14 on the grounds of racial discrimination until 2004, although it now appears to be more willing to accept that racial discrimination in violation of Article 14 has occurred, as is clear from the case law discussed in Chapter 2. Protocol 12 to the ECHR provides a freestanding right to equality and non-discrimination, but, to date, it has only been ratified by a small number of EU Member States. However, it has to be pointed out that, although the protection under international human rights instruments is not as strong as that under the Race Directive, the greater willingness of the European Court of Human Rights to find a breach shows that this Court is taking racial discrimination more seriously. This, together with its developing case law, could be influential in the ECJ's interpretation of the Race Directive.

It was suggested, in Chapters 5 and 6, that equality in all its types is needed to fight racism and racial discrimination and that legislation should aim at all four concepts of equality in order to ensure real equality for all, or, in Fredman's words, should aim at redressing racist stigma, stereotyping, humiliation and violence (formal equality); at breaking the cycle of disadvantage associated with groups defined by race or ethnicity (substantive equality: equality of opportunity and equality of results); and at positively affirming the accommodation of difference as a part of the right to equal concern and respect (pluralist concept of equality) (Fredman 2001a: 15).

If we see this as the ultimate goal of legislation against racial and ethnic origin discrimination or, put in another way, as the end goal of a road to racial equality for all, then the Race Directive, although an important step on the

1 For information on the different measures in existence in the 15 Member States which were Members when the Race Directive was adopted in 2000 see European Commission 2000.

road towards this goal, is 'only the end of the beginning. Much has still to be done to ensure the right to non-discrimination for all the peoples of Europe' (Brown 2002: 227). In its provisions against direct discrimination, against unfavourable or unequal treatment, it has made a huge step towards fulfilling the first requirement. Such legislation based on the formal equality concept is useful and indeed necessary as a minimum requirement. The Directive has made a step towards the second concept of equality of opportunity by permitting positive action, but, considering the Commission's Report on the Race Directive, it appears to be unlikely that this will go further towards a concept of equality of results. However, there will be no progress at all towards substantive equality in this respect if Member States do not take any positive action. The Directive has also made a cautious step towards substantive equality in prohibiting indirect discrimination. In a very tentative way, the Directive could also be said to go some way towards a pluralist concept of equality in that it contributes to a more tolerant society because it fights discrimination and intolerance. However, it does not contain any provisions for positive duties or for a duty to mainstream equality and diversity.

Therefore, the value which the EU provisions add to the existing national and international measures against discrimination lies in the setting of minimum, enforceable standards of protection against racial and ethnic origin discrimination across the EU. As Chopin *et al.* (2004: 1) write 'through the European Union legislator, standards have been significantly raised in at least 25 countries'. And, as mentioned in Chapter 1, all but one Member State have transposed the Race and Framework Directives (COM (2008) 426: 3) and the Commission has sent reasoned opinions for lack of complete or correct transposition to a number of Member States and is in contact with these States about this, so the Commission is working to achieve full and correct transposition in all Member States.

Whether the recent shift in the language about equality at EU level will lead to (legislative or other) measures which will move the EU further towards achieving equality of opportunity, equality of results and pluralism or, in other words, further towards performing all three functions which are required of equality if it is to fight racism and racial discrimination, remains to be seen. The emphasis on mainstreaming equal opportunities and the incorporation of a mainstreaming duty in relation to all Article 13 EC grounds in the Treaty of Lisbon is encouraging in this respect. A study of the legislation on positive duties which exists in some of the Member States might also suggest possible future steps EU legislation could take.

The Race Directive is 'only the end of the beginning' because, at present, it does not yet ensure full, factual equality for 'all the peoples in Europe' (Brown 2002: 227). We have highlighted a number of areas where the Directive falls short of providing full protection: the exception of nationality made in its Article 3(2); the omission of religion or belief under its grounds; the permissive and possibly restricted scope of positive action; and the fact that its main aim is to establish formal equality rather than a more substantive concept of equality because of an absence of more proactive and preventative provisions, which affords only limited protection to disadvantaged groups in society. The next part of this Chapter will make some suggestions as to how to deal with these shortcomings.

7.4 Proposals for change

As all but one Member State have transposed the Race Directive, it can be said that there is now a minimum standard of protection against racial and ethnic origin discrimination across the EU. Although some Member States may fall in some ways below this minimum standard because of incomplete or incorrect implementation, all but one have legislation against racial discrimination in place and the Commission is working towards getting all Member States to conform to the minimum standards laid down. Nevertheless, there are a number of improvements which could be made to the Directive in order to make it a stronger instrument against such discrimination. In this book, we have concentrated on legislative measures against racism and racial discrimination and, in particular, on the EU legislation in this area, i.e. the Race Directive. Nevertheless, the other EU measures against discrimination based on Article 13 EC have been mentioned where this was considered necessary. The same will apply in this part of Chapter 7 and, although we will not suggest any detailed changes to the other Equality Directives, many of the proposed changes to the Race Directive could and should also be made in the same way in the other Equality Directives. This is based on our opinion that all Directives, and possible future Directives adopted on the basis of Article 13, should, wherever possible, contain the same definitions, provisions and exceptions and unnecessary differences in wording should be avoided, as this would only create confusion and make interpretation more difficult. The 2008 Proposal (COM (2008) 426) to extend the coverage of the protection against discrimination on the grounds of religion or belief, disability age and sexual orientation is a step towards achieving this.

7.4.1 Nationality discrimination

In Chapter 4, it was mentioned that the Race Directive has been criticized for not defining key terms like race or racial origin, racism and ethnic origin. Member States are free to decide on whether they want to include definitions of these terms in their national legislation, as the Directive contains minimum requirements only. Some examples of definitions were given, but we would suggest that it would be preferable to define racial discrimination in legislation but to omit a definition of racism because of the problematic nature of this term.

The Race Directive prohibits discrimination on the ground of 'racial or ethnic origin' and we argued, in Chapter 4, that these terms can and should be interpreted as including colour and descent. However, Article 3(2) of the

Directive contains an explicit exception of nationality from its coverage, despite Article 3(1) declaring that the Directive applies to 'all persons'. The omission of nationality is problematic because, first, the distinction between nationality and racial origin discrimination is not always easy to draw. And, second, third-country nationals are only given limited protection, as they are not protected against nationality discrimination under Article 12 EC and Article 3(2) of the Race Directive limits their protection against racial discrimination in relation to immigration laws or other legal acts covering entry, residence and legal status.

As described in Chapter 4, the negotiations on the proposed scope of the Race Directive show that this is a very sensitive area as it touches on a State's sovereignty and the division of power between the Member States and the Union (Tyson 2001: 209–10). But is Article 3(2) really necessary? According to the Commission, admission policies were not included in the material scope of the Directive, so national systems as regards immigration and asylum would not be covered (Ibid). Therefore, Article 3(2) does not appear to be necessary and, as it could be used to deny third-country nationals protection in a very wide range of situations, it should be taken out of the Directive.

Alternatively, two other possible ways of building in safeguards for the protection of third-country nationals can be found in Articles 1(2) and 1(3) of the ICERD and the Race Directive could follow either of these. As all 27 EU Member States have signed and ratified the ICERD, it appears to be logical to look at that Convention for guidance. One alternative would be to only allow the exceptions mentioned in Article 3(2) if they are objectively justified by a legitimate aim and the means of achieving that aim are appropriate and necessary. This would follow the interpretation of Article 1(2) ICERD given by the CERD in point 1, 4 of its General Recommendation 30 on discrimination of non-citizens, discussed in Chapter 2. A similar objective justification test could be added to Article 3(2) of the Race Directive. This could also cover the police, law enforcement officials, border control officials, and the army and prison personnel in all their activities, including law enforcement in relation to immigration and asylum. These officials could then use the exceptions of Article 3(2) only as long as that use was objectively justified. So an amendment on these lines would build in an objective test, which could be scrutinized by the courts.

The other alternative would be to follow Article 1(3) ICERD, which reads:

> Nothing in this Convention may be interpreted as affecting in any way the legal provisions of State Parties concerning nationality, citizenship or naturalization, provided that such provisions do not discriminate against any particular nationality.

The first alternative would provide more protection for third-country nationals against discrimination than the second alternative, but both would be an improvement on the present situation. However, removal of Article 3(2) would provide the surest protection for non-EU nationals against abuse of the exceptions and thus give them the widest protection. After all, as Recital 3 of the Directive explicitly states: 'The right to equality before the law and protection against discrimination for all persons constitutes a universal right' and Article 3(1) also states that the Directive applies to 'all persons'. Of course, it should be remembered that the Member States can go beyond the Race Directive's minimum requirements and thus can leave the exception out of their national legislation against race discrimination or determine that the legislation also covers nationality.

7.4.2 *Discrimination on the grounds of religion and belief*

We have also argued for including religion and belief in the grounds protected by the Race Directive because religion is often closely related to racial and ethnic origin and it can be difficult to draw a distinction between the two. This is problematic because, at present, the protection provided by the Race Directive is more extensive than that provided by the Framework Directive. However, once the 2008 proposal (COM (2008) 426) is adopted, the protection against discrimination on the ground of religion and belief will extend to all areas outside the employment field covered by the Race Directive; and there will be a duty to designate a body or bodies for the promotion of equal treatment of all persons irrespective of their religion or belief, disability, age or sexual orientation. Does this not provide protection against religion or belief discrimination which is very close to the protection under the Race Directive against racial discrimination and, therefore, make it no longer necessary to include religion and belief in the Directive? Although the protection will be much closer to the protection offered by the Race Directive, one important difference remains: the justification of direct race discrimination is limited to two specific situations while justification of direct discrimination on the grounds of religion and belief is covered by the general exception of Article 2(5) and an additional genuine occupational requirement in Article 4(2) of the Framework Directive. Article 2(5) – and Article 2(8) of the 2008 Proposal which is identical to Article 2(5) – determines:

> This Directive shall be without prejudice to measures laid down by national law which, in a democratic society, are necessary for public security, for the maintenance of public order and the prevention of criminal offences, for the protection of health and the protection of the rights and freedoms of others.

Skidmore (2001: 129–30) calls this 'the most surprising and also most worrying permitted derogation from the equality principle' in the Framework Directive and writes that it is 'questionable, why this extra derogation, not considered necessary in sex or race discrimination law, was included'. He advocates that the ECJ 'is vigilant in the use of this derogation' because otherwise 'there is a risk that it could be used by Member States to perpetuate discrimination'. As we saw in Chapter 4, the need for Article 4(2) of the Framework Directive has also been questioned but both articles are present and applicable to discrimination on the grounds of religion and belief, and, therefore, the protection against such discrimination, even after adoption of the 2008 Proposal, is less strong than the protection against race discrimination under the Race Directive and this forms the basis for our argument that religion or belief should still be added to the grounds covered by that Directive. Support for this argument can also be found in the fact that the Framework Decision 2008 covers both race and ethnic origin and religion.

7.4.3 *Concepts of equality*

The formal equality concept is probably the concept most strongly represented in the Race Directive, but there are also some indications that the Directive goes beyond this towards a more substantive concept of equality in its provisions against indirect discrimination and for positive action.

In relation to the title and purpose, it would be better if all the other Directives followed the Recast Directive and mention 'the implementation of the principle of equal opportunities and equal treatment'; or, alternatively, 'the implementation of the principle of equality', as this appears to reflect more closely that the purpose of all EU Equality Directives goes beyond formal equality toward more substantive equality. It also reflects the often expressed opinion of the ECJ that the principle of equality (and the Court mentions equality rather than equal treatment), is a fundamental principle of Community law; and it is more in line with the shift in language that has been taking place at the EU level.

7.4.3.1 *Indirect discrimination*

Legislation prohibiting indirect discrimination aims beyond formal equality towards a more substantive concept, which contains elements of both equality of opportunity and equality of results. The Race Directive's provision against indirect discrimination thus shows a move towards substantive equality but the provision for justification should, as we have argued, be interpreted strictly and the ECJ should apply a very exacting test before it accepts justifications for indirect race discrimination.

7.4.3.2 *Positive action*

Article 5 of the Race Directive allows the Member States to provide for positive action and this is another move toward a substantive concept of equality, but whether this is equality of opportunity or equality of results depends on the interpretation by the ECJ. The ECJ's interpretation of Article 2(4) of the Equal Treatment Directive and Article 141(4) EC has always been quite restrictive as to what measures are allowed and its case law has thus 'been framed largely by the notion of equality of opportunities' (Poiares Maduro 2005: 25). We advanced some arguments for a broader interpretation of Article 5, but the European Commission's report under Article 17 of the Race Directive (COM (2006) 643: 7–8) seems to suggest that broader measures will not be allowed.

In the Report, the Commission itself points out that attitudes towards positive action vary hugely across the Member States (Ibid: 8). Ellis (2002: 298) writes that the differences in wording of Article 5 of the Race Directive, Article 2(4) of the Equal Treatment Directive and Article 141(4) EC and the 'notoriously inscrutable' case law of the ECJ on the equivalent sex discrimination provisions, are 'evidence of deep political and philosophical tensions which surround the whole matter of positive action'. She argues that:

> because of the legitimate scope for a wide diversity of views on the role of positive action, this is an area where it is unacceptable to leave the resolution of the meaning of the law entirely in judicial hands.

This suggests that Ellis is in favour of a path requiring more detailed guidance from the EU legislator on what measures are allowed.

In contrast, the existence of a wide variety of views in this area leads Caruso (2003: 333) to argue for a path where more discretion is given to the Member States. She writes that the ECJ is likely to interpret the positive action clauses of the new directives 'along the lines of its previous scrutiny of gender programs'. This is 'a chapter of E.U. history that should not be written' (Ibid). Caruso argues strongly for a policy of restraint in the ECJ's scrutiny of positive action cases. Poiares Maduro (2005: 26) also suggests giving the Member States a certain margin of discretion. He writes:

> It cannot be excluded that the reference in Article 141 EC to compensatory measures has as its aim providing a broader margin of discretion to Member States in adopting measures of positive discrimination. The issue here for the ECJ, and the decision that it has to take regarding admissibility of affirmative action and positive discrimination measures adopted by the Member States, is not actually whether affirmative action is the best way to fight discrimination and to reinstate equality in the labour market, but whether to give Member States a margin of discretion to decide what is compatible with the principle of equality. ... In my view, in an area such as this that is subject to intense discussion and scrutiny, it may be appropriate for the court to allow for some diversity

of national political choice regarding the extent to which Member States adopt affirmative action measures.

As mentioned, the ECJ sees positive action as a derogation of the principle of equal treatment. In the *Lommers* case, the ECJ held that its case law on derogations from an individual right was applicable to positive action measures. This case law had introduced a proportionality test for such derogations. As the ECJ considered:

> According to settled case law, in determining the scope of any derogation from an individual right such as the equal treatment of men and women laid down by the Directive, due regard must be had to the principle of proportionality, which requires that derogations must remain within the limits of what is appropriate and necessary in order to achieve the aim in view and that the principle of equal treatment be reconciled as far as possible with the requirements of the aim thus pursued.
>
> (Para 39)

Therefore, a proportionality test is already applicable to positive action measures within the EU. Allowing the Member States a margin of discretion might lead to the development of some interesting and innovative measures that could be used as examples of good practice for other Member States. The proportionality test introduced by the ECJ would ensure that the Member States cannot take just any measure they see fit because they must be able to objectively justify any positive action legislation. It is submitted that, rather than limiting positive action measures to what has thus far been permitted in the ECJ sex discrimination case law, like the Commission appears to do in the Report mentioned, or providing more guidance as to what measures are allowed in more detailed legislation at EU level, as Ellis seems to advocate, it is preferable to allow the Member States some discretion provided this is subject to a proportionality test. More detailed legislation at this level is likely to limit, rather than expand, the measures permitted.

Suggestions have also been made to make positive action mandatory, as it is under the ICERD, rather than permissive as it is at present. This means that there could be significant differences between the individual Member States with some taking extensive positive action measures while others do not. As we have seen, the EU Commission expressed the opinion that positive action may be necessary to compensate for the structural barriers and deep-rooted inequalities that some groups face and that measures to promote participation and social inclusion are important. It could therefore be argued that Member States who do not take any positive action measures would appear to act against this. And, if the Commission is of the opinion that positive measures are necessary, would this not be an argument for making these measures mandatory?

Paragraph 5 of ECRI's General Recommendation 7 does not appear to provide for mandatory positive action. However, it mentions that

> the law should provide that the prohibition of racial discrimination does not prevent the maintenance or adoption of temporary special measures designed either to prevent or compensate for disadvantages suffered by certain persons ... or to facilitate their full participation in all fields of life.

The EU Member States could follow this text and add the latter part of this paragraph to their legislation. Such a duty, including the facilitation of participation, mandatory or permissive, would certainly go further towards substantive and pluralist concepts of equality.

7.4.3.3 Mainstreaming

The Treaty of Lisbon will establish a mainstreaming duty in relation to all grounds of Article 13 EC. However, this mainstreaming duty is imposed on the Union, and not on the Member States. A gender equality mainstreaming duty is imposed on the Member States by Article 29 of the Recast Directive, which echoes an amendment made to Article 1 the 1976 Equal Treatment Directive by the Equal Treatment (Amendment) Directive and reads as follows:

> Member States shall actively take into account the objective of equality between men and women when formulating and implementing laws, regulations, administrative provisions, policies and activities in the areas referred to in this Directive.

This duty could and should be extended to cover all the Article 13 grounds by adding a similar paragraph to both Race and Framework Directives. There appears to be no reason why such a duty should only exist in relation to gender discrimination. The Race and Framework Directives were influenced by the then existing sex discrimination legislation and, in turn, the Equal Treatment (Amendment) Directive was adopted in order to bring the equal treatment provisions in relation to sex discrimination more in line with those Directives. In other words, the Race and Framework Directives have been influenced by, but have also been influential upon, EU sex discrimination legislation. Parmar (2004: 135) writes that 'there now seems to be a *reflexive cross-fertilisation* [her italics] process between EU race and gender equality law in particular, in which legislative definitions are borrowed, adapted and integrated'. The Race Directive (and the Framework Directive) could, therefore, 'borrow, adapt and integrate' Article 1(1) of the Equal Treatment (Amendment) Directive/Article 29 Recast Directive. The fact that the Treaty of Lisbon extends the mainstreaming duty to those other grounds seems to indicate that extending the duty to all the Article 13 EC grounds would not meet with major objections. The changes brought by the Treaty of Lisbon and the suggested change to the Race and Framework would put both the Union and the Member States under a duty to mainstream equality issues in all their policies and activities.

The Member States themselves could also follow ECRI's recommendation that national law 'should place public authorities under a duty to promote equality and to prevent discrimination in carrying out their functions'[2] and impose a mainstreaming duty on (public) authorities in their countries. A good example is the positive duty introduced by the British Race Relations (Amendment) Act 2000. This Act places a general duty on public authorities, in performing their public functions, to 'have due regard to the need: (a) to eliminate unlawful racial discrimination; and (b) to promote equality of opportunity and good relations between persons of different racial groups' (S 71(1) Race Relations Act 1976 as amended). The Act contains a very wide list of public authorities caught by the duty.

A mainstreaming duty, a duty to promote equality, participation and good relations, would move the Race Directive firmly towards substantive equality and pluralism.

7.5 ECJ case law

As the Race and Framework Directives were adopted in 2000 and should have been implemented before the end of 2003, the ECJ has had a number of opportunities to interpret some of their provisions. In Chapter 2, it was mentioned that the ECJ in both the *Mangold* (para 75) and the *Chacon Navas* (para 56) cases mentioned the principle of non-discrimination as a general, fundamental principle of Community law. In the *Mangold* case, the ECJ held that 'the principle of non-discrimination on the ground of age must thus be regarded as a general principle of Community law'. In the European Anti Discrimination Law Review (No. 3, 2006: 46), it is stated that:

> The principle of non-discrimination as a general principle of Community law, on the grounds of age and, by analogy, on the other grounds of Community law means that 'it is the responsibility of the national court, hearing a dispute involving the principle of non-discrimination in respect of age, to provide, in a case within its jurisdiction, the legal protection which individuals derive from the rules of Community law and to ensure that those rules are fully effective, setting aside any provision of national law which may conflict with that law' [para 77]. This new jurisdiction creates the possibility of the evolution of a body of non-discrimination

2 ECRI General Policy Recommendation 7: para 8 (ECRI 2007: 52). Point 27 of the Memorandum to the Recommendation elaborates on the duty and mentions that 'it would be desirable were the private sector also placed under a similar obligation' (Ibid: 63).

> law going beyond the existing secondary legislation through the direct application of the general principle of non-discrimination, if the ECJ is prepared to continue in the direction taken in this decision.[3]

In this case, the measure in question was held to be directly discriminatory on the ground of age and not to be objectively and reasonably justified. To be objectively and reasonably justified, the measure must have a legitimate aim and the means of achieving this aim must be proportionate; in other words, must be objectively necessary to attain this aim (para 65). Schiek *et al.* (2007: 152) mention that this makes clear that the ECJ 'will not apply a marginal test of arbitrariness to age distinctions' but will 'apply at least an intermediate intensity of review'.

This seems to be confirmed in the case of *Felix Palacios,* where the question put to the ECJ was whether the prohibition of direct age discrimination under the Framework Directive precluded a national law from allowing compulsory retirement clauses to be included in collective agreements. The ECJ held that the Framework Directive was applicable to the situation and that there was unfavourable treatment on the grounds of age. Such treatment constitutes discrimination unless it is 'objectively and reasonably justified by a legitimate aim, including legitimate employment policy, labour market and vocational training objectives, and if the means of achieving that aim are appropriate and necessary' (para 52).[4]

In the case of *Tadao Maruko,* a compulsory occupational pension scheme afforded a widower's pension for spouses but not for same-sex registered partners. It was held that such a pension scheme was to be classified as pay under Article 141 EC and that Recital 22 of the Framework Directive, which determines that 'the Directive is without prejudice to national laws on marital status and the benefits dependent thereon', did not prevent the application of anti discrimination law. The refusal to grant the survivor's pension to life partners thus constituted direct discrimination on grounds of sexual orientation.

In the *Coleman v Attridge Law* case, Mrs. Coleman claimed that she was discriminated against and harassed by her employer because she had a disabled son. The ECJ held that the Framework Directive's prohibition of discrimination and harassment is not limited only to people who are themselves disabled (para 38). In other words, the ECJ held that discrimination by association with a disabled person was also covered by the Framework Directive. And as the definitions of discrimination and harassment on the

3 However, the national provision must fall within the scope of Community law, as is clear from the *Chacon Navas* (para 56) and the *Birgit Bartsch* (para 25) cases.

4 See on this also the so-called *Heyday* case: *R on behalf of the Incorporated Trustees of the National Council on Ageing (Age Concern England) v Secretary of State for Business, Enterprise and Regulatory Reform.*

grounds of religion or belief, age, sexual orientation and racial or ethnic origin are the same, it can be argued, by analogy, that discrimination by association on all grounds covered by the Race and Framework Directives is prohibited.

The ECJ has, so far, only delivered one judgment in relation to the Race Directive. This was the case of *Centrum voor Gelijkheid van Kansen en voor Racismebestrijding v NV Firma Ferijn*. In this case, one of the directors of the Ferijn company publicly stated that his company did not wish to recruit immigrants because his customers were reluctant to give them access to their private residence for the period of the works. The Centre for Equal Opportunities and Opposition to Racism, the Belgian body designated under Article 13 of the Race Directive, brought the case. Under Belgian law, the Centre can be a party to judicial proceedings where discrimination exists or could exist without a prior complaint being necessary in this regard. The ECJ held that:

> The fact that an employer states publicly that it will not recruit employees of a certain ethnic or racial origin constitutes direct discrimination in respect of recruitment within the meaning of Article 2(2)(a) of Directive 2000/43, such statements being likely strongly to dissuade certain candidates from submitting their candidature and, accordingly, to hinder their access to the labour market.
>
> (Para 28)

The ECJ also held that the statements were enough for a presumption of the existence of a discriminatory employment policy, and that thus the burden of proof shifted to the employer, who had to prove that its recruitment policy was not discriminatory. Finally the ECJ held that in a case such as this '*where there is no direct victim of discrimination* [our italics], but a body empowered by law to do so seeks a finding of discrimination and an imposition of a penalty', the sanctions must be, in accordance with Article 15 of the Race Directive, effective, proportionate and dissuasive. This is an important case because it makes it possible to complain about discriminatory advertisements without a direct victim.

These cases suggest that the ECJ is prepared to give an interpretation to the Race and Framework Directives which could extend the possible reach of these Directives to include discrimination by association and cases where there is no direct victim. They also show that the ECJ is likely to require at a minimum 'an intermediate intensity of review' for justification of direct age discrimination (Schiek *et al.* 2007: 152). And if the ECJ applies an intermediate scrutiny to justifications of direct age discrimination, where the legislation allows a fairly wide range of justifications, it might apply a more intensive scrutiny test for justifications in relation to the Race Directive, which only allows for justification of indirect discrimination. This would be a positive development.

7.6 Concluding remarks

The Race Directive has made a significant contribution to establishing a minimum standard of protection against racial discrimination in all Member States and in this it is performing Fredman's (2001a: 15) first function of equality, in that it redresses racist stigma, stereotyping, humiliation and violence. The Directive has also made some contribution towards the second function of breaking the cycle of disadvantage associated with groups defined by race or ethnicity by allowing for indirect discrimination and positive action, but there is little in the Directive in relation to the third function of positively affirming the accommodation of difference as a part of the right to equal concern and respect.

In the last part of this Chapter, we have proposed changes to the Race Directive which would go further towards the second and third functions because we are of the opinion that equality and non-discrimination should perform all three functions to be an effective tool in the fight against racism and racial discrimination, in other words it should aim at all the concepts of equality distinguished in the previous chapters.

We suggested three alternative ways of dealing with Article 3(2) of the Directive and its exception for nationality discrimination. All three would provide third-country nationals with better protection against race discrimination, although dropping the paragraph altogether would provide the strongest protection.

Religion and belief should be added to the grounds covered by the Race Directive as, even if the protection against religious discrimination is levelled-up to cover all areas covered by the Race Directive, the existing justifications for direct discrimination on the grounds of religion and belief under Article 2(5) and 4(2) of the Framework Directive make this protection weaker.

We also suggested a number of ways in which the aim and purpose of the Race Directive could move further towards substantive and pluralist concepts of equality. One of these was that the ECJ should apply a very exacting test before it accepts justifications for indirect race discrimination. This would make the protection against indirect discrimination stronger. Putting the Member States under a duty to take positive action would ensure that they will all take some measures. We have argued that it would be preferable if the EU legislator and the ECJ allowed the Member States a certain measure of discretion as this could lead to some innovative positive measures. Imposing a duty to take positive action measures to make up for historical disadvantage on the Member States will increase the use of such measures. Leaving some discretion to the Member States as to how far these measures can go, provided these measures remain within the limits of what is appropriate and necessary in order to achieve the aim of ensuring full equality in practice, will allow Member States some freedom to aim for both equality of opportunity and equality of results through positive action but with an opportunity for scrutiny by the ECJ.

The Race Directive could also follow paragraph 5 of ECRI's General Recommendation 7 and add 'or to facilitate the full participation of groups disadvantaged on the grounds covered by this Directive in all fields of life'. This would bring an element of the pluralist concept of equality into the Race Directive. Adding a mainstreaming duty similar to the duty in Article 29 of the Recast Directive would add another element.

The ECJ's case law to date, although mainly on the Framework Directive, shows some signs that the ECJ is prepared to give both Race and Framework Directives a broad interpretation.

With the proposed changes, the Race Directive would aim towards achieving all four concepts of equality and would represent a big step towards promoting equality rather than just equal treatment. However, we would strongly argue that, although legislative measures against discrimination aiming to achieve all four concepts of equality are necessary, law should never be seen as the only way to fight racism and racial discrimination, it should be one of a number of tools that each complement and strengthen each other. Therefore, the Directive (and the other Equality Directives based on Article 13 EC), even with the suggested changes, cannot be the only tool at EU level to fight (racial) discrimination and promote (racial) equality. The legislation should be supported by other, non-legislative measures, not only dealing with (racial or other) discrimination, but also with, for example, human rights, employment, social inclusion and integration of immigrants. Some examples of such measures at EU level, most of which have been mentioned already, are: the stress in the Employment Guidelines since 1999 on preventive and active policies to promote an inclusive labour market; the policies for combating social exclusion via the European Structural Funds like the European Social Fund and via the open method of coordination;[5] the Action Programme 2001–2006, adopted in November 2000 and dealing with discrimination on all Article 13 EC grounds. After it was finished, a similar programme was incorporated in the social policy programme Progress (Decision No. 1672/2006/EC); the European Charter of Fundamental Rights; the creation of a Group of Commissioners responsible for fundamental rights, anti-discrimination and equal opportunities in 2004 (Barroso 2004: 3); the impact assessment the Commission carries out for all new proposals (SEC (2001) 380 and COM (2005) 172); the Communication from June 2005 on a Framework Strategy for Non-discrimination and Equal Opportunities for All (COM (2005) 224); the Proposal to designate 2007 as the European Year of Equal Opportunities for All (COM (2005) 225); and the establishment of a High-level Advisory Group on Social Integration of Ethnic Minorities and their Full Participation in the Labour Market (Commission Decision 2006). The 2005 Communication contains a number of supportive measures: it

5 This was decided on by the Lisbon European Conference in 2000. See para 32 of the *Presidency Conclusions* 2000. See also COM (2005) 706 and Bell 2008a: 118–127.

stresses the importance of mainstreaming non-discrimination and equal opportunities for all. It mentions that the Commission will aim to ensure that a range of EU funding instruments contribute to the promotion of non-discrimination and equal opportunities for all, especially through promoting exchanges of good practice, cooperation and networking between national authorities, specialized equality bodies, organizations working with victims of discrimination, and other stakeholders. The Commission also proposes an annual high-level Equality Summit to bring together key stakeholders (COM (2005) 224: 7–9). And in order to support policy development to tackle discrimination and social exclusion faced by disadvantaged ethnic minorities, the Commission plans to establish a high-level advisory group on social and labour market integration of these disadvantaged ethnic minorities (Ibid: 10).

A concerted effort on all fronts is necessary to move the fight against discrimination and the establishment of real equality in the EU forward. It appears that the EU is trying to make that effort in a number of ways mentioned above. The Race and the other Equality Directives are part of this process. Therefore, the Race Directive represents a significant step, but it should be seen as only the first step towards greater racial equality for all. It is important because it moved the EU along on its journey to equality and, thereby, laid the foundation for the protection against racial or ethnic origin discrimination for everyone in the EU. The challenge is now to build on this foundation in all policies and activities of the Union, including both the legislative framework and other policy initiatives. From the shift in language within the EU and the proposal to extend the areas in which discrimination on the grounds of religion or belief, disability, age and sexual orientation is prohibited, it appears that the Commission is keen to progress further along the road towards equality on all Article 13 EC grounds. The ECJ appears to be willing to do its bit towards this as well. Therefore, although the road is long and progress often very slow, the EU is moving towards more equality for all.

Bibliography

Agreement between the European Community and the Council of Europe for the Purpose of establishing, in accordance with Article 7(3) of Council Regulation (EC) No. 1035/97 of 3 June 1997 establishing a European Monitoring Centre on Racism and Xenophobia, Close Cooperation between the Centre and the Council of Europe [1999] OJ L 44/34.

Agreement between the European Community and the Council of Europe on Cooperation between the European Union Agency for Fundamental Rights and the Council of Europe [2008] OJ L186/7.

Alibhai-Brown, Y. (2000) "Race Relations in New Britain" in: Anwar, M., Roach, P. and Sondhi, R. (eds) *From Legislation to Integration? Race Relations in Britain* (Basingstoke: Macmillan Press) 178–95.

Allen, R. (1999) "Article 13 and the Search for Equality in Europe: An Overview" in: Europaforum Wien (eds) *Article 13 – Antidiscrimination: the Way Forward* (Vienna: Europaforum).

Allen, R. (2007) "Article 13 EC, Evolution and Current Context" in: Meenan, H. (ed.) *Equality Law in an Enlarged European Union Understanding the Article 13 Directives* (Cambridge: Cambridge University Press) 38–72.

Allott, A. (1980) "Limits on the Utility of Law for Social Transformation" in: Allot, A. *The Limits of Law* (London: Butterworth) 161–237.

Annual Plan of Work and Budget Breakdown A13/002/2005 January to December 2006 http://www.antigone.gr/listpage/community_documents/action_programmes/070517.pdf (accessed 20 April 2009).

Austria Fails to Implement EU Race Anti-discrimination Law 4 May 2005 http://ec.europa.eu/employment_social/news/2005/may/austria_en.html (accessed 20 April 2009).

Bacik, I. (1997) "Combating Discrimination: The Affirmative Action Approach Developments in Affirmative Action Law in Ireland and Europe" in: Byrne, R. and Duncan, W. (eds) *Developments in Discrimination Law in Ireland and Europe* (Dublin: Irish Centre for European Law) 119–30.

Bagley, C. (1973) *The Dutch Plural Society: A Comparative Study in Race Relations* (London/Oxford: Institute of Race Relations/Oxford University Press).

Ballard, R. (1994) "The Emergence of Desh Pardesh" in: Ballard, R. (ed.) *Desh Pardesh: The South Asian Presence in Britain* (London: Hurst and Company) 1–34.

Ballard, R. (1996) "Negotiating Race and Ethnicity: Exploring the Implications of the 1991 Census" 30, 3, *Patterns of Prejudice* 3–33.

Banton, M. (1983) "Changing Conceptions of Race" in: Banton, M. *Racial and Ethnic Competition* (Cambridge: Cambridge University Press) 32–59.

Banton, M. (1985) *Promoting Racial Harmony* (Cambridge: Cambridge University Press).

Banton, M. (1992) "The Nature and Causes of Racism and Racial Discrimination" 7, 1, *International Sociology* 69–84.

Banton, M. (1994) *Discrimination* (Buckingham: Open University Press).

Banton, M. (1996) *International Action against Racial Discrimination* (Oxford: Clarendon Press).

Banton, M. (2002a) *The International Politics of Race* (Cambridge: Polity Press).

Banton, M. (2002b) "International Report Lessons from the 2001 World Conference Against Racism" 28, 2, *Journal of Ethnic and Migration Studies* 355–66.

Barnard, C. (1998) "The Principle of Equality in the Community Context: *P, Grant, Kalanke and Marschall*: Four Uneasy Bedfellows?" 57, 2, *Cambridge Law Journal* 352–73.

Barnard, C. (1999) "Article 13: Through the Looking Glass of Union Citizenship" in: O'Keeffe, D. and Twomey, P. (eds) *Legal Issues of the Amsterdam Treaty* (Oxford: Hart Publishing) 375–95.

Barnard, C. (2001) "The Changing Scope of the Fundamental Principle of Equality?" 46, 4, *McGill Law Journal* 955–77.

Barnard, C. and Hepple, B. (2000) "Substantive Equality" 59, 3, *Cambridge Law Journal* 562–85.

Barroso, J. (2004) SPEECH/04/474 Speech to the European Parliament, 26 October 2004.

Barry, E. (2003) "Different Hierarchies – Enforcing Equality Law" in: Costello, C. and Barry, E. (eds) *Equality in Diversity The New Equality Directives* (Dublin: Irish Centre for European Law/Irish Equality Authority/Ashfield Publishing) 409–34.

Bell, M. (2000) "The New Article 13 EC Treaty: a Platform for a European Policy against Racism?" in: Moon, G. (ed.) *Race Discrimination. Developing and Using a New Legal Framework* (Oxford/Portland, Oregon: Hart Publishing) 81–112.

Bell, M. (2001) "Meeting the Challenge? A Comparison between the EU Racial Equality Directive and the Starting Line" in: Chopin, I. and Niessen, J. (eds) *The Starting Line and the Incorporation of the Racial Equality Directive into the National Laws of the EU Member States and Accession States* (Brussels/London: Migration Policy Group/Commission for Racial Equality) 22–54.

Bell, M. (2002a) *Anti-Discrimination Law and the European Union* (Oxford: Oxford University Press).

Bell, M. (2002b) "Combating Racism through European Laws: A Comparison of the Racial Equality Directive and Protocol 12" in: Chopin, I. and Niessen, J. (eds) *Combating Racial and Ethnic Discrimination: Taking the European Legislative Agenda Further* (Brussels/London: Migration Policy Group/Commission for Racial Equality) 7–35.

Bell, M. (2003a) "The Right to Equality and Non-Discrimination" in: Hervey, T. and Kenner, J. (eds) *Economic and Social Rights under the EU Charter of Fundamental Rights – A Legal Perspective* (Oxford/Portland, Oregon: Hart Publishing) 91–110.

Bell, M. (2003b) "European Union Strategies to Combat Racism and Xenophobia as a Crime" in: Nickel, R., Coomber, A., Bell, M., Hutchinson, T. and Zahi, K. (eds)

European Strategies to Combat Racism and Xenophobia as a Crime (Brussels: European Network Against Racism) 31–8.

Bell, M. (2004) "Equality and the European Constitution" 33, 3, *Industrial Law Journal* 242–60.

Bell, M. (2005) "Combating Racial Discrimination through the European Employment Strategy" in: Bell, J. and Kilpatrick, C. (eds) 6, *Cambridge Yearbook of European Legal Studies 2003–2004* (Oxford/Portland, Oregon: Hart Publishing) 55–71.

Bell, M. (2007) "EU Anti-Racism Policy; the Leader of the Pack?" in: Meenan, H. (ed.) *Equality Law in an Enlarged European Union Understanding the Article 13 Directives* (Cambridge: Cambridge University Press) 178–201.

Bell, M. (2008a) *Racism and Equality in the European Union* (Oxford: Oxford University Press).

Bell, M. (2008b) *Extending EU Anti-Discrimination Law: Report of an ENAR Ad Hoc Expert Group on Anti-Discrimination Law* (Brussels: European Network Against Racism).

Bell, M. and Waddington, L. (2003) "Reflecting on Inequalities in European Equality Law" 28, *European Law Review* 349–69.

Bell, M., Chopin, I. and Palmer, F. (2007) *Developing Anti-Discrimination Law in Europe. The 25 EU Member States compared* (Luxembourg: OOPEC).

Benedict, R. (1983) *Race and Racism* (London: Routledge & Kegan Paul).

Bernard, N. (1996) "What are the Purposes of EC Discrimination Law" in: Dine, J. and Watt, B. (eds) *Discrimination Law: Concepts, Limitations and Justifications* (London: Longman) 77–99.

Blom, J. (2000) "Pillarisation in Perspective" 23, 3, *West European Politics* 153–64.

Boyle, K. and Baldaccini, A. (2001) "A Critical Evaluation of International Human Rights Approaches to Racism" in: Fredman, S. (ed.) *Discrimination and Human Rights The Case of Racism* (Oxford: Oxford University Press) 135–92.

Brennan, F. (2002/2003) "The Race Directive: Recycling Racial Inequality" 5, *Cambridge Yearbook of European Legal Studies* 311–31.

Brennan, F. (2004) "The Race Directive, Institutional Racism and Third Country Nationals" in: Takis, T. and Nebbia, P. (eds) *European Union Law for the Twenty-First Century* (Volume 2) (Oxford/Portland Oregon: Hart Publishing) 371–86.

Brown, C. (2002) "The Race Directive: Towards Equality for *All* the Peoples of Europe?" 21, *Yearbook of European Law* 195–227.

Bryan, I. (2002) "Equality and Freedom from Discrimination: Article 13 EC Treaty" 24, 2, *Journal of Social Welfare and Family Law* 223–38.

Bryant, C. (1981) "Depillarisation in the Netherlands" 32, 1, *British Journal of Sociology* 56–74.

Bryant, C. (1997) "Citizenship, National Identity and the Accommodation of Difference: Reflections on the German, French, Dutch and British Cases" 23, 2, *New Community* 157–72.

Bulmer, M. and Solomos, J. (1999) (eds) *Racism* (Oxford: Oxford University Press).

Cahn, C. (2005) "Towards Realising a Right to Positive Action for Roma in Europe: Connors v UK" 1, *Roma Rights Quarterly* www.errc.org/cikk.php?cikk=2160 (accessed 17 April 2009).

Caruso, D. (2003) "Limits of the Classic Method: Positive Action in the European Union after the New Equality Directives" 44, *Harvard International Law Journal* 331–86.

Centre for Strategy and Evaluation Services (2007) *Non-Discrimination Mainstreaming – Instruments, Case Studies and Way Forwards* (Sevenoaks: European Commission DG for Employment, Social Affairs and Equal Opportunities and CSES).

Charter of Fundamental Rights of the European Union [2000] OJ C 364/1.

Charter of European Parties for a Non-Racist Society, adopted at Utrecht, 28 February 1998 www.art1.nl/artikel/2017-Charter_of_European_Political_Parties_for_a_non-racist_society (accessed 17 April 2009).

Chopin, I. (1999) "The Starting Line Group: A Harmonized Approach to Fight Racism and to Promote Equal Treatment" 1, *European Journal of Migration and Law* 111–29.

Chopin, I. and Niessen, J. (1998) (eds) *Proposals for Legislative Measures to Combat Racism and to Promote Equal Rights in the European Union* (London: Belmont Press).

Chopin, I., Cormack, J. and Niessen, J. (eds) (2004) *The Implementation of European Anti Discrimination Legislation: Work in Progress* (Brussels: Migration Policy Group).

Cohen, B. (2005) "Positive Obligations: Shifting the Burden in Order to Achieve Equality" 1, *Roma Rights Quarterly* (2005) www.errc.org/cikk.php?cikk=2161 (accessed 17 April 2009).

Coliver, S. (ed.) (1992) *Striking a Balance, Hate Speech, Freedom of Expression and Non-Discrimination* (London/Colchester: Article 19/Human Rights Centre University of Essex).

COM (1988) 318, *Proposal for a Council Resolution on the Fight against Racism and Xenophobia.*

COM (1989) 471, *Community Charter of Fundamental Social Rights.*

COM (1994) 333, *European Social Policy – a Way Forward for the Union*: a White Paper.

COM (1995) 653, *Communication of the Commission on Racism, Xenophobia and Anti-Semitism, and Proposal for a Council Decision designating 1997 as European Year against Racism.*

COM (1996) 615, *Proposal for a Council Regulation (EC) establishing a European Monitoring Centre for Racism and Xenophobia.*

COM (1998) 183, *Communication from the Commission An Action Plan against Racism.*

COM (1999) 268, *Report from the Commission on the Implementation of the European Year against Racism* (1997).

COM (1999) 564, *Communication from the Commission to the Council, the European Parliament, the Economic and Social Committee and the Committee of the Regions on Certain Community Measures to Combat Discrimination.*

COM (1999) 565, *Proposal for a Council Directive establishing a General Framework for Equal Treatment in Employment and Occupation.*

COM (1999) 566, *Proposal for a Council Directive implementing the Principle of Equal Treatment between Persons irrespective of Racial or Ethnic Origin.*

COM (1999) 567, *Proposal for a Council Decision establishing a Community Action Programme to combat Discrimination (2001–2006).*

COM (2000) 328, *Amended Proposal for a Council Directive implementing the Principle of Equal Treatment between Persons irrespective of Racial or Ethnic Origin* (presented by the Commission pursuant to Article 250(2) of the EC Treaty).

COM (2001) 291, *Communication from the Commission, Contribution to the World Conference against Racism, Racial Discrimination, Xenophobia and Related Intolerance* (Durban, South Africa, 31 August 2001–7 September 2001).

COM (2001) 664, *Proposal for a Council Framework Decision on Combating Racism and Xenophobia.*

COM (2002) 157, *Proposal for a Council Decision on the Signature of a Euro-Mediterranean Association Agreement between the European Community and their Member States, of the one Part, and the People's Democratic Republic of Algeria on behalf of the European Community.*

COM (2003) 657, *Proposal for a Council Directive implementing the Principle of Equal Treatment between Men and Women in the Access to and Supply of Goods and Services.*

COM (2004) 379, *Green Paper on Equality and Non-discrimination in an Enlarged European Union.*

COM (2004) 693, *Communication from the Commission, The Fundamental Rights Agency Public Consultation Document.*

COM (2005) 172, *Communication from the Commission, Compliance with the Charter of Fundamental Rights in Commission Legislative Proposals.*

COM (2005) 224, *Communication from the Commission to the Council, the European Parliament, the European Economic and Social Committee and the Committee of the Regions, Non-Discrimination and Equal Opportunities for All – A Framework Strategy.*

COM (2005) 225, *Proposal for a Decision of the European Parliament and the Council on the European Year of Equal Opportunities for All (2007) – Towards a Just Society.*

COM (2005) 706, *Communication from the Commission, Working Together, Working Better: A New Framework for the Open Coordination of Social Protection and Inclusion Policies in the European Union.*

COM (2006) 643, *Communication from the Commission to the Council and the European Parliament. The Application of Directive 2000/43/EC of 29 June 2000 implementing the Principle of Equal Treatment Between Persons irrespective of Racial or Ethnic Origin.*

COM (2008) 420, *Communication from the Commission Non-Discrimination and Equal Opportunities: A Renewed Commitment.*

COM (2008) 426, *Proposal for a Council Directive on Implementing the Principle of Equal Treatment between Persons Irrespective of Religion or Belief, Disability, Age or Sexual Orientation.*

Commission Decision 2006/33/EC of 20 January 2006 *Establishing a High-Level Advisory Group on Social Integration of Ethnic Minorities and Their Full Participation in the Labour Market* [2006] OJ L 21/20.

Commissioner P. Flynn, Closing Address, European Conference on Anti-Discrimination: "*The Way Forward*", Vienna, 3–4 December 1998 http://europa.eu/rapid/pressReleasesAction.do?reference=SPEECH/98/282&format=HTML&aged=1&language=EN&guiLanguage=en (accessed 18 April 2009).

Committee on Economic, Social and Cultural Rights (1994) *Concluding Observations on Romania*, 30 May 1994, E/C.12/12/1994/4.

Committee on Economic, Social and Cultural Rights (1999) *General Comment No. 13*.

Committee on Economic, Social and Cultural Rights (2000) *Concluding Observations on Belgium*, 1 December 2000, E/C.12/1/Add. 54.

Committee on the Elimination of Racial Discrimination (1993) General Recommendation 14, *Definition of Discrimination Art 1, par 1*, 22 March 1993.

Committee on the Elimination of Racial Discrimination (2004) General Recommendation 30, *Discrimination against Non-Citizens*, CERD/C/64/Misc.11/rev.3.

CONF 2500/96, Presidency: *Outline for a Draft Revision of the Treaties*, 5 December 1996 www.unizar.es/euroconstitucion/Treaties/Treaty_Amst_Neg.htm (accessed 18 April 2009).

Consolidated Versions of the Treaty on European Union and the Treaty on the Functioning of the European Union [2008] OJ C 115/1.

Contribution from the Commission Services to the Regional European Conference, *"All Different – All Equal": From Theory to Practice*, 17 April 2000.

CONV 828/1/03 REV 1, *Updated Explanations Relating to the Complete Text of the Charter of Fundamental Rights of the European Union (as Amended by the European Convention and Incorporated as Part II of the Treaty on a Constitution of Europe)* 18 June 2003.

Coomber, A. (2003) "The Council of Europe: Combating Racism and Xenophobia" in: Nickel, R., Coomber, A., Bell, M., Hutchinson, T. and Zahi, K. (eds) *European Strategies to Combat Racism and Xenophobia as a Crime* (Brussels: European Network Against Racism) 17–26.

Cormack, J. and Niessen, J. (2005) "The Independence of Equality Bodies" 1, *European Anti-Discrimination Law Review* 23–8.

Costello, C. (2003) "Positive Action" in: Costello, C. and Barry, E. (eds) *Equality in Diversity The New Equality Directives* (Dublin: Irish Centre for European Law/Irish Equality Authority/Ashfield Publishing) 177–212.

Council Decision (1963) 64/732/EEC of 23 December1963 on the *Conclusion of the Agreement establishing the Association between the European Economic Community and Turkey* [1964] OJ 217/3685.

Council Decision (2000a) 2000/750/EC of 27 November 2000 *establishing a Community Action Programme to combat Discrimination (2001 to 2006)* [2000] OJ L 303/23 (Action Programme).

Council Decision (2000b) of 13 March 2000 on *Guidelines for the Member States' Employment Policies for the year 2000* [2000] OJ L 72/15.

Council Decision (2001) of 19 January 2001 on *Guidelines for the Member States' Employment Policies for the year 2001* [2001] OJ L 22/18.

Council Decision (2002) of 21 February 2002 on *Guidelines for the Member States' Employment Policies for the year 2002* [2002] OJ L 60/60.

Council Decision (2003) of 22 July 2003 on *Guidelines for the Member States' Employment Policies* [2003] OJ L 197/13.

Council Directive 76/207/EEC of 9 February 1976 on *the Implementation of the Principle of Equal Treatment for Men and Women as Regards Access to Employment, Vocational Training and Promotion, and Working Conditions* [1976] OJ L 39/40 (Equal Treatment Directive).

Council Directive 79/7/EEC on *the Progressive Implementation of the Principle of Equality for Men and Women in Matters of Social Security* [1979] OJ L 6/24.

Council Directive 86/378/EEC on *the Implementation of the Principle of Equality for Men and Women in Occupational Social Security Schemes* [1986] OJ L 225/40.

Council Directive 86/613/EEC on the *Application of the Principle of Equal Treatment between Men and Women engaged in an Activity, including Agriculture, in a Self-employed Capacity, and on the Protection of Self-employed Women during Pregnancy and Motherhood* [1986] OJ L 359/56.

Council Directive (1997) 97/80/EC of 15 December 1997 on *the Burden of Proof in Cases of Discrimination based on Sex* [1997] OJ L 14/6.

Council Directive 2000/43/EC of 29 June 2000 *implementing the Principle of Equal Treatment between Persons irrespective of Racial or Ethnic Origin* [2000] OJ L 180/22 (Race Directive).

Council Directive 2000/78/EC of 27 November 2000 *establishing a General Framework for Equal Treatment in Employment and Occupation* [2000] OJ L 303/16. (Framework Directive).

Council Directive 2002/73/EC of the European Parliament and of the Council of 23 September 2002 *amending Council Directive 76/207/EEC on the Implementation of the Principle of Equal Treatment for Men and Women as Regards Access to Employment, Vocational Training and Promotion, and Working Conditions* [2002] OJ L 269/15 (Equal Treatment (Amendment) Directive).

Council Directive 2003/109/EC of 25 November 2003 *Concerning the Status of Third-Country Nationals who are Long-Term Residents* [2004] OJ L 16/44.

Council Directive 2004/113/EC of 13 December 2004 *implementing the Principle of Equal Treatment between Men and Women in the Access to and Supply of Goods and Services* [2004] OJ L 373/37 (Equal Treatment (Goods) Directive).

Council Directive 2006/54/EC of 5 July 2006 on *the Implementation of the Principle of Equal Opportunities and Equal Treatment of Men and Women in Matters of Employment and Occupation (recast)* [2006] OJ L 204/23 (Recast Directive).

Council Framework Decision on *Combating Certain Forms and Expressions of Racism and Xenophobia by Means of Criminal Law* 2008/913/JHA [2008] OJ L 328/55.

Council of the European Union (2000a) *Outcome of Proceedings of the Social Questions Working Party*, 6435/00, Brussels, 1 March 2000.

Council of the European Union (2000b) *Outcome of Proceedings of the Social Questions Working Party*, 6942/00, Brussels, 31 March 2000.

Council of the European Union (2000c) *Outcome of Proceedings of the Social Questions Working Party*, 8454/00, Brussels, 16 May 2000.

Council of the European Union (2000d) *Outcome of Proceedings of the Social Questions Working Party*, 9423/00, Brussels 20 June 2000.

Council Regulation 1035/97/EC of 2 June 1997 *establishing a European Monitoring Centre on Racism and Xenophobia* [1997] OJ L 151/1.

Council Regulation 168/2007 of 15 February 2007 *establishing a European Union Agency for Fundamental Rights* [2007] OJ L 53/1.

Council Resolution (1990) of 29 May 1990 on the *Fight against Racism and Xenophobia* [1990] OJ C 157/1.

Council Resolution (1999) on *the 1999 Employment Guidelines* [1999] OJ C 69/2.

Council Resolution (2007) of 5 December 2007 *on the Follow-up of the European Year of Equal Opportunities for All (2007)* [2007] OJ C 308/1.

Council of Europe *Statute of the European Commission against Racism and Intolerance (ECRI)* www.coe.int/t/dghl/monitoring/ecri/about/ECRI_statute_en.asp (accessed 27 April 2009)

Council of Europe, ETS No. 177, *Explanatory Report on Protocol 12 to the Convention for the Protection of Human Rights and Fundamental Freedoms.*

Cox, L. (2002) "The Fight against Discrimination and the International Labour Organisation" 16, 238, *Discrimination Law Association Briefings* 3–8.

de Burca, G. (1997) "The Role of Equality in Community Law" in: Dashwood, A. and O'Leary, S. (eds) *The Principle of Equal Treatment in EC Law* (London: Sweet and Maxwell) 13–34.

Decision No. 1672/2006/EC of the European Parliament and of the Council of 24 October 2006 *establishing a Community Programme for Employment and Social Solidarity — Progress* [2006] OJ L 315/1.

Declaration (1998) by the Council and the Representatives of the Governments of the Member States meeting within the Council of 16 December 1997 on *Respecting Diversity and Combating Racism and Xenophobia* [1998] OJ C 1/1.

de Rooy, P. (1997) "Farewell to Pillarisation" 33, 1, *The Netherlands Journal of Social Sciences* 27–41.

de Schutter, O. (2005) *The Prohibition of Discrimination under European Human Rights Law Relevance for EU Racial and Employment Equality Directives* (Luxembourg: OOPEC).

de Vos, M. (2007) *Beyond Formal Equality Positive Action under Directives 2000/43/EC and 2000/78/EC* (Luxembourg: OOPEC).

Dine, J. and Watt, B. (1996) (eds) *Discrimination Law: Concepts, Limitations and Justifications* (London: Longman).

Discrimination in Europe Eurobarometer 57.0, Special Survey, May 2003.

DROIPEN 34 8544/07 *Proposal for a Council Framework Decision on Combating Racism and Xenophobia*, 17 April 2007.

Drzemczewski, P. (2001) "The Council of Europe's Position with Respect to the EU Charter of Fundamental Rights" 22, 1–4, *Human Rights Law Journal* 14–31.

Dummett, A. (1994) "The Starting Line: A Proposal for a Draft Council Directive Concerning the Elimination of Racial Discrimination" 20, 3, *New Community* 530–8.

Dummett, A. (2000) "Tackling Racism: Britain in Europe" in: Anwar, M., Roach, P. and Sondhi, R. (eds) *From Legislation to Integration? Race Relations in Britain* (Basingstoke: Macmillan Press) 107–23.

Duncan, W. (1997a) "Racism, Discrimination and Amendment of the European Community Treaty and the Treaty on European Union" in: Byrne, R. and Duncan, W. (eds) *Developments in Discrimination Law in Ireland and Europe* (Dublin: Irish Centre for European Law) 43–54.

Duncan, W. (1997b) "Racism and Xenophobia in Europe" in: Barrett, G. (ed.) *Justice Cooperation in the European Union* (Dublin: Institute of European Affairs) 183–94.

Dworkin, R. (1978) "Reverse Discrimination" in: Dworkin, R. *Taking Rights Seriously* (London: Duckworth) 223–39.

Ellis, E. (2002) "The Principle of Non-Discrimination in the Post-Nice Era" in: Arnull, A. and Wincott, D. (eds) *Accountability and Legitimacy in the European Union* (Oxford: Oxford University Press) 291–305.

Ellis, E. (2005) *EU Anti-Discrimination Law* (Oxford: Oxford University Press).

ENARgy, Newsletter from the European Network Against Racism.

Equal Rights in Practice, News Review of the Community Action Programme to Combat Discrimination.

Equal Voices, Newsletter from the European Monitoring Centre on Racism and Xenophobia.

Eurobarometer Opinion Poll, no. 47.1, *Racism and Xenophobia in Europe*. Results presented at the Closing Conference of the European Year against Racism, Luxembourg, 18–19 December 1997.

Euro-Mediterranean Agreement *establishing an Association between the European Communities and their Member States, of the one Part, and the Republic of Tunisia of the other Part* [1998] OJ L 97/2.

Euro-Mediterranean Agreement *establishing an Association between the European Communities and their Member States, of the one Part, and the Kingdom of Morocco of the other Part* [2000] OJ L 70/2.

European Anti-Discrimination Law Review, European Network of Legal Experts in the Non-Discrimination Field.

European Commission (2000) *Report on Member States Legal Provisions to Combat Discrimination* (Luxembourg: OOPEC).

European Commission (2003a) DG for Employment and Social Affairs *Annual Report on Equality and Non-discrimination 2003 Towards Diversity.*

European Commission (2003b) DG for Employment and Social Affairs *Equality, Diversity and Enlargement Report on Measures to Combat Discrimination in Acceding and Candidate Countries.*

European Commission (2003c) DG for Employment, Industrial Relations and Social Affairs *The Costs and Benefits of Diversity A Study on Methods and Indicators to Measure the Cost-Effectiveness of Diversity Policies and Enterprises.*

European Commission (2004a) DG Employment and Social Affairs *Equality and Non-discrimination Annual Report 2004.*

European Commission (2004b) DG for Employment and Social Affairs *Anti-discrimination, Fundamental Rights and Civil Society, Experts Reports on the Implementation of EU Anti-Discrimination Laws regarding Race and Religion.*

European Commission (2005a) DG for Employment and Social Affairs *Anti-discrimination, Fundamental Rights and Civil Society, Experts Reports on the Implementation of EU Anti-Discrimination Laws* Jan-March 2005.

European Commission (2005b) DG Employment, Social Affairs and Equal Opportunities *Equality and Non-Discrimination Annual Report 2005.*

European Commission (2006) Directorate General for Employment, Social Affairs and Equal Opportunities *Equality and Non-discrimination Annual Report 2006.*

European Commission (2007) DG for Employment, Social Affairs and Equal Opportunities *Tackling Multiple Discrimination Practices, Policies and Laws.*

European Commission (2008) DG for Employment, Social Affairs and Equal Opportunities *On-going Evaluation of the 2007 European year of Equal Opportunities for All.*

European Commission against Racism and Intolerance (2007) *Compilation of ECRI's General Policy Recommendations* (Strasbourg: Council of Europe).

European Commission against Racism and Intolerance, CRI (2009) 5 *General Policy Recommendation N°12: Combating Racism and Racial Discrimination in the Field of Sport* Adopted by ECRI on 19 December 2008.

European Council Consultative Commission on Racism and Xenophobia (1995) *Final Report*, Brussels, 6906/1/95, RAXEN 24 REV 1 http://aei.pitt.edu/archive/00001588/ (accessed 20 April 2009)

European Network Against Racism (2005) General Policy Paper 1: *Fighting Religious Discrimination.*

European Parliament (1985) *Committee of Inquiry on the Rise of Fascism and Racism in Europe* (Evrigenis Report) A2-0160/85.

European Parliament (1986) *Resolutions on the Rise of Racism and Fascism in Europe* [1986] OJ C 36/142 and 36/143.

European Parliament (1987) *Resolution on the Growing Number of Crimes Connected with Fascism, Racism and Xenophobia in the Community Countries* [1987] OJ C 190/108.

European Parliament (1988) *Written Declaration on the Fight against Xenophobia and Racism* [1988] OJ C 187/117.

European Parliament (1989) *Resolution on the Proposal from the Commission to the Council on a Resolution concerning the Fight against Racism and Xenophobia* [1989] OJ C 69/43.

European Parliament (1990a) *Committee of Inquiry on Racism and Xenophobia* (Ford Report) A3-0195/90.

European Parliament (1990b) *Resolution on Measures to Combat Racism and Xenophobia* [1990] OJ C 175/178.

European Parliament (1990c) *Resolution on the Report by the Committee of Inquiry on Racism and Xenophobia* [1990] OJ C 284/57.

European Parliament (1990d) *Resolution on the Intergovernmental Conferences in the Context of the European Parliament's Strategy for the European Union* [1990] OJ C 324/219.

European Parliament (1991) *Resolution on Racism and Xenophobia* [1991] OJ C 280/146.

European Parliament (1992a) *Resolution on Support for Demonstrations in Favour of Democracy and Tolerance and against Racism and Xenophobia* [1992] OJ C 94/269.

European Parliament (1992b) *Resolution on the Riots in Rostock-Lichtenhagen and other Cities in the New Lander* [1992] OJ C 284/99.

European Parliament (1992c) *Resolution on Racism, Xenophobia and Anti-Semitism* [1992] OJ C 305/590.

European Parliament (1992d) *Resolution on the Resurgence of Racism and Xenophobia in Europe and the Danger of Right Wing Extremist Violence* [1993] OJ C 150/127.

European Parliament (1993) *Resolution on Racism and Xenophobia* [1993] OJ C 342/19.

European Parliament (1994) *Resolution on Racism, Xenophobia and Anti-Semitism* [1994] OJ C 323/154.

European Parliament (1995a) *Resolution on Racism, Xenophobia and Anti-Semitism* [1995] OJ C 126/75.

European Parliament (1995b) *Resolution on Racism, Xenophobia and Anti-Semitism* [1995] OJ C 308/140.

European Parliament (1996) *Resolution on the Communication from the Commission on Racism, Xenophobia and Anti-Semitism (COM (1995) 653)* [1996] OJ C 152/57.

European Parliament (1997) *Resolution on Racism, Xenophobia and Anti-Semitism and the European Year against Racism* [1997] OJ C 55/17.

European Parliament (1998) *Resolution on Racism, Xenophobia and Anti-Semitism and the Results of the European Year Against Racism (1997)* [1998] OJ C 56/35.

European Parliament (1999) *Resolution on Countering Racism and Xenophobia in the European Union (COM (1999) 268)*, A5-0049/2000.

Feldman, D. (2002) *Civil Liberties and Human Rights in England and Wales* (2nd ed. Oxford: Oxford University Press) 135–65.

Finland and Luxembourg are Found Guilty of Failing to Implement EU Race Anti-Discrimination Law 24 February 2005 http://ec.europa.eu/employment_social/news/2005/feb/anti-discrimination_en.html (accessed 20 April 2009)

Finlay, M. (2003) "Indirect Discrimination and the Article 13 Directives" in: Costello, C. and Barry, E. (eds) *Equality in Diversity The New Equality Directives* (Dublin: Irish Centre for European Law/Irish Equality Authority/Ashfield Publishing) 135–50.

Flynn, L. (1999) "The Implications of Article 13 EC – After Amsterdam, will some Forms of Discrimination be more Equal than Others?" 36, *Common Market Law Review* 1127–52.

Fottrell, D. (1999) "Ever Decreasing Circles: Affirmative Action and Special Measures under International Law" in: Fottrell, D. and Bowring, B. (eds) *Minority and Group Rights in the New Millennium* (The Hague: Martinus Nijhoff Publishers) 183–203.

Fredman, S. (ed.) (2001a) *Discrimination and Human Rights: The Case of Racism* (Oxford: Oxford University Press).

Fredman, S. (2001b) "Equality: A New Generation?" 30, 2, *Industrial Law Journal* 145–68.

Fredman, S. (2002) *Discrimination Law* (Oxford: Oxford University Press).

Fredman, S. (2005) "Double Trouble: Multiple Discrimination and EU Law" 2, *European Anti-Discrimination Law Review* 13–20.

Fredman, S. and Szyszczak, E. (1992) "The Interaction of Race and Gender" in: Hepple, B. and Szyszczak, E. (eds) *Discrimination: The Limits of Law* (London: Mansell) 214–46.

Furedi, F. (1998) *The Silent War: Imperialism and the Changing Perception of Race* (London: Pluto Press).

Gearty, C. (1999) "The Internal and External 'Other' in the Union Legal Order: Racism, Religious Intolerance and Xenophobia in Europe" in: Alston, P. (ed.) *The EU and Human Rights* (Oxford: Oxford University Press) 327–58.

Gelber, K. (2002) *Speaking Back, The Free Speech versus Hate Speech Debate* (Amsterdam/Philadelphia: John Benjamins Publishing Company) 93–115 and 135–7.

Gerards, J. (2004a) "Intensity of Judicial Review in Equal Treatment Cases" 51, *Netherlands International Law Review* 135–83.

Gerards, J. (2004b) "The Application of Article 14 ECHR by the European Court of Human Rights" in: Niessen, J. and Chopin, I. (eds) *The Development of Legal Instruments to Combat Racism in a Diverse Europe* (Leiden/Boston: Martinus Nijhoff Publishers) 3–60.

Germany has failed to Implement EU Race Anti-Discrimination Law 29 April 2005 http://ec.europa.eu/employment_social/news/2005/apr/courtruling_en.html (accessed 20 April 2009)

Goldberg, D. (1999) "The Semantics of Race" in: Bulmer, M. and Solomos, J. (eds) *Racism* (Oxford: Oxford University Press) 362–77.

Goldschmidt, J. (1999) "Back to the Future – an Agenda for a More Equal Future" in: Loenen, T. and Rodrigues, P. (eds) *Non-Discrimination Law: Comparative Perspectives* (The Hague: Kluwer) 437–49.

Goldston, J. (1999) "Race Discrimination in Europe: Problems and Prospects" 5, *European Human Rights Law Review* 462–83.

Goldston, J. (2001) "European Law: New Possibilities in the Fight against Discrimination" 13, 3, *Interights Bulletin* 127–9.

Gregory, J. (1987) *Sex, Race and the Law: Legislating for Equality* (London: Sage).

Grief, N. (2002) "Non-Discrimination under the European Convention on Human Rights: A Critique of the United Kingdom Government's Refusal to Sign and Ratify Protocol 12" 27, *European Law Review*, Human Rights Survey, HR/3-HR/18.

Guild, E. (2000a) "The EC Directive on Race Discrimination: Surprises, Possibilities and Limitations" 29, 4, *Industrial Law Journal* 416–23.

Guild, E. (2000b) "The European Union and Article 13 of the Treaty Establishing the European Community", in: Moon, G. (ed.) *Race Discrimination. Developing and Using a New Legal Framework* (Oxford/Portland, Oregon: Hart Publishing) 65–80.

Guillaumin, C. (1999) "The Changing Face of Race" in: Bulmer, M. and Solomos, J. (eds) *Racism* (Oxford: Oxford University Press) 355–62.

Hannett, S. (2003) "Equality at the Intersections: The Legislative and Judicial Failure to Tackle Multiple Discrimination" 23, 1, *Oxford Journal of Legal Studies* 65–86.

Henrard, K. (2007) *Equal Rights versus Special Rights? Minority Protection and the Prohibition of Discrimination* (Luxembourg: OOPEC).

Hepple, B. (1992) "Have Twenty Five Years of the Race Relations Acts in Britain been a failure?"in: Hepple, B. and Szyszczak, E. (eds) *Discrimination: The Limits of Law* (London: Mansell) 19–34.

Hepple, B. (2000) "Freedom of Expression and the Problem of Harassment" in: Beatson, J. and Cripps, Y. (eds) *Freedom of Expression and Freedom of Information* (Oxford: Oxford University Press) 177–96.

Hepple, B. (2004) "Race and Law in Fortress Europe" 67, 1, *Modern Law Review* 1–15.

Hervey, T. (1999) "Putting Europe's House in Order: Racism, Race Discrimination and Xenophobia after the Treaty of Amsterdam" in: O'Keeffe, D. and Twomey, P. (eds) *Legal Issues of the Amsterdam Treaty* (Oxford: Hart Publishing) 329–49.

Higgins, I. (2003) "Enforcement and the New Equality Directives" in: Costello, C. and Barry, E. (eds) *Equality in Diversity The New Equality Directives* (Dublin: Irish Centre for European Law/Irish Equality Authority/Ashfield Publishing) 391–409.

High Level Advisory group of Experts on the Social Integration of Ethnic Minorities and their Full Participation in the Labour Market (2007) *Ethnic Minorities in the Labour Market: An Urgent Call for Better Social Inclusion* http://www.iza.org/downloads/Ethnic_Minorities_in_the_Labour_Market.pdf (accessed 16 April 2009)

House of Lords Select Committee on European Union, *EU Proposals to Combat Discrimination*, Session 1999-2000, 9th Report, 16 May 2000 www.publications.parliament.uk/pa/ld199900/ldselect/ldeucom/68/6802.htm (accessed 17 April 2009)

Howard, E. (2005) "Anti Race Discrimination Measures in Europe: An Attack on Two Fronts" 11, 4, *European Law Journal* 468–86.

Howard, E. (2006) "The European Union Agency for Fundamental Rights" 4, *European Human Rights Law Review* 445–55.

Howard, E. (2007a) "The Case for a Considered Hierarchy of Discrimination Grounds in EU Law" 13, 4, *Maastricht Journal of European and Comparative Law* 443–68.

Howard, E. (2007b) "The EU Race Directive: Time for Change?" 8, 4, *International Journal of Discrimination and the Law* 237–61.

Howard, E. (2008) "The European Year of Equal Opportunities for All – 2007: Is the EU Moving away from a Formal Idea of Equality?" 14, 2, *European Law Journal* 168–85.

Howard, E. (2009) "School Bans on the Wearing of Religious Symbols: Examining the Implications of Recent Case Law from the UK" 4, 1, *Journal for Religion and Human Rights* 7–24.

Human Rights Committee, General Comment 18: *Non-Discrimination*, 10 November 1989.

Human Rights Committee *Rules of Procedure*, 4 August 2004, CCPR/C/3/Rev. 7.

Iganski, P. (2001) "Hate Crimes Hurt More" 45, 4, *American Behavioral Scientist* 626–38.

Iganski, P. (2002) (ed.) *The Hate Debate: Should Hate be Punished as a Crime* (London: Profile Books/Institute for Jewish Policy Research).

Institute of Race Relations (2008) "Cultural Cleansing" *European Race Bulletin* 18-25.

International Council on Human Rights Policy (2000) *The Persistence and Mutation of Racism* http://www.ichrp.org/files/reports/26/112_report_en.pdf (accessed 17 April 2009).

International Labour Organisation (1988) *Report of the Committee of Experts, Equality in Employment and Occupation*, International Labour Conference, 75th Session, Report III.

International Labour Organisation (1996) *Report of the Committee of Experts, Equality in Employment and Occupation*, International Labour Conference, 83th Session, Report III.

Jacobs, F. (2002) "The EU Charter of Fundamental Rights" in: Arnull, A. and Wincott, D. (eds) *Accountability and Legitimacy in the European Union* (Oxford: Oxford University Press) 275–90.

Jacobs, J. and Potter, K. (1998) *Hate Crimes, Criminal Law and Identity Politics* (Oxford: Oxford University Press).

Jenkins, R. (1967) *Essays and Speeches* (London: Collins) 267.

Johansson, P. (2004) "Comparing National and Community Anti-Discrimination Law" in: Niessen, J. and Chopin, I. (eds) *The Development of Legal Instruments to Combat Racism in a Diverse Europe* (Leiden/Boston: Martinus Nijhoff Publishers) 155–210.

Joint Action (1996), 96/443/JHA, of 15 June 1996 adopted by the Council on the basis of Article K.3 of the Treaty on European Union, *Concerning Action to Combat Racism and Xenophobia* [1996] OJ L 185/5.

Joint Declaration (1986) of the European Parliament, the Council, the Representatives of the Member States meeting within the Council, and the Commission against Racism and Xenophobia [1986] OJ C 158/1.

Joint Statement (2008) of the EU Fundamental Rights Agency and the Council of Europe's Commissioner for Human Rights *on the Durban Review Conference 2008* http://fra.europa.eu/fraWebsite/material/pub/speeches/JointStat-Durban-Review-Conf-051208_en.pdf (Accessed 2 April 2009)

Joint Statement (2009a) *on the Occasion of the International Day for the Elimination of Racial Discrimination (21 March 2009)* Office for Democratic Institutions and Human Rights, the European Commission against Racism and Intolerance and the EU Fundamental Rights Agency http://fra.europa.eu/fraWebsite/attachments/evt-21March-jointstatement-09_en.pdf (accessed 2 April 2009)

Joint Statement (2009b) *on the Occasion of the International Roma Day (8 April 2009)* made by the FRA, the Council of Europe Commissioner for Human Rights, the ODIHR and the OSCE High Commissioner on National Minorities http://fra.europa.eu/fraWebsite/attachments/Roma-day-joint-statement-0409_en.pdf (accessed 21 April 2009)

Jones, T. (2003) "The Race Directive: Redefining Protection from Discrimination in EU Law" 5, *European Human Rights Law Review* 515–26.

King, J. (1995) "Ethnic Minorities and Multilateral European Institutions" in: Hargreaves, A. and Leaman, J. (eds) *Racism, Ethnicity and Politics in Contemporary Europe* (Aldershot: Edward Elgar) 179–91.

Kruger, H. and Polakiewicz, J. (2001) "Proposals for a Coherent Human Rights Protection System in Europe" 22, 1–4, *Human Rights Law Journal* 1–13.

Lacey, N. (1987) "Legislation Against Sex Discrimination: Questions from a Feminist Perspective" 14, 4, *Journal of Law and Society* 411–21.

Lacey, N. (1992) "From Individual to Group?" in: Hepple, B. and Szyszczak, E. (eds) *Discrimination: The Limits of Law* (London: Mansell) 99–123.

Lester of Herne Hill, Lord A. (2000) "New European Equality Measures" *Public Law* 562–7.

Liegl, B., Perching, B. and Weyss, B. (2004) *Combating Religious and Ethnic Discrimination in Employment from the EU and International Perspective* (Brussels: European Network against Racism).

Lijphart, A. (1975) *The Politics of Accomodation: Pluralism and Democracy in the Netherlands* (2nd ed. Berkeley: University of California Press).

Lijphart, A. (1995) "Self-Determination versus Pre-Determination of Ethnic Minorities in Power-Sharing Systems" in: Kymlika, W. (ed.) *The Rights of Minority Cultures* (Oxford: Oxford University Press) 275–87.

Lustgarten, L. (1986) "Racial Inequality and the Limits of Law" 49, *Modern Law Review* 68–85.

Lustgarten, L. (1992) "Racial Inequality, Public Policy and the Law: Where are we Going?" in: Hepple, B. and Szyszczak, E. (eds) *Discrimination: The Limits of Law* (London: Mansell) 455–71.

MacEwen, M. (1995) *Tackling Racism in Europe: An Examination of Anti-Discrimination Law in Practice* (Oxford/Washington: Berg) 1–88 and 174–200.

MacEwen, M. (1997) (ed.) *Anti-Discrimination Law Enforcement: A Comparative Perspective* (Aldershot: Avebury).

McColgan, A. (2003) "Principles of Equality and Protection from Discrimination in International Human Rights Law" 2, *European Human Rights Law Review* 157–75.

McColgan, A. (2005) *Discrimination Law: Text, Cases and Materials* (2nd ed. Oxford/Portland, Oregon: Hart Publishing).

McColgan, A. (2007) "Reconfiguring Discrimination Law" *Public Law* 74–94.

McCrudden, C. (2003) "The New Concept of Equality", 4, 3, *ERA-Forum* 9–29.

McGoldrick, D. (2006) *Human Rights and Religion: the Islamic Headscarf Debate in Europe* (Oxford/Portland, Oregon: Hart Publishing).

McInerney, S. (2002) "Bases for Action against Race Discrimination in EU Law" 27, *European Law Review* 72–9.

McInerney, S. (2003) "Legal Protection against Discrimination based on Racial and Ethnic Origin under European Union Law – Necessary but not Sufficient?" 6, 1, *International Journal of Discrimination and the Law* 3–43.

Mahoney, P. (2002) "The Charter of Fundamental Rights of the European Union and the European Convention on Human Rights from the Perspective of the European Convention" 23, 8–12, *Human Rights Law Journal* 300–3.

Makkonen, T. (2002) *Multiple, Compound and Intersectional Discrimination: Bringing the Experiences of the Most Marginalized to the Fore* (Institute for Human Rights Abo Akademi University).

Martiniello, M. (2004) *How to combine Integration and Diversities: The Challenge of an EU Multicultural Citizenship* (Vienna: European Union Monitoring Centre for Racism and Xenophobia).

Mason, D. (1995) *Race and Ethnicity in Modern Britain* (Oxford: Oxford University Press).

Memo 04/189, *Background Note on Procedures to enforce EU Anti-Discrimination Law*, 19 July 2004.

Menski, W. (1992) "The Indian Experience and its Lessons for Britain" in: Hepple, B. and Szyszczak, E. (eds) *Discrimination: The Limits of Law* (London: Mansell) 300–43.

Menski, W. (1993) "Asians in Britain and the Question of the Adaptation to a New Legal Order: Asian Law in Britain?" in: Israel, M. and Wagle, N. (eds) *Ethnicity, Identity, Migration: The South Asian Context* (Toronto: University of Toronto) 238–68.

Menski, W. (2001) "Muslim Law in Britain" 62, *Journal of Asian and African Studies* 127–63.

Menski, W. (2002a) "Chameleons and Dodgy Lawyers: Reflections on Asians in Britain and their Legal Reconstruction of the Universe" in: *Britain, India and the Diaspora: Changing Social and Historiographical Perceptions, XXVIII, Indo-British Review* (Millennium Issue) 89–103.

Menski, W. (2002b) "Immigration and Multiculturalism in Britain: New Issues in Research and Policy" 12, *KIAPS Bulletin of Asia-Pacific Studies* 43–66.

Miles, R. (1989) *Racism* (London/New York: Routledge).

Moon, G. (2006) *Multiple Discrimination – Problems Compounded or Solutions Found?* (London: JUSTICE) http://www.justice.org.uk/images/pdfs/multiplediscrimination.pdf (accessed 5 April 2009)

Moraes, C. (2000) "Race against Time" *The Guardian* 30 June 2000 www.guardian.co.uk/analysis/story/0,,338078,00.html (accessed 17 April 2009)

More, G. (1999) "The Principle of Equal Treatment: From Market Unifier to Fundamental Right?" in: Craig, P. and de Burca, G. (eds) *The Evolution of EU Law* (Oxford: Oxford University Press) 517–52.

Nathwani, N. (2002) "Atlantic Divide on Fight Against Racist Websites" 10, *Equal Voices* 11–9.

Nickel, R., Coomber, A., Bell, M., Hutchinson, T. and Zahi, K. (2003) (eds) *European Strategies to Combat Racism and Xenophobia as a Crime* (Brussels: European Network Against Racism).

Niessen, J. (2001a) "The Charter for Political Parties for a Non-Racist Society" 3, *European Journal of Migration and Law* 73–89.

Niessen, J. (2001b) "The Further Development of European Anti-Discrimination Policies" in: Chopin, I. and Niessen, J. (eds) *The Starting Line and the Incorporation of the Racial Equality Directive into the National Laws of the EU Member States and Accession States* (Brussels/London: Migration Policy Group/Commission for Racial Equality) 7–21.

Niessen, J. and Chopin, I. (2004) (eds) *The Development of Legal Instruments to Combat Racism in a Diverse Europe* (Leiden/Boston: Martinus Nijhoff Publishers).

O'Donovan, K. and Szyszczak, E. (1988) *Equality and Sex Discrimination Law* (Oxford: Basil Blackwell) 1–20.

O'Flaherty, M. (1997) "The UN Committee on the Elimination of Racial Discrimination as an Implementation Agency" in: MacEwen, M. (1997) (ed.) *Anti-Discrimination Law Enforcement: A Comparative Perspective* (Aldershot: Avebury) 209–33.

O'Hare, U. (2000) "Equality and Affirmative Action in International Human Rights Law and its Relevance to the European Union" 4, *International Journal of Discrimination and the Law* 3–45.

O'Hare, U. (2001) "Enhancing European Equality Rights: A New Regional Framework" 8, 2, *Maastricht Journal of European and Comparative Law* 133–65.

Opinion of the Committee of the Regions (2000) on: *the 'Communication from the Commission on certain Community Measures to combat Discrimination'; the 'Proposal for a Council Directive establishing a General Framework for Equal Treatment in Employment and Occupation'; the 'Proposal for a Council Directive implementing the Principle of Equal Treatment between Persons irrespective of Racial or Ethnic Origin'; and the 'Proposal for a Council Decision establishing a Community Action Programme to combat Discrimination 2001-2006'* [2000] OJ C 226/1.

Opinion of the Economic and Social Committee (1989) on *the Proposal for a Council Resolution on the Fight against Racism and Xenophobia* [1989] OJ C 23/33.

Opinion of the Economic and Social Committee (2000) on *the 'Communication from the Commission to the Council, the European Parliament, the Economic and Social Committee and the Committee for the Regions on certain Community Measures to Combat Discrimination'; the 'Proposal for a Council Directive establishing a General Framework for Equal Treatment in Employment and Occupation'; the 'Proposal for a Council Directive implementing the Principle of Equal Treatment between Persons irrespective of Racial or Ethnic Origin'; and the 'Proposal for a Council Decision establishing a Community Action Programme to combat Discrimination 2001-2006'* [2000] OJ C 204/82.

Opinion of the European Parliament (2000) on *COM (1999) 566, the Proposal for a Council Directive implementing the Principle of Equal Treatment between Persons irrespective of Racial or Ethnic Origin* A5-0136/2000.

Parekh, B. (1998) "Integrating Minorities" in: Blackstone, T., Parekh, B. and Sanders, P. (eds) *Race Relations in Britain: A Developing Agenda* (London/NewYork: Routledge) 1–21.

Parmar, S. (2004) "The European Court of Justice and Anti-Discrimination Law: Some Reflections on the Experience of Gender Equality Jurisprudence for the Future Interpretation of the Racial Equality Directive" in: Niessen, J. and Chopin, I. (eds) *The Development of Legal Instruments to Combat Racism in a Diverse Europe* (Leiden/Boston: Martinus Nijhoff Publishers) 131–54.

Pennings, P. (1997) "The Evolution of Dutch Consociationalism, 1917-1997" 33, 1, *The Netherlands Journal of Social Sciences* 9–26.

Petrova, D. (2001) "Racial Discrimination and the Rights of Minority Cultures" in: Fredman, S. (ed.) *Discrimination and Human Rights. The Case* of *Racism* (Oxford: Oxford University Press) 45–76.

Pitt, G. (1992) "Can Reverse Discrimination be Justified?" in: Hepple, B. and Szyszczak, E. (eds) *Discrimination: The Limits of Law* (London: Mansell) 281–99.

Poiares Maduro, M. (2005) "The European Court of Justice and Anti-Discrimination Law" 2, *European Anti-Discrimination Law Review* 21–6.

Political Declaration by the Governments of the Member States of the Council of Europe on the Occasion of the European Conference *All Different – All Equal: From Principle to Practice*, European Contribution to the WCAR, Strasbourg, 11–13 October 2000.

Poulter, S. (1990) "Cultural Pluralism and its Limits: A Legal Perspective" in: Commission for Racial Equality *Britain: A Plural Society* (London: Commission for Racial Equality) 3–28.

Poulter, S. (1998) *Ethnicity, Law and Human Rights: The English Experience* (Oxford: Clarendon Press) 1–57, 67–119 and 379–91.

Presidency Conclusions, Lisbon European Council 23-24 March 2000 http://ue.eu.int/ueDocs/cms_Data/docs/pressdata/en/ec/00100-r1.en0.htm (accessed 26 April 2009)

Presidency Conclusions, Brussels, 12–13 December 2003 http://europa.eu/european_council/conclusions/index_en.htm (accessed 20 April 2009)

Press Release IP/99/895, *Commission: A Step Forward for the EU – Empowering Victims of Discrimination*, 25 November 1999.

Press Release IP/03/1047, *Commission concerned at Member States' Failure to Implement New Racial Equality Rules*, 18 July 2003.

Press Release IP/04/947, *Commission goes to the European Court of Justice to enforce EU Anti-Discrimination Law*, 19 July 2004.

Press Release IP/04/1408, *Fight Against Discrimination: Strong Demand for More EU Action*, 26 November 2004.

Press Release IP/05/494, *President Barroso Proposes a New Framework to 'lock-in' a Culture of Fundamental Rights in EU Legislation*, 27 April 2005.

Press Release IP/06/149, *Expert Group to Promote Inclusion of Ethnic Minorities in the EU,* 13 February 2006.

Report from the Opening Conference of the European Year against Racism, 30–31 January 1997, The Hague, including the Declaration of Intent: *'Europe against Racism'*, and the speeches of this conference.

Resolution of the Council and the Representatives of the Governments of the Member States meeting within the Council of 23 July 1996 *concerning the European Year against Racism (1997)* [1996] OJ C 237/1.

Rex, J. (1986) *Race and Ethnicity* (Milton Keynes: Open University Press).

Schiek, D. (2002) "A New Framework on Equal Treatment of Persons in EC Law?" 8, 2, *European Law Journal* 290–314.

Schiek, D., Waddington, L. and Bell, M. (eds) (2007) *Cases, Materials and Text on National, Supranational and international Non-Discrimination Law* (Oxford/Portland, Oregon: Hart Publishing).

Schokkenbroek, J. (2000) "Towards a Stronger European Protection Against Discrimination: The Preparation of a New Additional Protocol to the European Convention of Human Rights" in: Moon, G. (ed.) *Race Discrimination. Developing and Using a New Legal Framework* (Oxford/Portland, Oregon: Hart Publishing) 29–37.

Schokkenbroek, J. (2004) "A New European Standard Against Discrimination: Negotiating Protocol No 12 to the European Convention on Human Rights" in: Niessen, J. and Chopin, I. (eds) *The Development of Legal Instruments to Combat Racism in a Diverse Europe* (Leiden/Boston: Martinus Nijhoff Publishers) 61–80.

SEC (2001) 380, *Memorandum on the Application of the Charter of Fundamental Rights of the European Union*.

Shaw, J. (2004) *Mainstreaming Equality in European Union Law and Policymaking* (Brussels: European Network Against Racism).

Sierra, M. (2002a) (ed.) *Towards Equal Treatment Transposing the Directive – Analysis and Proposals* (Brussels: European Network Against Racism).

Sierra, M. (2002b) "The World Conference Against Racism and the Role of the European NGOs" 4, *European Journal of Migration and Law* 249–60.

Skidmore, P. (2001) "EC Framework Directive on Equal Treatment in Employment: Towards a Comprehensive Community Anti-Discrimination Policy?" 30, 1, *Industrial Law Journal* 126–32.

Small, J. (2003) "Structure and Substance: Developing a Practical and Effective Prohibition on Discrimination under the European Convention on Human Rights" 6, 1, *International Journal of Discrimination and the Law* 45–67.

Solomos, J. (1993) *Race and Racism in Britain* (2nd ed. Basingstoke: McMillan).

Spencer, M. (1995) "Racism, Discrimination and Social Rights" in: Spencer, M. *States of Injustice. A Guide to Human Rights and Civil Liberties in the European Union* (London/Boulder, Colorado: Pluto Press) 126–52.

Spidla, V. (2004) *Equality in the Europe of Tomorrow*, Opening Address at the EU Dutch Presidency Conference on Anti-Discrimination, Scheveningen, 22 November 2004 http://ec.europa.eu/employment_social/speeches/2004_en.html (accessed 20 April 2009)

Spidla, V. (2005) *Mainstreaming Diversity* Opening Address at the EU Luxembourg Presidency Conference on Anti-Discrimination, Mondorf-les-Bains, 27 June 2005 http://ec.europa.eu/employment_social/speeches/2004_en.html (accessed 20 April 2009)

Starting Line Group (1997) *The Starting Point* (Starting Line Group).

Steiner, J., Woods, L. and Twigg-Flesner, C. (2006) *Textbook on EC Law* (9th ed. Oxford: Oxford University Press).

The Stephen Lawrence Inquiry (1999) Report of an Inquiry by Sir William MacPherson of Cluny (Cm 4262-I).

Sunstein, C. (1991) "Three Civil Rights Fallacies" 79, 1–3, *California Law Review* 751–74.

Swann Committee Report (1985) *Education of Children from Ethnic Minority Groups* (Cmnd 9453).

Tobler, C. (2008) *Limits and Potential of the Concept of Indirect Discrimination* (Luxembourg: OOPEC).

Toggenburg, G. (2001/2) "The Race Directive: A New Dimension in the Fight against Ethnic Discrimination in Europe" 1, *European Yearbook of Minority Issues* 231–44.

Toonen, T. (2000) "Governing a Consensus Democracy: The Interplay of Pillarisation and Administration" 23, 3, *West European Politics* 165–78.

Townshend-Smith, R. (1998) *Discrimination Law: Text, Cases and Materials* (London: Cavendish Publishing) 4-8 and 61–86.

Treaty of Lisbon amending the Treaty on European Union and the Treaty establishing the European Community [2007] OJ C 306/10.

Treaty of Nice [2001] OJ C 80/1.

Tyson, A. (2001) "The Negotiation of the European Community Directive on Racial Discrimination" 3, *European Journal of Migration and Law* 199–229.

UNESCO (1969) *Four Statements on the Race Question* (Paris: UNESCO) http://unesdoc.unesco.org/images/0012/001229/122962eo.pdf (accessed 27 April 2009) van Boven, T. (2001) "Discrimination and Human Rights Law: Combating Racism" in: Fredman, S. (ed.) *Discrimination and Human Rights: The Case of Racism* (Oxford: Oxford University Press) 111–34.

Verma, G. (1990) "Pluralism: Some Theoretical and Practical Considerations" in: Commission for Racial Equality *Britain: A Plural Society* (London: Commission for Racial Equality) 44–57.

Verzuiling www.parlement.com/9291000/modules/g72bd2vo (accessed 8 April 2009).

Vickers, L. (2006) *Religion and Belief Discrimination in Employment – the EU Law* (Luxembourg: OOPEC).

Vienna Convention on the Law of Treaties http://members.yline.com/~waltergehr/trea/wvkengl.html (accessed 17 April 2009).

Waddington, L. (1999) "Testing the Limits of the EC Treaty Article on Non-Discrimination" 28, 2, *Industrial Law Journal* 133–51.

Waddington, L. (2000) "Article 13 EC: Setting Priorities in the Proposal for a Horizontal Employment Directive" 29, 2, *Industrial Law Journal* 176–81.

Waddington, L. (2003a) *The Expanding Role of the Equality Principle in European Union Law*, Policy Paper, European University Institute, Robert Schuman Centre of Advanced Studies www.iue.it/RSCAS?e-texts/CR2003-04.pdf (accessed 27 April 2009)

Waddington, L. (2003b) "The New Equality Directives: Mixed Blessings", in: Costello, C. and Barry, E. (eds) *Equality in Diversity: The New Equality Directives* (Dublin: Irish Centre for European Law/Irish Equality Authority/Ashfield Publishing) 39–54.

Waddington, L. (2004) "Taking Stock and Looking Forward: The Commission Green Paper on Equality and Non-discrimination in an Enlarged European Union" 33, 4, *Industrial Law Journal* 367–73.

Waddington, L. and Bell, M. (2001) "More Equal than Others: Distinguishing European Union Equality Directives" 38, *Common Market Law Review* 587–611.

Watson, C. (2000) *Multiculturalism* (Buckingham/Philadelphia: Open University Press).

Winant, H. (1998) "Racism Today: Continuity and Change in the Post-Civil Rights Era" 21, 4, *Ethnic and Racial Studies* 755–66.

Wintle, M. (2000) "Pillarisation, Consociation and Vertical Pluralism in the Netherlands Revisited: A European View" 23, 3, *West European Politics* 139–52.

World Conference against Racism, Racial Discrimination, Xenophobia and Related Intolerance, Durban, South Africa, 31 August-8 September 2001, *Declaration* and *Action*.

Index